JÜNGEL

BLOOMSBURY GUIDES FOR THE PERPLEXED

Bloomsbury's Guides for the Perplexed are clear, concise and accessible introductions to thinkers, writers and subjects that students and readers can find especially challenging. Concentrating specifically on what it is that makes the subject difficult to grasp, these books explain and explore key themes and ideas, guiding the reader towards a thorough understanding of demanding material. Guides for the Perplexed available from Bloomsbury include:

Atonement: A Guide for the Perplexed, Adam Johnson
Balthasar: A Guide for the Perplexed, Rodney Howsare
Barth: A Guide for the Perplexed, Paul Nimmo
Benedict XVI: A Guide for the Perplexed, Tracey Rowland
Bonhoeffer: A Guide for the Perplexed, Joel Lawrence
Calvin: A Guide for the Perplexed, Paul Helm
De Lubac: A Guide for the Perplexed, David Grummett
Luther: A Guide for the Perplexed, David M. Whitford
Pannenberg: A Guide for the Perplexed, Timothy Bradshaw
Pneumatology: A Guide for the Perplexed, Daniel Castelo
Political Theology: A Guide for the Perplexed, Elizabeth Philips
Postliberal Theology: A Guide for the Perplexed, Ronald T. Michener
Prayer: A Guide for the Perplexed, Ashley Cocksworth
Predestination: A Guide for the Perplexed, Jesse Couenhoven
Schleiermacher: A Guide for the Perplexed, Theodore Vial
Scripture: A Guide for the Perplexed, William Lamb
Tillich: A Guide for the Perplexed, Andrew O' Neil
Wesley: A Guide for the Perplexed, Jason A. Vickers
Žižek: A Guide for the Perplexed, Sean Sheehan

Forthcoming Guides for the Perplexed available from Bloomsbury include:
Catholic Social Teaching: A Guide for the Perplexed, Anna Rowlands
God-Talk: A Guide for the Perplexed, Aaron B. James and Ryan S. Peterson
Resurrection: A Guide for the Perplexed, Lidija Novakovic
Salvation: A Guide for the Perplexed, Ivor J. Davidson
Schillebeeckx: A Guide for the Perplexed, Stephan van Erp

JÜNGEL

A GUIDE FOR THE PERPLEXED

R. David Nelson

t&tclark

LONDON • NEW YORK • OXFORD • NEW DELHI • SYDNEY

T&T CLARK
Bloomsbury Publishing Plc
50 Bedford Square, London, WC1B 3DP, UK
1385 Broadway, New York, NY 10018, USA

BLOOMSBURY, T&T CLARK and the T&T Clark logo are
trademarks of Bloomsbury Publishing Plc

First published in Great Britain 2020

Cover design: Terry Woodley
Cover image © Shaun Brierley/Getty

A catalogue record for this book is available from the British Library.

A catalog record for this book is available from the Library of Congress.

ISBN: HB: 978-0-5676-6005-3
         PB: 978-0-5676-6003-9
       ePDF: 978-0-5676-6002-2
       ePUB: 978-0-5676-6004-6

Typeset by Integra Software Services Pvt. Ltd.

To find out more about our authors and books visit www.bloomsbury.com
and sign up for our newsletters.

In memory of John Webster
1955–2016

CONTENTS

PREFACE

The most pivotal season of Eberhard Jüngel's early intellectual and theological formation almost never happened. The year was 1957, and the young theologian was nearing the end of his first round of studies at the Kirchliche Hochschule in Berlin. At the behest of his teachers Ernst Fuchs and Heinrich Vogel, Jüngel had arranged to spend the upcoming winter semester studying abroad in Switzerland. Gerhard Ebeling, Fuchs's long-time collaborator and one of the 'Old Marburgers' who had studied with Rudolf Bultmann in the early 1930s, had agreed to serve as Jüngel's mentor. Jüngel would live and work in Zürich, attending doctoral seminars at the university and meeting with Ebeling and other professors from the faculty of theology. Vogel, meanwhile, had mediated contact with his old friend Karl Barth, securing for Jüngel a seat in Barth's famed seminar and discussion group. Once a week, Jüngel would venture west by train to visit the 'grand old man of Basel'. Jüngel also planned to pay monthly visits to Freiburg im Briesgau to hear Martin Heidegger deliver his lectures on the nature of language.

At the time, the political situation in Berlin was rapidly deteriorating. The wall would not go up until 1961, and at the end of the 1950s citizens of both zones still could move about the city with some ease. International travel, however, was heavily regulated for those living in the east. Jüngel, hailing from Magdeburg in the DDR and a citizen of East Berlin, would need to pull some strings for the semester in Switzerland to happen. He made the formal academic arrangements for his time abroad through the seminary campus in West Berlin, rather than through the Sprachenkonvikt – the 'Language House', where seminarians took courses in Hebrew, Greek and Latin – in the east. The ploy technically violated existing policies governing student travel and would have been impossible just a few years later and once the city was divided by the wall. It is unclear what consequences Jüngel would have faced had he been caught. It is likely that, in 1957, while citizens of the DDR still could enjoy a few fading freedoms even as the political climate was becoming suffocating, Jüngel's plot would be viewed as a pardonable infraction. Still, Jüngel was putting much at stake to study with Ebeling, Barth and Heidegger.

After the official travel documentation had been filed, there remained the dilemma of how to slip away south to Switzerland. In an interview from 2005, Jüngel recounts hatching a clever scheme to get around border control. He bought a ticket to Wittenberg and crossed the checkpoint, but then alighted the S-Bahn early at Berlin-Tempelhof. 'When the conductor checked my ticket', Jüngel recalls, 'I lied and said, "Yes, I will continue on to Wittenberg." But instead I got off at the airport.' He caught a flight to Zürich, embarking upon an industrious six-month journey of study and conversation that would continue to impact his theology long thereafter. Of course, once Jüngel was on the ground and fast at work in Zürich, he had to address an additional detail for his ruse to succeed: 'I had to explain my absence in Berlin … So I let the rumor spread that I had suffered a nervous breakdown and was on my way to the Harz to recover in a sanatorium. The bad thing was that some people said, "Well, we saw it coming!"'[1]

Jüngel's quick-wittedness is on full display in this tale, both in his outfoxing of ministers of education and border control agents and in his tongue-in-cheek remark on how his absence was received in Berlin, which almost assuredly abbreviates real sentiments shared among some of his peers at the Kirchliche Hochschule – for Jüngel has a long-standing reputation for possessing a swaggering, cavalier and occasionally insolent personality. But there is something else we must not miss in this brief episode in the backdrop of his 'illegal' semester with Ebeling, Barth and Heidegger in 1957–1958. Jüngel spent his childhood amid the chaos of Nazi Germany and his adolescence in the stifling shadow of Stalinism in the DDR. He later would remark that his experiences growing up in such hellish political circumstances left a 'permanent stamp' on his life and theology. In the ruins of the war, and as the totalitarianism of Soviet communism was descending upon the Eastern Bloc just as he was coming of age, Jüngel discovered 'the Protestant church as the only place within Stalinist society accessible … at that time in which one could hear and speak the truth with impunity'.[2] As I show throughout this guide, Jüngel's relentless pursuit of the truth of the Christian gospel as a word of freedom which interrupts and overturns all worldly hegemonies, political and otherwise, is at the heart of his theological witness.[3] It is fitting, I think, that Jüngel's plan to study abroad with three leading luminaries was hard won. For the sake of a chance to cut his teeth as a theologian, he had to defy heavy-handed decrees imposed by an encroaching tyranny, deceive the powers-that-be while making his escape, fake a mental illness to excuse his absence and, through it all, jeopardize his well-being.

Eberhard Jüngel still has much to say to us. Several decades have passed since his theological career was in full swing, and the political circumstances of the German reconstruction, the long Cold War, the violent 1960s, the conflict in Vietnam, the nuclear crisis, the burgeoning of European secularization and the dissolution of the Soviet Union – all of which shape the background of his theological existence and development – are a fading memory. And yet the world remains besieged by powers and principalities (Eph. 6:12). Empires and despots come and go, but evil and deception and injustice abidingly reign. Jüngel urges us that the light of Jesus Christ shines forth in the midst of the world's oppressing darkness. The clarity and conviction of his theological voice continue to stand out in an academic culture in which theology so easily can become bureaucratic, banal, bourgeois and even blasphemous. While we may discover many reasons to disagree with Jüngel on this or that topic – and I express a number of my own demurrals in the course of this guide – the prophetic edge of his writing and his commitment to what he calls the 'truth of life' and to the freedom of theology warrant our consideration. If the analysis set forth in this guide does nothing more than to draw attention to the enduring significance of Jüngel's theological witness, I yet will have succeeded.

It is demonstrable that Jüngel's work is underappreciated and underexplored among anglophone theologians today. While many of his most important contributions to modern theology have been rendered into English, his path-breaking dissertation on Paul and Jesus, the German text of which is now in its seventh revised edition (2004), has never been translated, nor have scores of key essays, popular level articles, lecture theses, interviews and sermons. Moreover, the English texts already available are, as a rule, tough going. Jüngel's written German relies upon potent rhetorical devices – alliterations, hyperboles, neologisms, wordplays and poetic cadences, to name but a few – which, often enough, go missing in translation. On a couple of occasions elsewhere I have described Jüngel's writing as 'sermonic' in an effort to express the persuasive power of the German originals and to draw attention to the close connection Jüngel envisages between theological discourse and Christian preaching.[4] Unfortunately, the sermonic character of Jüngel's theological voice is difficult to capture in English. Instead, most of the available translations, even while executed quite capably and sometimes beautifully by leading scholars of German theology, are something of a slog. In addition to all of this is the matter of anglophone secondary literature on Jüngel's theology, which, in general, has focused on specific texts and themes. I do not at all wish to disparage any of the fine scholarship on Jüngel's thought undertaken by theologians in the English-speaking world during the past few decades. But because there are available mainly specialized studies of some aspect of his theology or another, and, likewise, there endures a scarcity of general introductions to his life and work, and because, too, only a fragment of his oeuvre is available in English, anglophone students of modern theology are without a panoramic survey of Jüngel's intellectual and theological formation and key writings. I have written the present guide to address this need.

This project originated in a lively discussion with Anna Turton of T&T Clark in Nottingham, England, in April 2013, at the annual meeting of the Society for the Study of Theology. That brief moment of brainstorming and vision-casting set in motion several initiatives on the part of this historic and prestigious theological press to make available in English new works by and about Eberhard Jüngel. Readers of modern Christian theology owe much to Anna and the rest of the team at T&T Clark. And I am ever indebted to Anna for the interest she has shown in my own work and for her friendship, generosity and cross-bench discussions on theological publishing.

My perspective on Jüngel's theology has taken shape over many years and as a result of hundreds of conversations and correspondences. While I hold no one else but myself responsible and accountable for the analysis unfolding in these pages, I express my gratitude especially to the following friends and dialogue partners: Mike Allen, Kimlyn Bender, John Betz, André Birmelé, Carl Braaten, Dave Bruner, Ray Carr, Deborah Casewell, David Congdon, Paul DeHart, Theo Dieter, Hans-Anton Drewes, Mark Elliott, Sven Ensminger, David Ford, Steve Garrett, David Gilland, Gary Green, Tom Greggs, Paul Hinlicky, Chris Holmes, Tom Holsinger-Friesen, Reinhard Hütter, Matt Jenson, Joshua Kira, Matt Levering, Brian Lugioyo, Mark Mattes, Bruce McCormack, Travis McMaken, Paul Molnar, Arnold Neufeldt-Fast, George Newlands, Ben Reynolds, Ben Rhodes, Cindy Rigby, Phil Rolnick, Mike Root, Christoph Schwöbel, Ry Sigglekow, Archie Spencer, Roland Spjuth, Justin Stratis, Chris Tilling, Geoffrey Wainwright, John White, David Yeago, Phil Ziegler and Jens Zimmermann.

In particular, I am grateful to Piotr Małsz for his friendship and for his partnership as co-chair of the Eberhard Jüngel Research Colloquium, which has convened four times since 2014 and remains an invaluable network for anglophone scholars undertaking research in Jüngel's thought. I thank Dirk Evers and Malte Krüger for inviting me to contribute the essay 'Eberhard

Jüngels Theologie der Sakramente' to a German-language collection of short studies on various aspects of Jüngel's theology. The assignment allowed me to make new connections with European scholars interested in Jüngel's work and its significance. George Hunsinger and Keith Johnson kindly invited me to compose a chapter on 'Barth and Jüngel' for the *Wiley Blackwell Companion to Karl Barth*. Stephen Plant mediated contact with the Karl Barth-Archiv in Basel while I was seeking unpublished materials pertaining to the theological friendship between Barth and Jüngel. I am grateful to Peter Zocher of the Archiv for sending along several items, including a scan of a letter of reference Barth wrote on Jüngel's behalf following the latter's 'illegal' semester in Switzerland. My friends Joe Mangina and Paul Nimmo read some of my work on Barth and Jüngel and offered patient, helpful feedback. Hans-Peter Großhans, who years ago served as Jüngel's assistant in Tübingen, fielded several questions regarding Jüngel's record of university service and passed along three helpful biographical pieces.

I am indebted to my family for being a significant and constant source of strength and support throughout my own theological career. My parents, grandmother and extended family have enthusiastically cheered on all of my academic efforts. My greatest debt, though, is to Dacia and to our children: Robert, Reace and Liam. I would not have completed this journey without the love and patience the four of you have shown me every step of the way.

I dedicate this book to the memory of John Webster, who passed away unexpectedly on 25 May 2016. My research on Jüngel's theology in pursuit of a doctorate, which John supervised in Aberdeen beginning in 2004, originated in an accident of history. I arrived at my first in-person meeting with John with a list of Barth projects in hand. To my dismay, he rejected the lot of them, remarking at one point in our conversation that he would rather me take up 'something more interesting' than a thesis on Barth. On the way to our meeting I had scribbled down 'Jüngel on the sacraments' as an afterthought. John latched onto the topic as soon as he laid eyes on it, and the matter, in effect, was settled. That exchange with him in Atlanta, GA, in November of 2003 officially launched my scholarly preoccupation with Eberhard Jüngel's theology, and also established a close working relationship with John that extended through my time in the programme at Aberdeen and into my role as his editor for several projects for Baker Academic, none of which – alas! – ever came to fruition.

A couple of reflections from my time studying Jüngel with John are worth mentioning in the prefatory remarks to this guidebook. I vividly recall a frigid, rain-soaked, quintessentially Aberdonian September afternoon in 2004, when I hiked the mile from John's office in King's College to our little flat on Seaforth Road, struggling along the way to tote his 'Jüngel box' – a heavy, unwieldy bankers box filled to the brim with handwritten notes, photocopied articles and book chapters, reams of duplications of Jüngel's class lecture outlines and sundry other items of Jüngel memorabilia John had collected over the years. While, at the time, I thought it an odd way to commence my journey into Jüngel's theology (John urged me to 'dig through the box' before continuing to explore Jüngel's corpus beyond what I already had read in seminary), looking back I realize that my encounter with John's stash of Jüngel souvenirs early on decisively impacted my perspective and the course of my research. For by sifting through the rarities in John's personal archive, I gained an appreciation for Jüngel's biography, intellectual formation and vocation as a teacher. To put it another way, those days spent with John's box provided a unique window into the *person* of Jüngel beyond his theological *work*, and this, in turn, impacted my understanding of his *ideas*. In the present guide I have endeavoured to give due attention both to the man and to his theological contribution. I credit John for inspiring this approach.

Even as I was embarking upon a pathway through Jüngel's theology, John was looking back on his own journey as he would a fading memory. When I arrived in Aberdeen in 2004, he was fast at work on the manuscript for *Barth's Earlier Theology*,[5] the anthology which, upon its publication, effectively closed the phase of his career marked by close critical readings of key texts from the modern period (mainly from Jüngel and Barth). His planned-but-never-ventured, multi-volume *Systematic Theology* was on the distant horizon and, in anticipation of that Herculean task, John increasingly was committing his energy and time to issues in the areas of theological prolegomena and the doctrine of God. He still enjoyed discussing Jüngel's theology, and, as a rule, our supervisory meetings consisted of animated conversations about the key texts and issues pertaining to my research. But it had been several years since John had read Jüngel closely, and he no longer was actively engaged in scholarship on Jüngel's theology. John's interests, more or less, had moved on.

Along these lines, I recall here a revealing conversation we had sometime around the mid-point of my stay in Aberdeen. I just had read for the first time John's 1997 essay 'Jesus in the Theology of Eberhard Jüngel', a penetrating and, on full measure, sharply disapproving analysis of Jüngel's Christology.[6] John told me that he considered the essay his 'last word' on Jüngel, summarizing both his admiration for and deep ambivalence about Jüngel's programme.[7] In the same breath, he reflected on the shelf life of his own little guidebook, *Eberhard Jüngel: An Introduction to His Theology*.[8] John recognized that he had written the book at about the halfway point of Jüngel's own theological career, and that Jüngel had gone on in the 1980s and 1990s to address new topics in Christian dogmatics. In particular, John was well aware that the *Introduction* covered topics mostly falling within the first and second regions of Christian teaching (that is, the doctrine of God and Christology) and hardly any beneath the creedal third article. And yet, many of Jüngel's most arresting contributions to Christian theology written after the publication of John's *Introduction* are on themes such as ecclesiology, sacramental theology and eschatology. John acknowledged that the 1986 book could carry readers only so far into Jüngel's thought. As a student of John's writing a dissertation on Jüngel, it was both fascinating and instructive to hear him speak so frankly about the limitations of his own bygone research.

I have reflected upon that key conversation with John on many occasions during the preparation of this *Guide for the Perplexed*. I am ever alert to the fact that my own reading of Jüngel, such as it is, is shaped profoundly and lastingly by my apprenticeship under John in a season during which he had moved well beyond Jüngel as a source of interest and inspiration. In the bookends to his 'Jüngel period' – his doctoral dissertation,[9] which differs from the *Introduction*, and the essay 'Jesus in the Theology of Eberhard Jüngel' – John's appraisal of Jüngel's theology is highly critical and in some spots even outright disparaging. For all he might have gained intellectually and theologically from his early work on Jüngel, by the mid-1990s he had developed a strong distaste for several features of Jüngel's programme.[10] My dissertation reflects some of the unease he expressed during our many supervisory meetings. It was unavoidable that I would adopt a number of John's judgements, even as our readings of Jüngel's contribution to modern theology differ considerably in important respects.[11] In any event, I consciously have attempted in this book to mitigate the critical tone and to present as clearly and as straightforwardly as possible the main texts and themes marking Jüngel's theology.

John's *Introduction* reads effortlessly. Admirers of his written work will discover in the book all the hallmarks of his theological oeuvre – confident and commanding prose, careful exegesis of source materials, charitability in dealing with viewpoints diverging from his own and so on. Additionally, the book remains *the* magisterial resource in English for the study of Jüngel's theology, even after three decades in print. The present *Guide for the Perplexed* is not at all intended as a replacement for John's *Introduction*. I happily point the reader to John's book as the best primer on Jüngel's thought in English, particularly on the arc of Jüngel's career spanning from his doctoral dissertation, *Paulus und Jesus* (1962), to *God as the Mystery of the World* (1977). However and as already mentioned, John's analysis stops in the mid-1980s and therefore does not include commentary on key works from the final two decades of Jüngel's career. It is hoped that this guide will find its niche in the secondary literature on Jüngel as the first introduction in English to cover the span of his written output. If there is any advantage to this book when compared to the Webster *Introduction*, it lies here.

I miss John's friendship and mentorship terribly. I am grateful to have known him. It is only fitting that I dedicate this book to his memory and in appreciation of his abiding theological witness.

R. David Nelson
Candlemas, 2019

ACKNOWLEDGEMENTS

A few sections of this guidebook draw from remarks published elsewhere and in other form. In all such instances, I have restated and reconceived previously written materials for inclusion here. I am grateful to Bloomsbury T&T Clark for permission to make use of the following:

R. David Nelson, *The Interruptive Word: Eberhard Jüngel on the Sacramental Structure of God's Relation to the World*, T&T Clark Studies in Systematic Theology 24 (London: Bloomsbury T&T Clark, 2013).

Nelson, 'Foreword to the English Text', in Jüngel, *God as the Mystery of the World: On the Foundation of the Theology of the Crucified One in the Dispute between Theism and Atheism* (London: Bloomsbury T&T Clark, 2014), xv–xxiv.

Nelson, 'Foreword to the 2014 English Edition', in Jüngel, *Justification – The Heart of the Christian Faith: A Theological Study with an Ecumenical Purpose* (London: Bloomsbury T&T Clark, 2014), xlii–li.

Bloomsbury T&T Clark also has kindly permitted me to cite at length from the five volumes of Jüngel's works in English published over the years and reprinted in 2014. Full bibliographical information on these volumes is found below.

Some of my comments on Jüngel's intellectual, theological and personal relationship to Karl Barth revise portions of the chapter 'Barth and Jüngel' in George Hunsinger and Keith L. Johnson, eds., *Wiley Blackwell Companion to Karl Barth* (Malden, MA: Wiley Blackwell, 2020).

A Note on Translation

All English quotations with references to German sources are my own translations. Any quotation that references an English edition is from that edition unless otherwise stated.

ABBREVIATIONS

Throughout this book, I have used inline references for Jüngel's key publications. For articles, essays, published lecture theses and reviews, I point the reader to one of several collections of Jüngel's shorter writings if an anthologized edition is available. The following abbreviations are used for Jüngel's works in the parenthetical citations and also in the endnotes whenever appropriate:

Barth   *Barth-Studien* [Ökumenische Theologie 9] (Zürich: Benziger; Gütersloh: Mohn; Reprint ed., Tübingen: Mohr Siebeck, 2003).

Becoming   *God's Being Is in Becoming: The Trinitarian Being of God in the Theology of Karl Barth – A Paraphrase*, trans. John B. Webster (Edinburgh: T&T Clark). Reprint (London: Bloomsbury T&T Clark, 2014).

Essays I   *Theological Essays*, trans. J.B. Webster (Edinburgh: T&T Clark, 1989). Reprint (London: Bloomsbury T&T Clark, 2014).

Essays II   *Theological Essays II*, ed. J.B. Webster, trans. Arnold Neufeldt-Fast (Edinburgh: T&T Clark, 1994). Reprint (London: Bloomsbury T&T Clark, 2014).

Justification   *Justification: The Heart of the Christian Faith*, trans. Jeffrey F. Cayzer, with an Introduction by John Webster (Edinburgh: T&T Clark). Reprint (London: Bloomsbury T&T Clark, 2014).

Leidenschaft   *Die Leidenschaft, Gott zu denken. Ein Gespräch über Denk- und Lebenserfahrungen*, ed. Fulvio Ferrario (Zürich: TVZ, 2009).

Mystery   *God as the Mystery of the World: On the Foundation of the Theology of the Crucified One in the Dispute between Theism and Atheism*, trans. Darrell L. Guder (Edinburgh: T&T Clark; Grand Rapids: Wm. B. Eerdmans, 1983). Reprint (London: Bloomsbury T&T Clark, 2014).

P&J   *Paulus und Jesus. Eine Untersuchung zur Präzisierung der Frage nach dem Ursprung der Christologie* (Tübingen: Mohr Siebeck; 7th ed., 2004).

Abbreviations

TE I	*Unterwegs zur Sache. Theologische Erörterungen I* (Tübingen: Mohr Siebeck; 3rd ed., 2000).
TE II	*Entsprechungen: Gott – Wahrheit – Mensch. Theologische Erörterungen II* (Tübingen: Mohr Siebeck; 3rd ed., 2002).
TE III	*Wertlose Wahrheit: Zur Identität und Relevanz des christlichen Glaubens. Theologische Erörterungen III* (Tübingen: Mohr Siebeck; 2nd ed., 2003).
TE IV	*Indikative der Gnade – Imperative der Freiheit. Theologische Erörterungen IV* (Tübingen: Mohr Siebeck).
TE V	*Ganz Werden. Theologische Erörterungen V* (Tübingen: Mohr Siebeck).

Additional abbreviations in inline references:

CD	Karl Barth, *Church Dogmatics*, 4 volumes, eds. Geoffrey W. Bromiley and Thomas F. Torrance, trans. Geoffrey W. Bromiley, et al. (Edinburgh: T&T Clark, 1956–1975).
DEC	*Decrees of the Ecumenical Councils*, 2 volumes, ed. Norman P. Tanner, S.J. (London: Sheed & Ward; Washington, DC: Georgetown University Press; 1990).
Denzinger	Heinrich Denzinger, *Compendium of Creeds, Definitions, and Declarations on Matters of Faith and Morals*, 43rd edition, ed. Peter Hünermann, English edition ed. Robert Fastiggi and Anne Englund Nash (San Francisco: Ignatius Press, 2012).
JDDJ	Lutheran World Federation and the Roman Catholic Church, *Joint Declaration on the Doctrine of Justification* (Grand Rapids: Eerdmans, 2000).
LW	Martin Luther, *Luther's Works*, 55 volumes, eds. Jaroslav Pelikan and Helmut T. Lehmann (St Louis: Concordia; Philadelphia and Minneapolis: Fortress: 1955).
WA	Martin Luther, D. *Martin Luthers Werke. Kritische Gesamtausgabe*, 73 volumes (Weimar: Herman Bohlaus Nachfolger, 1883–2009).

Endnotes and the bibliography use SBL guidelines for abbreviations of periodicals.

CHAPTER 1
INTRODUCTION

This T&T Clark *Guide for the Perplexed* is designed to serve as a companion for readers exploring the theology of Eberhard Jüngel, one of the most significant Protestant theologians of the period after Barth. Over the course of an academic career spanning nearly five decades, Jüngel produced several highly influential monographs and hundreds of carefully crafted short pieces. Although he never attempted a comprehensive and systematic exposition of the Christian faith, the occasional writings filling out his literary oeuvre span the entire range of the theological topics. The goal of this guide is to help both the casual reader and the serious student of Jüngel's theological writings grasp a sense of the lay of the land. Attention is devoted to Jüngel's location along the trajectory of modern Protestant thought, to the origins of his theology and his intellectual formation, to minor adjustments and changes of mind within the development of his written work and to the abiding significance of his thought and the questions his writings continue to pose to his readers. At all points along the way, we will pay close heed to the primary sources. In two of the three chapters at the heart of the book, I comment upon the content and structure of Jüngel's key monographs (Chapter 3) and analyse eleven of Jüngel's most important theological essays (Chapter 4). Especially now, as English renderings of previously untranslated works from Jüngel's pen are in preparation, and dissertations and short essays on Jüngel's thought are appearing with some regularity, it is my hope that this guide will find use as a companion and primer to Jüngel's thought and his legacy. Of course, a book such as this cannot take the place of careful and critical engagement with the original texts. On the contrary, the extent to which this book succeeds in accomplishing its task depends upon whether it leads readers further into Jüngel's own theological works. Let the discerning reader be the judge.

On the cover of the print edition of this book is a stock photograph of clockwork. When I was shown a selection of images for the cover early on in the life of the book, I chose the clockwork theme sheerly for its aesthetic value, as I found it more visually striking than the other designs on offer.

But I have come to regard it as an appropriate illustration for the book at least in two senses. First, Jüngel's written contributions to Christian theology often are described using adjectives such as complex, involved, circuitous and even, as our title has it, perplexing. The gears, ratchets and other mechanisms powering a clockwork device are evocative of intricacy, and for this reason the imagery is well suited for an introductory volume on a notoriously difficult theologian. One of my goals in this guide is to dispel the notion that Jüngel is too hard to understand and in any case hardly worth the effort. Of course, to figure out how a watch works, one must carefully examine the movement and get a feel for the engineering. Likewise, having a sense of the whole engenders an appreciation for the delicate parts. This guide will introduce the reader to particular texts while simultaneously providing a broad orientation for appreciating Jüngel's career and written work.

Second, clockwork also serves as an apt metaphor for capturing one of Jüngel's key theological commitments. Ironically, however, as a metaphor it conveys precisely the opposite decision about God and God's relation to creatures from that which Jüngel urges us to see at the heart of the New Testament witness and the theology emerging from it. Ever since the European Enlightenment and the rise of modern science and philosophy, appeals to the idea of God as the cosmic watchmaker have become commonplace, both in scholarly discourse and in popular parlance. Perhaps most famously, in his *Natural Theology*, William Paley invokes the watchmaker analogy in support of his teleological argument for the existence of God.[1] For Paley, the complexity, order, mechanism and motion of the watch are signatures of the watch's designer. Likewise, Paley insists, when we by natural reason observe the intricacies of the world, and the good order and sublime movement of heavenly bodies, and the scientific laws according to which all material things operate, and so on, we are able to arrive by way of inference at the idea of God as Creator. As the cosmic watchmaker, so the analogy goes, God designs and creates the world and sets its mechanism in motion.

Jüngel has no interest in the conception of God as the cosmic watchmaker, nor does he wish to commit himself to any understanding of the world as a closed system of laws, mechanisms and processes originating in God's design and prime directive and evolving naturally over the course of time. Indeed, as we shall discover throughout this guide, Jüngel frequently describes God as the one who *interrupts* the world, whose coming to the world in events of self-disclosure profoundly upsets the world and its actualities. The attention Jüngel has devoted throughout his career to this way of conceiving

God – that is, to the idea of God as the one who interrupts the world in the word – puts him at odds with numerous alternative visions for theology emerging since the Enlightenment. He is fiercely opposed to naturalistic readings of theological problems. He is a stout enemy, moreover, of the natural theologies of modernity, which, to his mind, far too easily and wilfully neutralize the distinction between God and creatures. For Jüngel, theological naturalism and natural theology alike jeopardize the New Testament witness of God as the one who freely determines to be God only as God-for-us. If clockwork imagery is appropriate for a book on Jüngel, it is so just because it is suggestive of the watchmaker god – for Jüngel, an imaginary god of human making against which the Christian gospel is marshalled.

Eberhard Jüngel – theologian of Christian freedom: A brief intellectual biography

Jüngel's childhood and adolescence

Eberhard Jüngel was born on 5 December 1934 in Magdeburg. He was born a twin to a sister named Hannelore. 'I am a twin', he quips in a late retrospective interview, 'so actually I am only half a person' (Jüngel, *Leidenschaft*, 9). Eberhard and Hannelore had an older brother named Rainer and, much later, a younger sister named Margarete. His comments on the other men of the family betray the tensions marking the Jüngel household during Eberhard's childhood and adolescence. His father was 'very smart but not very kind, and his temper often troubled us children – and my mother as well'. Eberhard and his brother Rainer did not see eye to eye about much of anything, with the latter growing into adulthood as a Marxist and an avowed atheist. On the other hand, Jüngel remembers his mother with great fondness. She was 'an extremely kind and intelligent woman' who possessed a 'natural' piety, even though the family was only nominally religious. His mother's latent faith and strength of character came through during the chaos of the war. A sizeable and strategic city on the Elbe, Magdeburg was heavily and repeatedly bombed by the Allies. The Jüngels converted an old ice cellar in the garden into an air raid shelter, and the sturdy structure became a refuge for the entire neighbourhood when the klaxons blared. On one occasion, Allied bombs fell close nearby, and the bunker began to shake and threatened to collapse. Jüngel recalls that everyone in the shelter came unglued. 'But it was, above all, the men among us who performed rather miserably that day', he remarks. 'I'll never forget how grown men cried' as the bombs exploded just outside. But Jüngel's mother was unfazed. She 'prayed in a loud voice the Lord's Prayer and the room went still' (*Leidenshaft*, 9–10).

The Jüngels, though, were not active churchgoers, and religion rarely was discussed in the home. 'My father never went to church unless we were being confirmed', Jüngel comments. 'And even then the only thing in the service he really liked was when the pastor railed against the socialist government.' His mother's private piety never translated into an eager interest in the religious formation of her children beyond ensuring that they received basic catechetical instruction in their confirmation classes. As a rule of thumb, Jüngel explains, 'my parents were business people who had little time for their children'. Fortunately, an 'honorary aunt' (*Wahltante*), a friend of the family given charge over the Jüngel children, took Rainer and Eberhard under her wing and endeavoured to give them an informal education, teaching them the basics of religion, grammar, art and poetry. In time Jüngel developed a passion particularly for theatre and opera. The pastor of the local parish was a writer before pursuing a call to the ministry, and he worked hard to engender in the children of the congregation a love for drama and performance (*Leidenschaft*, 10–11). In school Jüngel read classics and memorized poetry (in 2005 he recalled reciting by heart Schiller's 430-line 'Song of the Bell' from start to finish!); in confirmation classes he committed to memory the catechism and some traditional hymns (*Leidenschaft*, 11).

In due course the young Jüngel decided to follow the academic and vocational path which would lead to ordination and, eventually, his career in theology. In his retrospective comments on his adolescence, he never mentions any particular moment of conversion precipitating this decision. Ongoing tensions with his father appear to have played a minor role: 'I wanted to annoy my father', Jüngel writes, perhaps with tongue in cheek. 'My brother also wanted to annoy our father, and so became a Marxist. But I became a theologian, and this too annoyed our father. "You should become a lawyer," he said, "but not a theologian."' The more significant motivation, however, was 'a far deeper experience',[2] namely, Jüngel's discovery of the church as a haven for the truth in the midst of the communist authoritarianism and state atheism descending upon East Germany in the wake of the war. 'As a student', Jüngel reflects, 'and in the context of an increasingly despotic "socialist" school, I came to know the church as the only place where one could speak the truth freely. I learned that the "the truth will set you free" (John 8:32) long before I ever read that verse in the Gospel of John' (*Leidenschaft*, 12).

Jüngel's encounter with the truth as a word of *freedom* had a profound and immediate impact. He comments at length about this encounter:

> What a liberating experience this was by comparison with the ideological and political tyranny which prevailed at school! Friends were arrested; I myself was interrogated several times by the security services and taken to court – simply because we dared to say what we thought. One day before my ... examination, directly before the workers' revolt in 1953, I was removed from my school as an 'enemy of the republic.' My fellow pupils were required immediately to break all contact with us. As I left the hall of the Humboldt School in Magdeburg ... the honest men and women among the teachers there turned away in helpless silence. This was a symbolic scene in which the truth of the sentence from Cicero which these same teachers had instilled in us dawned on me like a flash. *Cum tacent, clamant*: by keeping silent, they cry out. However, in the Christian church one was free to break through that oppressive silence and the pressure to lie, which was becoming increasingly marked. Here people dared to witness to the truth of the gospel, and to do so in the political situation in such a way that the liberating power of this truth could also be experienced in a very secular, indeed a very political, way.[3]

Theological studies in Naumburg (Saale), Berlin and Switzerland

This conviction that the word of truth must speak forth in a world of lies and tyranny provoked Jüngel to pursue theological studies and, eventually, a career in public ministry as a theologian and preacher. 'I was eager to get to know the liberating truth [of the gospel] and the place where it thrives', he writes in one place, reflecting on his vocational origins. 'I believed, and therefore I wanted to understand *what* I believed.'[4] He enrolled in the newly established Kirchliche Proseminar programme at the Katechetische Oberseminar in Naumburg (Saale). Because he was expelled from the public Humboldt School in Magdeburg the day before taking his graduation exam, Jüngel was not awarded a high school diploma and for this reason was prohibited from matriculating at any of the state universities of the DDR. The Proseminar offered 'emergency' exams for public school students who had been disqualified by the state for political reasons. Jüngel passed the surrogate exam and advanced into the theological curriculum at the Oberseminar.

Oddly enough, but squarely in line with the surreal political conditions marking the DDR in the 1950s, Jüngel eventually got the chance to take the standard state exam, which he passed with ease ('the church examiners graded us much more strictly than the state examiners!', he recalls in *Leidenschaft*, 15). Due to widespread protests against the policy, the government had revoked its decision to withhold diplomas from high school students deemed 'enemies of the state'. Years later, and as he handed out exams to his own students in Tübingen, Jüngel would relate this anecdote, ending with the remark: 'In this world there are no fair exams. Only the final exam on the day of judgement – the *iudicium extremum* – will be a fair exam!' (*Leidenschaft*, 16).

Jüngel studied in Naumburg from 1953 to 1955 and then at the Kirchliche Hochschule in Berlin from 1955 to 1959. While at the first institution, he came under the influence of the philosopher Gerhard Stammler (1889–1971), who impressed upon Jüngel the importance of strict logic ('the stricter the better!'[5]) in theological and philosophical discourse. He also crossed paths with the controversial New Testament theologian Walter Grundmann (1906–1976), an ardent anti-Semite and member of the Nazi party from its rise to power to the end of the war. In spite of his serious misgivings concerning his professor's notoriety and objectionable viewpoints, it was from Grundmann that Jüngel first learned the ropes of New Testament exegesis. Jüngel especially was drawn to the patristic scholar and church historian Rudolf Lorenz (1914–2003), an expert in Augustine's theology who went on to have a long career as professor of church history at Mainz. Jüngel remembers Lorenz as a gifted teacher whose informative lectures helped students see the connections between the early church and the challenges facing Christianity in modernity. For Lorenz, Jüngel wrote a paper on the theme of doubt in Augustine and Descartes, two figures with whom he would continue to wrestle once his theological career was under way (*Leidenschaft*, 33).

It is difficult to measure with any accuracy the impact these early teachers had on Jüngel's mature theology. On one hand, Jüngel's time in Naumburg laid a foundation in the disciplines of biblical exegesis, Christian dogmatics, church history and practical theology. His courses in these and related subjects were his first encounters with the academic study of the Christian faith. Jüngel assuredly was *formed*, both theologically and vocationally, while a student at the Oberseminar, and with good reason we may conclude that many of the lessons he learned during these first years of formal academic work in theology tarried with him as his education moved forward. Interestingly, however, in the various retrospective pieces in which he mentions (always briefly) his years in Naumburg, Jüngel never indicates that his teachers exposed the seminarians to contemporaneous trends in German Protestant thought. It was only later, after Jüngel transitioned to the Kirchliche Hochschule in Berlin, that he began to read Barth, Bultmann, Luther and others in earnest, and to confront the challenges of modern theology and philosophy.

Two of Jüngel's teachers from his time in Berlin deserve special mention in this regard. Heinrich Vogel (1902–1989) was a systematic theologian, Lutheran pastor and composer of sacred music who had been teaching theology in Berlin for several decades when Jüngel arrived in 1955. Vogel had joined the Confessing Church soon after its founding in 1934 and during the early years of Nazi rule earned a reputation as a fiery opponent of the German Christians. In 1935 he joined the faculty of the newly established Kirchliche Hochschule für reformatorische Theologie in Berlin, serving as principal from 1937 to 1941. The war years were especially difficult for Vogel, who was arrested and jailed on several occasions and, from 1941, censored by the Nazi regime. Vogel and Barth had become good friends after years of fighting a common enemy. Barth affectionately dubbed Vogel 'that special little Lutheran bird' ('*Vogel*' is the German word for 'bird') and in one spot comments with characteristic warmth and good humour about Vogel's penchant for getting agitated while attempting to arouse pastors to withstand the tide of Nazism. 'Wizened and worked up', Barth writes, 'there [Vogel] is all the time, waving his arms like a windmill and shouting "Confess! Confess!" And in his own way, this is just what he does'.[6]

Unfortunately, the bulk of Vogel's works, including *Gott in Christo*, his massive text on Christian dogmatics,[7] remain untranslated. Anglophone readers can, however, get a good sense of Vogel's contribution in the form of the little book *Consider Your Calling*,[8] a primer to the study of theology he wrote for his students in Berlin in 1957, the year prior to when Jüngel commenced his coursework at the Kirchliche Hochschule. Vogel covers the theme of theology as a vocation in the church, the scientific conditions of theological work, the significance of truth in theology and five characteristics of theology – theology as exegetical, dogmatic, historical, practical and doxological. The book is marked by a pastoral tone, and three of the four main sections of the text end with short, personal letters to his student readers. In several passages – notably, throughout the unit on truth and in the section on the dialogical character of theology – we encounter hints of Vogel's fondness for the use of *paradox* in theological discourse. Since, for Vogel, the truth of the gospel is contrary to all human or worldly truths, we can be said to lay hold of it only as it subverts human knowledge and intelligence. For all he learned otherwise from Vogel, Jüngel never quite could accommodate paradoxical reasoning in his approach to theological epistemology. Looking back on his time in Berlin, he refers to Vogel's theology as 'paradoxically sealed' and states that 'he could not at that time nor later on adopt the view' of his teacher. And yet, in the course of the same reflection, Jüngel acknowledges the genuine insight of Vogel's appeal to paradox: namely, that theology, when understood as an instantiation of paradoxical reasoning, poses a crisis to 'one-dimensional thinking'.[9] We might say that in his early studies with Vogel, Jüngel encountered an understanding of the truth of the Christian message as alien and interruptive, and antagonistic to the normal course of human knowledge. This understanding of the basic structure of theological truth obtains throughout Jüngel's writings, even as he discovers a (to his mind) better conceptual framework for nuancing the problem in the doctrine of analogy.

During his years in Berlin, Jüngel also came under the wing of Ernst Fuchs (1903–1983), an 'Old Marburger' who had studied under Bultmann in the mid-1920s, writing a dissertation on the early Christian document, 'Shepherd of Hermas'. By the time Jüngel encountered him in Berlin, Fuchs was well known for his innovative, though at times opaque, writings on New Testament exegesis and had developed notoriety for his bombastic and mercurial personality. In one spot Jüngel describes Fuchs's intellectual manner as ever punctuated by *schwäbischen Eruptionen*[10] – Swabian eruptions, a playful allusion to the volcanism which gave shape to the Swabian Jura dominating the landscape of Fuchs's southwestern German homeland. Fuchs had arrived in Berlin from Tübingen in 1955 to chair the faculty of theology at Humboldt University. In the late 1950s, students at the Kirchliche Hochschule were permitted to take courses at the state universities. Jüngel encountered Fuchs at Humboldt and later arranged for him to supervise his doctoral thesis, which he completed at the Sprachenkonvikt in 1961. The relationship between the two got off to an inauspicious start. 'In the beginning there was only noise', Jüngel recalls (*Leidenschaft*, 17), going on in the same paragraph to describe an early and rather unusual argument that erupted between teacher and student during a seminar on 1 John. Fuchs made an offhand, dismissive remark describing Barth and philosopher Nicolai Hartmann as peddlers of *Hausfrauenontologie* – literally, 'housewives ontology', used pejoratively in this instance to convey something like 'homemade' or 'domestic' ontology. Jüngel objected to the condescending barb, but also worried – himself having just started the *Church Dogmatics* and recently completed Hartmann's *Zur*

Grundlegung der Ontologie – that his teacher had repudiated the work of Barth and Hartmann too clumsily and without sufficiently attending to the issues at stake as they unfold in the primary sources. Jüngel pressed Fuchs on the matter, and Fuchs, in turn, challenged Jüngel to write for credit a paper on how Barth and Hartmann differentiate *ontisch* and *ontologisch* (*Leidenschaft*, 17–18). This early encounter sparked a long-standing, even if occasionally awkward, working relationship between advisor and apprentice which culminated in Jüngel's thesis *Paulus und Jesus*.

In Chapter 2 on Jüngel's intellectual and theological formation, we explore the so-called New Hermeneutic, shorthand for the programme for hermeneutical theology spearheaded by Fuchs and his close friend and collaborator Gerhard Ebeling (1912–2001) of Zürich. For this biographical sketch it will suffice to remark that over the course of his time in Berlin, Jüngel became convinced that the New Hermeneutic signalled a promising way forward for theology and the interpretation of Christian scripture. In *Paulus und Jesus* he attempts to unpack the full range of repercussions of the New Hermeneutic for the question of the relationship between Paul's preaching of the gospel of justification by faith and the Evangelists' portraits of Jesus of Nazareth. The dissertation reveals the significance of the teacher–student relationship for Jüngel's early theology, as even some of the vocabulary found in the work points back to Fuchs's technical studies of Paul. More than anything else, though, it was while researching and writing under Fuchs's tutelage that Jüngel discovered the necessity of coordinating the method of historical-critical exegesis and the task of Christian preaching. 'According to Fuchs', he writes, 'the historical-critical method has done its work only "when the necessity for preaching arises from the text." For it is in the sermon alone that we come to grasp the connection between the text's claim to truth and the human condition.'[11] The conviction that exegesis and theological reflection are subservient to proclamation runs through Jüngel's oeuvre from beginning to end.

In the preface to this guidebook, I narrated the story of Jüngel's 'illegal' semester spent abroad during the winter of 1957–1958. I will not reiterate here the details of his escape south, nor will I comment at length on the impact of his time with Ebeling, Barth and Heidegger on his subsequent career in theology, for such is a topic we will examine in Chapter 2. For our present purposes, it is worth noting that Jüngel studied with these luminaries right at the mid-point of his first round of coursework at the Kirchliche Hochschule. Taking into consideration the entirety of Jüngel's Berlin period, we get a good sense for what was, as it were, in the air during this particular season of post-war theology in German-speaking Europe. In Christian dogmatics, Barth was the centre of gravity, regardless of whether one perceived him as a muse or as a foil; in New Testament exegesis and hermeneutics, the school of Bultmann continued to exert enormous influence; in philosophy, Heidegger's thought, particularly what is found in later works written after he had turned his attention to the problem of language, was generating considerable attention. The young Jüngel took all of this in while advancing through the seminary curriculum. Influential teachers such as Vogel and Fuchs provoked the students to stay on top of the current theological discussions and shepherded them through matters of special intellectual difficulty. And, in Jüngel's case, it was Vogel and Fuchs who mediated contact with Barth and Ebeling, respectively, thus making possible Jüngel's semester in Switzerland. Should we expect anything other than that these looming figures from Jüngel's student days in the late 1950s and early 1960s – Vogel, Fuchs, Ebeling, Barth, Heidegger and, just slightly further afield, Bultmann and Käsemann – would remain key dialogue partners as his theological vocation unfolded? Indeed, we discover that Jüngel's time in Berlin at the Kirchliche Hochschule was profoundly significant for his intellectual and theological development. The concerns and interests which gave shape to that critical period in the history of modern German theology continued to inform his thought long thereafter.

Theology 'behind the wall' – lecturing at the Kirchliche Hochschule Ost-Berlin, 1961–1966

Jüngel completed his qualifying studies in the summer of 1961, and almost immediately the deteriorating political situation – in particular, the raising of the wall beginning that August – imposed itself upon the vocational maneuverings of the young doctor of theology. As Jüngel explains:

> I became a theological teacher literally overnight as a result of the building of the Berlin Wall. When Erich Honecker built the Berlin Wall on the orders of Walter Ulbricht and thus firmly cemented the division of Germany, the students of the Kirchliche Hochschule living in East Berlin were cut off from their professors, who lived in West Berlin. In order to meet the emergency which thus arose, Kurt Scharf, who later became a bishop, appointed me a theological teacher. I had only gained my doctorate in theology a few weeks before and

therefore was hopelessly badly prepared. It was the same for my friend Hermisson, and the then Bishop of Magdeburg, my friend Demke, found the same thing. A time of hard lubrications began. What nights we worked! Often I did not know in the evening what I would be lecturing on in the morning.[12]

Jüngel approached the rigours of academic responsibility with a clear-headed commitment to his vocation and to the mission of the church as a beacon of truth encircled by the darkness of Stalinism. At one point soon after the wall went up, he was offered a means of escape by a Jewish friend with connections in the Israeli intelligence community. 'My place is here now, in East Berlin', Jüngel responded.[13] Ultimately, it was his dedication to his students and to the cause of Christian theology that enabled Jüngel to carry on with confidence. The young lecturer and his students established 'a common theological existence', as he later put it, starting each day 'by returning once again to the beginning given to us' in the word of the gospel.[14]

Jüngel began his teaching career at the hastily reorganized Kirchliche Hochschule Ost-Berlin (which was housed in the Sprachenkonvikt in the area of the city now known as Berlin-Mitte) as lecturer in New Testament studies, the discipline of his doctoral dissertation. Due to the political circumstances, he expedited his Habilitationsschrift on the origins of the problem of analogy in the writings of the pre-Socratic philosophers Parmenides and Heraclitus (published in 1964; available in *TE II*, 52–102), completing the work in early 1962, just six months after the commencement of his lectureship. Jüngel also was ordained in 1962 as a rostered minister in the Evangelische Kirche in Berlin-Brandenburg. Upon receiving his promotion, he transitioned from lecturing in New Testament to systematic theology in 1963, remaining in that position until his departure three years later. Jüngel nearly left Berlin in 1964 to take a position on the faculty at the University of Greifswald, still in the DDR, but the arrangements failed to materialize. He finally left the city in 1966 after receiving an appointment as full professor for systematic theology and church history at the University of Zürich. In all, Jüngel was in Berlin for eleven formative years (1955–1966), first as a seminarian, then as a doctoral student, next as a lecturer in the newly reorganized seminary and finally, during what would be his last full academic year, as rector of the Sprachenkonvikt. Among his students during this period was Wolf Krötke, just a few years Jüngel's junior, who would go on to have a long and celebrated career in Christian theology, first at the Sprachenkonvikt and later at Humboldt University.

Jüngel's Berlin period offers us a glimpse, as it were, behind the wall, revealing some interesting insights into the intellectual and theological climate of the eastern sector of the city and of the DDR as a whole during the height of the Stalinist hegemony. On one hand, the study of theology at the Sprachenkonvikt unfolded at its normal pace and according to well-established standards for pedagogy, research and academic writing. We already have noted that Jüngel and his students devoted themselves to 'beginning anew each morning': that is, to carrying on with the tasks of theology notwithstanding the stifling political circumstances. Also, aside from his remarkable industriousness and the technical proficiency characterizing his prose, Jüngel's writings from the Berlin period exhibit a trend of early career publishing familiar to students of modern theology in both its European and Anglo-American contexts – a dissertation, a Habilitationsschrift, an additional technical monograph (*Gottes Sein ist im Werden*; ET: *Becoming*) and two dozen or so short pieces. The thematic range spanning these texts is hardly astonishing, with Jüngel devoting his critical energies to the quest for the historical Jesus, the problem of analogy, Barth's trinitarian theology, the relationship between law and gospel, hermeneutics, sacramental theology and the scientific character of Christian dogmatics, all topics of wide interest in European theology in the 1950s and 1960s.

In spots, however, we discover Jüngel homing in on the theme of freedom, specifically on the significance of the concept of Christian freedom for theological existence in profoundly *un*free times. For chief instance, soon after receiving his appointment as full professor at Zürich, Jüngel composed an essay on 'Der Freiheit der Theologie' – 'The Freedom of Theology' (*TE II*, 11–33), a piece originating as a lecture he presented to an Evangelische Kirche in Deutschland (EKD) committee on 'Scripture and Proclamation'. EVZ-Verlag published the lecture as a free-standing tract in its acclaimed Theologische Studien series. In the essay he endeavours to show how the *liberating* truth of the gospel impacts the nature and tasks of theology at every point. Of particular note, Jüngel argues that the mark of freedom affords the theologian the *courage* to faithfully think, speak, write, act and hope. Such a claim gains significance when read against the backdrop of Jüngel's formative years in Berlin, during which time his own theological existence was ever threatened by the oppressiveness of the East German state. Demonstrably so, he never laid aside this commitment to freedom as the most prominent feature of Christian theology.

Jüngel's career as public theologian, churchman and scholar

From the time he transitioned from Berlin to Zürich until roughly his eightieth birthday, Jüngel's vocational life unfolded as one might expect for a professor of theology in the European research university system. Rather than chronicling these decades year-by-year or even season-by-season, for the sake of our purposes here I summarize the highlights of Jüngel's career in three categories: academic service and honours, church service and ecumenical work, and publications.

Jüngel spent three years in Zürich before moving in 1969 to Tübingen to take the position of full professor of systematic theology and philosophy of religion on the faculty of Protestant theology. He received a simultaneous appointment as director of the Institut für Hermeneutik, established in Tübingen three years earlier by Ebeling as a centre of research for the then burgeoning discipline of hermeneutical theology. The transition to Tübingen moved Jüngel to the very centre of the theological world of post-war Germany. Jüngel recalls receiving a postcard while he was still in Zürich from New Testament theologian Ernst Käsemann, who taught at Tübingen throughout the 1960s. 'In Zürich you sit in your ivory towers', Käsemann had written. 'But in Tübingen you will be in the middle of the arena – right where you belong. So come!'[15] Indeed, arriving as he did on the heels of the student riots of 1968 and early 1969, Jüngel discovered in Tübingen a lively, even raucous academic atmosphere. Moreover, full professors of Christian theology at Tübingen frequently were called upon to speak publicly on issues at the intersection of faith and contemporary culture. Alongside other prominent colleagues such as Jürgen Moltmann, Hans Küng and Walter Kasper, Jüngel often found himself wearing the hat of 'public intellectual'. With increasing regularity as his career at Tübingen advanced, Jüngel supplemented his normal academic work with a variety of activities at the 'popular' level – public lectures, published sermons, magazine articles, newspaper interviews and so on.

Jüngel served as professor of theology at Tübingen from 1969 until his retirement in 2003. Over the years he lectured on a host of topics in systematic theology: prolegomena, doctrine of God, creation, Christology, the doctrine of the Holy Spirit, justification, ecclesiology and eschatology, to name but a few. For the sake of his lecturing responsibilities he developed a rigorous routine for addressing whatever topic happened to be at hand. Jüngel began by drafting a set of theses on the topic, covering as much ground as he hoped to explore during the course of the semester. During class sessions he would use the collection of theses as a springboard for further elaboration, commentary and instruction. The method ensured that students received a comprehensive introduction to the topic. Jüngel published several theses collections over the years, and these pieces give us a window into his approach to theological pedagogy. Painstakingly detailed and carefully organized, the 'theses essays' demonstrate that Jüngel was committed to the task of regular dogmatics in the laboratory of the theological classroom.

As a full professor, Jüngel's contribution to the theological and pedagogical climate at Tübingen extended well beyond the lecture hall. Jüngel gave numerous papers and addresses representing the Protestant faculty of theology both within the context of the university and abroad. He supervised a number of doctoral students over the years, held various administrative responsibilities and served on committees both within and without the department of theology. In short, during his time in Tübingen Jüngel was a key decision maker in the department and in the university at large, a public figure who represented the university at the local and national levels, and, increasingly so as his career unfolded, an internationally recognized scholar whose work in constructive dogmatics contributed to the university's reputation as a leading centre for the academic study of Christian theology. As per a long-established practice in the German university system, Jüngel drafted assistants to help him complete his responsibilities in the department and for the academy. He developed notoriety for demanding of his apprentices late hours and heroic effort. Several of his assistants went on to have long and storied academic careers. To name but a few: Dr Hans-Anton Drewes was director of the Karl Barth-Archiv in Basel from 1998 to 2012; Prof. Dr Ingolf U. Dalferth, who has authored dozens of monographs in systematic and philosophical theology, is formerly full professor of theology and director of the Institute of Hermeneutics and Philosophy of Religion at the University of Zürich, and remains, at the time of this writing, Danforth Chair in Philosophy of Religion at Claremont Graduate University; Prof. Dr Hans-Peter Großhans served as study secretary for theology and church at the Lutheran World Federation (LWF) before receiving an appointment as full professor of theology at Münster; and Prof. Dr Dirk Evers, who has made numerous contributions to the evergreen discussion between theology and science, is full professor of systematic theology and philosophy of religion at Martin-Luther-Universität Halle-Wittenberg.

In 1987 Jüngel was appointed director of the Evangelische Stift Tübingen, remaining in that role until 2005. Founded in the sixteenth century and housed in a building once used as an Augustinian monastery, the Stift, which is operated by the Evangelische Landeskirche in Württemberg, offers students of Protestant theology an opportunity to live and work in close community during their years preparing for Christian ministry. Johannes Kepler, J.A. Bengel, Friedrich Hölderlin, G.W.F. Hegel, Friedrich Schelling, F.C. Baur and D.F. Strauß all took up residence at the Stift while at Tübingen. As director, Jüngel was responsible for representing the Stift in the university and in the public at large, mediating between the community of students and the governing body of the Landeskirche, awarding the entry scholarship to seminarians, giving shape to day-to-day operations and activities, and shepherding students as they advanced through the seminary curriculum.

Over the course of Jüngel's career at Tübingen he was awarded numerous academic and civic accolades and honours: memberships in several international learned societies (the Heidelberg Academy of Sciences and Humanities [from 1981], the Norwegian Academy of Science and Letters [from 1987], the European Academy of Sciences and Arts [from 1991], the Göttingen Academy of Sciences and Humanities [as corresponding member since 2001] and the Institute for Advanced Study in Berlin [as fellow from 1999 to 2000]); enrolment in the Ordens pour le mérite for Sciences and the Arts in 1992, joining Adolf von Harnack, Albert Schweitzer, Gerhard von Rad, Rudolf Bultmann and Karl Rahner as the only Christian theologians ever invited to join that august company; and honorary doctorates from Aberdeen (1985), Griefswald (2001) and Basel (2002). He was named dean of the Protestant faculty on two occasions, serving in this capacity from 1970 to 1972 and from 1992 to 1994. In 1985 he was appointed as deputy judge on the constitutional court of the State of Baden-Württemberg. The following year, Jüngel was honoured as the inaugural recipient of the Karl Barth Prize, a prestigious award bestowed every other year by the Union Evangelischer Kirchen to scholars whose work, in the spirit of Barth, has advanced the cause of Christian dogmatics and ecumenical theology. In 1994 he was awarded the großen Verdienstkreuzes mit Stern – the Great Cross of Merit, with Star; one of the classes of the Order of Merit of the Federal Republic of Germany. In 2000 Jüngel received the Order of Merit of the State of Baden-Württemberg. In the years following his retirement from Tübingen he was recipient of consecutive appointments in Heidelberg (as director of the Forschungsstätte der Evangelischen Studiengemeinschaft, from 2003 to 2006; and as Hans-Georg Gadamer Chair in Theology, from 2007). From 2009 to 2013 he served as chancellor of the Ordens pour le mérite for Sciences and the Arts.

During the long plateau of his university career, Jüngel received a number of official ecclesial appointments. As I already have mentioned, he was ordained in the Evangelische Kirche in Berlin-Brandenburg in 1962, and from the very start of his professional life he conceived his academic work and university service as equally ingredient to his vocational commitment to the church's mission and ministries. It is, therefore, hardly surprising that he would be tapped to support the church in several formal contexts. In 1972 he was elected to the synod of the Evangelische Kirche in Deutschland (EKD), the governing body of that federation of German churches. He served on the 126-member synod for 29 years. A decade later, in 1981, he became chairman of the theological commission of the Evangelische Kirche der Union (EKU). In 1992 he received two appointments in the EKD: chairman of the theology cabinet and membership on the cabinet for public action.

A few words on the EKD and the EKU are in order here, as the historical and confessional make-up of each body helps to shed light upon Jüngel's own public theological commitments. The EKD is an organization of Protestant – Lutheran, Reformed and Union – denominations and regional churches, formed in 1948 in an effort to unify German Protestantism following the difficult period of the Third Reich and the war. The EKD serves as an excellent example of a successful ecumenical federation. While member churches share a common public witness through the work of the synod, cabinets and committees, and through pulpit and altar fellowship, each church retains its own distinct polity and government, territorial jurisdiction and confessional and theological identity. The majority of member churches and individual members (including Jüngel) consider themselves to be Lutheran. At the level of the federation, however, ecclesial, confessional and theological distinctives are set aside for the sake of a united witness. The EKU, the Prussian Union of Churches, which formally dissolved in 2003 in order to join the newly formed Union Evangelischer Kirchen (UEK), originated in 1817 at the behest of Frederick William III as a union of Lutheran and Reformed churches in territories then governed by the Kingdom of Prussia. The EKU survived for nearly two centuries in spite of numerous internecine conflicts, several reorganizations and two schisms. The Prussian Union faced its greatest challenge with the rise of Nazism in 1933, when a host of pastors and congregations declared allegiance to Hitler, while many others broke away to help form the Confessing Church. During the last half of the twentieth century, the EKU struggled to maintain its fragile unity in the face of a divided Germany. In due course several of the regional churches elected to form independent polities, and the divisions by and large fell according to the doctrinal dissensuses of the sixteenth century between the Lutheran and Reformed wings of Protestantism. The story of the EKU thus embodies the uneasiness of the communion model of ecumenical engagement, where geographical, political and doctrinal tensions often can mitigate the spirit of ecumenical openness.

It is essential to have this lay of the German ecclesial landscape in mind when considering both Jüngel's identity as a Lutheran theologian and his contribution to recent developments in Lutheran dogmatics. Readers in Britain and North America are accustomed to modes of jurisdictional cartography which differ considerably from what one discovers upon surveying historical and contemporary trends in German Christianity. For instance, even though Protestant Christianity in North America today includes a handful of loose federations and communions between major denominations, nothing remotely resembling the EKD or the EKU or the UEK – that is, a single ecclesiastical organization encompassing regional churches of the various strands of magisterial Protantism – has emerged. Indeed, it is difficult to envision such a union of Protestant churches flourishing on North American soil. After all, many American and Canadian Protestant denominations arose from the European migration movements of the late nineteenth century, and to this day the echoes of ethnicity, culture and language resound. When likewise we consider long-standing differences over doctrine and polity, it hardly is surprising that the map of North American Protestantism features sharp boundaries between denominations and traditions. If there is an exception to this rule, it is the peculiar phenomenon of American evangelicalism, a coalition of Protestant churches and individual Christians loosely coordinated around a nest of theological, practical and political positions. American evangelicalism, however, has no ecclesiastical *Doppelgänger* in German Christianity, nor does it in any way bear a family resemblance to the EKD, the EKU or similar unions of European churches.

In the context of British and North American Protestantism, the distinctions between Lutheranism, Reformed Protestantism, Methodism, Anglicanism, and so on, are, as a rule, relatively clear-cut. Such is not the case in Europe, where very different historical, political and pedagogical circumstances have given rise to unique expressions of ecumenical cooperation. Jüngel's commitments to church and university must be considered in light of this contrast. During his years of professional activity, he was not a Lutheran theologian in the same way that a professor of Christian theology at a college or university affiliated with one of the North American

Lutheran denominations serves her or his church. Rather, as a professor at a major state-funded research university, and as an officer in the governing bodies of two pan-Protestant unions, Jüngel's highest commitment was to the public witness of united Protestantism. His published theological work also exhibits this arrangement of ecclesial interests. Rarely in his writings do we find Jüngel toeing the party lines laid out in the Lutheran confessional documents from the sixteenth century. Indeed, and perhaps surprisingly, citations from the documentary deposit of early Lutheranism are virtually absent from Jüngel's publications. Nor does he limit his roster of supportive interlocutors to theologians of Lutheran vintage. On the contrary, Jüngel's theological work is in dialogue with and contributes to the enterprise of modern German *Protestant* thought before it exemplifies developments within the trajectory of Lutheran dogmatics since the reformation.

All of this helps to explain as well the unusual role Jüngel played in the unfolding story of the modern ecumenical movement. 'Jüngel is not representative', Catholic theologian and ecumenist Otto Hermann Pesch once grumbled in the context of an interaction with Jüngel's examination of the question of the church's sacramentality.[16] The observation epitomizes the difficulty of locating Jüngel's ecumenical contribution. Liberated from the strictures of binding confessions and church constitutions, Jüngel approached ecumenical work as a constructive Protestant theologian engaged with the broader Christian tradition, rather than as a proxy for the Lutheran stream of historical Protestantism. André Birmelé, a French theologian and ecumenist who has served the LWF for decades at the level of the international bilateral dialogues, remarks that 'even though [Jüngel] has never been a member of any official dialogue commission, his ongoing, critical commentary on the ecumenical movement has played a decisive role'.[17] Along these lines, in one spot Jüngel describes himself as 'the thorn in the flesh of Protestant theology' (*Essays I*, 191), at least in regard to the ecumenical impasse under discussion. As we will explore later on, it is particularly for the sake of clarifying the terms of the late twentieth-century dialogue between Catholics and Lutherans over the doctrine of justification that Jüngel's activity as ecumenical provocateur and gadfly intrudes upon the scene. For the purpose of the present chapter, it will suffice to comment that we do well to esteem Jüngel as a major figure in the history of the modern ecumenical movement, even if his role was ever unsanctioned, peripheral and cantankerous.

Jüngel's identity as a churchman is not limited to the official positions he held in service to the EKD and the EKU nor to his unofficial participation in ecumenism. As an ordained minister, Jüngel often was called upon to preach in various contexts of Christian worship. Several volumes anthologizing his sermons are available, and these collections shed light upon the clarity and rigour of his homiletical work. One of the themes we will continue to revisit in this guidebook is the intimate connection between theology and proclamation, a prominent mark of Jüngel's thought and literary oeuvre. This feature strongly emerges in the published sermons, where we encounter Jüngel bringing theological insights to bear upon careful exegesis of the biblical texts, and vice versa. The sermon collections are notable also for featuring Jüngel's theological exegesis of the Old Testament. Citations from and interpretations of Old Testament passages are, as a rule, conspicuously uncommon in Jüngel's major theological writings. His anthologized sermons, however, demonstrate that Jüngel found much of interest in the Pentateuch (especially Exodus), the Psalms and the Major Prophets (mainly Isaiah).

Jüngel left behind a sizeable literary deposit. His key works have rightly taken their place within the canon of theological literature in the modern period. He has given us four major monographs, at least two of which – *God's Being Is in Becoming* and *God as the Mystery of the World* – are widely esteemed as essential texts in Christian theology from the latter half of the twentieth century. He published a host of shorter volumes and theological pamphlets, the latter contributing to the continuation of a literary tradition which had emerged in German theology between the wars.[18] For all the recognition his longer works have deservedly earned, it is, arguably, as a theological essayist that Jüngel was at his very best. During the long plateau of his academic career, he produced an extraordinary number of short pieces – articles, book chapters, published papers and reviews. As I will demonstrate, some of his most significant and enduring contributions fall within this segment of his oeuvre. In addition to these technical short works, he produced popular articles, a host of interviews, published sermons (as just mentioned) and lecture theses. Finally, we do well to note here that Jüngel served as editor for two leading German journals of Christian theology, *Zeitschrift für Theologie und Kirche* and *Zeitzeichen – Evangelische Kommentare zu Religion und Gesellschaft*. He also was a member of the editorial team of the fourth edition of the prestigious reference work, *Religion in Geschichte und Gegenwart*.[19]

I already have remarked that Jüngel's written prose tends either to delight or to exasperate his readers. Such reactions reflect the rhetorical idiosyncrasies which mark his writings at every point. Jüngel employed the written word to persuade rather than to teach or to explain, and from beginning to end he remained committed to a vision of theology lying at the crossroads of classical dogmatics and Christian proclamation. By consequence, Jüngel's prose bears its author's unique homiletical panache. As I mentioned in the preface to this guide, the German originals feature the stamps of Jüngel's skills at wordsmithery – alliterations, neologisms, wordplays, creative uses of italics, structural parallelisms, rhythmic cadences and so on. Jüngel also turns to devices such as irony, humour, hyperbole and even, on occasion, browbeating to achieve his points. To this reader of Jüngel's theology, at least, such features are among the primary reasons why his writings are so arresting.

Jüngel as a practitioner of 'irregular' dogmatics

My goal in this guidebook is to recommend, especially to readers encountering Jüngel's work for the first time, some strategies for reading his brilliant, but notoriously difficult, theological contributions. As I have indicated, for a variety of reasons anglophone readers just getting into Jüngel's oeuvre are likely to find him challenging, even impenetrable. But Jüngel rewards those who possess the patience, intellectual charity and imaginativeness necessary for pressing ahead. It is, of course, well beyond my capacity to cultivate such virtues in my own readers. What I can and will do instead is to attempt to tear down some of the obstacles which tend to inhibit readers from the very start. In the final section of this opening chapter, and in preparation for what lies ahead, let me advance an approach to Jüngel's thought by introducing a distinction which, to my mind, is essential for reading his publications well – namely, the distinction between what I will call, following Barth, 'regular' and 'irregular' dogmatics.[20]

In *CD* I/1, Barth draws a 'relative distinction' between what he dubs 'regular' and 'irregular' dogmatics. Barth's purpose in the passage is to acknowledge the 'regular' character of the *Church Dogmatics* and to outline the scientific conditions of any programme for the presentation of Christian dogma which, such as his own, 'aims at the completeness appropriate to the special task of the school, of theological instruction' (*CD* I/1, 275). In other words, for Barth, regular dogmatics 'is to be taught', and thus demands patient, orderly and comprehensive treatment of the theological topics, organized for the sake of pedagogical clarity. 'A regular or academic dogmatics', Barth thus writes, must cover the whole field in respect to the range of concepts and themes that are significant for Church proclamation, in respect of the biblical witness in which this proclamation has its concrete criterion, in respect of orientation to the history of dogmas and dogmatics, i.e., to the concrete forms of Church proclamation existing thus far, in respect of real and possible difficulties and contradictions that one will find in every individual question, and finally in respect of the implicit and explicit distinctness of the path of knowledge. (*CD* I/1, 276)

The statement neatly epitomizes the various tasks Barth undertakes and the concerns he addresses throughout the *Church Dogmatics*. It also helps to explain why Barth occasionally was accused of rekindling a *scholastic* vision for Christian theology. For Barth, the regular paradigm for dogmatics reflects the fact that 'it is part of the human reality of the Church that there has to be in it not just theology but also the theological school or the theology of the school (*theologia scholastica*), i.e., the theology which is practiced not just for free intellectual exchange but also for instruction' (*CD* I/1, 277).

Even a cursory overview of Jüngel's literary output reveals that he never attempted a programme of regular dogmatics. Jüngel taught theology for decades, lecturing and leading seminars on a number of theological *loci*. As I mentioned earlier, his literary deposit includes several published collections of 'theses' on particular topics, all of which originated as his outlines for comprehensive lecture series and seminars. Jüngel's published theses give us a tantalizing glimpse into how he addressed certain themes with depth and encyclopedic coverage in the context of university pedagogy. Apart from these fragmentary pieces, however, nothing in his oeuvre stands out as regular in approach and scope, at least as Barth describes the designation. Even Jüngel's major monographs are, as it were, occasional and provisional in character, homing in on timely, specialized topics (*Paulus und Jesus* and *God's Being Is in Becoming*) or bringing to close large trajectories of theological research (*God as the Mystery of the World* and *Justification*).

I propose that we get a good sense of the whole of Jüngel's contribution to modern theology, and also grasp the significance of particular contributions, by recognizing that his work falls into the second of Barth's categories: 'irregular' dogmatics. Barth's elaboration of this concept is worth citing at length:

By irregular dogmatics ... we mean the enquiry into dogma in which there is no primary thought of the task of the school and there is no primary concern for the completeness mentioned above. Dogmatics as free discussion of the problems that arise for Church proclamation from the standpoint of the question of dogma can and must be pursued in the Church outside of the theological school and apart from its special task. Such free dogmatics existed before there was the regular dogmatics of the school, and it will always have its own necessity and possibility alongside this. It will differ from it by the fact that it does not cover the whole ground with the same consistency, whether in respect of Church proclamation itself, the decisive biblical witness, the history of dogma, detailed systematics, or strictness and clarity of method. Perhaps for specific historical reasons it will take up a specific theme and focus on it. Perhaps it will be relatively free in relation to the biblical basis or its choice of results, and will take the form of theses or aphorisms, and will observe only partially or not at all the distinction between dogmatics and proclamation. Perhaps it will leave much to be desired as regards one respect or another, or even in many or all respects, it will be, and will mean to be, a fragment, and it will have to be evaluated as such. (*CD* I/1, 277)

Several aspects of Barth's description are pertinent to the study of Jüngel's theology, for they nicely encapsulate Jüngel's intellectual and theological manner. First, as Barth makes plain at the outset of the passage, irregular dogmatics is not *primarily* attentive to the needs of the classroom. To be sure, this does not mean that practitioners of irregular dogmatics fulfil their vocations only in non-academic contexts. Barth's point is that in irregular dogmatics, the focus of theological labour is on whatever particular problems happen to be at hand, rather than on the task of shepherding students through theological curricula. Consequently, works of irregular dogmatics seldom feature 'completeness' and 'consistency'. In what forms, then, do they appear? Rounding out the passage, Barth draws attention to several possibilities, at all points emphasizing the *freedom* of irregular dogmatics as compared to the rigidness of regular dogmatics. For instance, because the theologian is not encumbered by the need to unfold a comprehensive, coherent system of Christian thought, she or he is free to devote careful attention to specific themes. Hence, in the tradition some of the best examples of irregular dogmatics are tightly concentrated expositions of a topic or problem. Sometimes, though, works of irregular dogmatics take the form of 'theses or aphorisms', since the theologian has no need to commit herself or himself to a concrete, exhaustive programme for biblical exegesis or to some particular approach to the intersection of theology and preaching. The literary yield of an exercise in irregular dogmatics might even be *fragmentary*, Barth suggests, covering to some extent the item under consideration, but otherwise 'leav[ing] much to be desired as regards one respect or another, or even in many or all respects'. Barth's point in drawing this distinction hardly is to disparage the practice of writing irregular dogmatics. On the contrary, the passage directs the reader to one of the major demarcations in the literary deposit of theology, showing how texts falling on both sides of the divide satisfy particular intellectual conditions. Shortly: regular, *scholastic* (in Barth's sense) works of dogmatics are designed for the classroom; irregular works of *free* dogmatics may find ancillary use in the classroom but are written to address more immediate theological questions and concerns.

An earlier and, upon reflection, rather clumsy table of contents for this guidebook contained a unit in which I would attempt to 'systematize' Jüngel's thought by assimilating his insights beneath the headings of the classical theological *loci*. In due course I scuttled the outline. For Jüngel's theology resists systematization; he writes *irregular*, rather than regular, Christian dogmatics. Even though he taught theology throughout the duration of his career, he never wrote theology like a teacher. On the contrary, his published works more closely resemble extended theological *sermons* than they do textbooks, manuals and systematic expositions. As a rule, Jüngel aims in his written theology to persuasively advance the argument at hand and to arouse his readers to the significance of the mystery of God's self-disclosure in Jesus Christ. Only seldomly does he proceed into and through a given topic accumulatively, explaining to the reader the various building blocks of argumentation and clarifying the connections between them. He generally is unconcerned, too, with the task of tracing the lateral lines between different regions of Christian teaching. He assumes that, instead of explaining how, the 'body of divinity' hangs together. As a rule, Jüngel writes as if everything is at stake in the matter in front of him – his goal in the short space of an essay or pamphlet, or even in the capacious argument of a monograph, to convince the reader of this or that position. 'The urgent', to put it rather abstractly, determines the method, direction, pace, resources and outcome of each of his irregular theological exercises.

The sword cuts both ways, of course. For if the benefit of Jüngel's manner of writing theology is its power to persuade, its drawback is, as Webster puts it, a penchant towards intellectual 'monism'. Jüngel 'tends to adhere very closely to one intellectual strategy to the exclusion of others', Webster writes, 'and tends to emphasize the coherent, unitary nature of his material.'[21] Consequently, Webster observes, Jüngel's written works are marked by 'a fondness for the generalized proposition, a preference for the abstract, and an absence of exemplification',[22] among other stylistic features.

Webster offers such observations in his *Introduction* in order to express his 'fundamental anxiety about Jüngel's work'.[23] I reiterate them here in the hope of encouraging a particular pathway into Jüngel's publications. Jüngel, as I have argued, throughout his career wrote theology that fits comfortably within the paradigm of irregular dogmatics. If we recognize this from the start and read accordingly, we will overcome the gap between our expectations and what we actually find in the texts themselves – namely, we will come to expect, rather than be surprised by, the urgency of his prose, the colourfulness of his style and also the fragmentary character of his output. On the basis of anecdotal evidence and numerous anglophone reviews of Jüngel's works, I am convinced that the most common source of the bewilderment which often besets his readers is that he fails to meet their expectations. In particular, new readers tend to approach his work as if he were attempting to unfold a regular programme for Christian dogmatics. To be sure, over the course of his long career Jüngel wrote on just about every region of Christian doctrine. However, and as we shall see especially in our expositions of key texts in Chapters 3 and 4, his monographs and essays on particular topics are each, as it were, ad hoc – that is, written to address particular points or to contribute to hot conversations or to respond to alternative positions. And even though we can trace certain theological commitments and conceptual patterns across the canon of his written works, it hardly is possible to string his insights together in order to systematize his thought. I contend, rather, that the best way to fully appreciate what Jüngel is up to is to take each piece more or less on its own while keeping in mind the broad contours of his academic career and literary deposit. That is the strategy I employ in this guidebook. This chapter and the following one on Jüngel's intellectual and theological formation provide an overview of the man, his career and the backgrounds of his thought. This sets the stage for my expositions of Jüngel's four major monographs and eleven of his most important theological essays.

CHAPTER 2
JÜNGEL'S INTELLECTUAL AND THEOLOGICAL FORMATION

In this chapter, I endeavour to locate the genesis of Jüngel's theological contribution within the broad, complicated terrain of Christian theology in the modern period. For all intents and purposes, I deal here with the question of Jüngel's intellectual and theological *influences*. In the comments that follow, however, I deliberately avoid as much as possible using that word, 'influence', and its various inflected forms and related concepts. I hope to persuade you, rather, that there is yet a better way to think about Jüngel's intellectual and theological formation than to call attention to the debts he supposedly owes to particular influential forebears.

Let me move towards my own proposal for understanding the origins of Jüngel's thought by expressing some general cautions regarding what I will refer to here as 'genealogical' approaches to describing intellectual formation. Demonstrably so, such strategies are commonplace in the literature of anglophone scholarship in Christian theology, for it is not unusual to encounter talk of influences and indebtedness in secondary studies on key thinkers. And yet, one must exercise delicate care when employing genealogical metaphors for describing, framing or tracing the, ahem, origins of a theologian's thought. To be sure, it is ineluctably the case that every theologian – or anyone engaged in any intellectual labour, for that matter – is connected, we might say, by 'familial bonds' to others in antecedent, contemporaneous and subsequent generations. As such, it can be helpful for students of a given theologian to sketch a family tree, situating the individual at hand in the context of the intersecting lines of intellectual ancestry. Indeed, a careful consideration of the pedigree of a given theologian can yield a wealth of insight into the roots and implications of her or his theological interests, decisions and intellectual habits, and even can help to explain the genesis of certain stylistic and linguistic idiosyncrasies. On the other hand, an unhealthy or excessive fixation on genealogical theories can, at best, distract from the real business of dealing with the theologian's *theology* on its own terms, or, at worst, tacitly (or even explicitly) recommend that the theologian's theology is merely the product of some combination of her or his influences. As a rule of thumb, therefore, students of particular figures from the history of Christian theology, whether classical or modern, do well to employ genealogical metaphors cautiously, modestly and sparingly, utilizing them to highlight intellectual lineages whenever appropriate while keeping alert to the dangers that lurk when familial bonds and origin stories are overstated.

A number of anglophone studies of Jüngel's theology contain weighty comments on his theological and intellectual ancestry. Paul DeHart begins his fine volume on Jüngel's doctrine of God by detailing what he calls the 'theological "grand tour"' marking Jüngel's illegal semester abroad in 1957–1958, during which time, as I have detailed above, he visited Zürich, Basel and Freiburg, home to Ebeling, Barth and Heidegger, respectively.[1] DeHart underscores this significant episode from Jüngel's biography, arguing that the 'tour' neatly illustrates the fact that Ebeling, Barth and Heidegger, together also with Bultmann, Fuchs, Hegel and Luther, serve as the 'dominant intellectual influences' whose work decisively shaped Jüngel's theology.[2] Roland Spjuth offers a similar proposal in his comparative study of Jüngel and Scottish Reformed theologian Thomas F. Torrance, identifying Jüngel's 'theological mentors [as] Luther, Bultmann, and Barth', the analysis of whose thought is 'help(ed)' by 'Martin Heidegger's philosophy and the hermeneutics of Ernst Fuchs and Gerhard Ebeling'.[3] A bit differently, but moving in the same general direction, Mark Mattes suggests that Jüngel's indebtedness to Bultmann, Heidegger, Hegel, the New Hermeneutic theologians (Fuchs and Ebeling), and especially Barth, inevitably distorts his reading of Luther.[4] In the book *Vehicle for God*, Roland Zimany asserts that 'fundamentally, Jüngel's theology combines the thought of Karl Barth and Martin Heidegger … by uniting Heidegger's approach to language and thought with the content of Barth's theology'.[5] By so doing, Zimany argues, Jüngel successfully overcomes 'the half-century-old debate between the dialectical (Barthian) and existentialist (Bultmannian/early Heideggerian) poles of kerygmatic theology, by incorporating both of them into his own perspective'.[6] The thesis that Jüngel has drawn together the 'dialectical' and the 'existentialist' becomes the lens through which Zimany examines a number of particular aspects of Jüngel's thought. Moreover, he proposes that Jüngel, if read in just this way, has 'cultivated a fertile environment for sound theological thought in the future'.[7]

I hardly wish to dispute that forebears such as Luther, Hegel, Barth, Bultmann, Heidegger, Fuchs and Ebeling are significant for Jüngel's intellectual and theological formation and development. However, there is a common undercurrent running through the various genealogical theories of Jüngel's thought that gives me great pause. For in reading English-language secondary studies of Jüngel's work, one gets the impression that his theology is the yield of a relatively straightforward mixture of ingredients from his influences: Luther's forensic account of justification + Hegel's speculative Good Friday + Barth's doctrines of revelation and election + Bultmann's programme of demythologization + Heidegger's analysis of *Dasein* + the New Hermeneutic's turn towards language in theology = Jüngel; or some similar recipe. When laid out this way, the inadequacies and limitations of a clear-cut genealogical approach rise to the surface. To be sure, all of these forebears and the theological programmes and particular themes associated with them factor into the development of Jüngel's theology. But the careful reader of Jüngel's writings will discern that there is much more going on in his work than a clumsy hodgepodge of already tried and tested ideas.

More importantly and speaking generally, easy genealogical accounts of intellectual origins do not square with the extraordinarily complex phenomenon of theological formation. In his little book *The Practice of Catholic Theology*, Paul J. Griffiths explores some of the intellectual habits and contexts which give shape to emerging theology.[8] Griffiths nods to the fact that the earliest phases of theological development are marked by 'unoriginality' and 'pastiche'. Especially while they are learning to write their own theology, theologians evolve by imitating their literary and intellectual mentors. Such mimicry is far from controversial; indeed, Griffiths observes that imitation is part and parcel of other intellectual and artistic endeavours marked by advancement and the acquisition of skills: musical composition, poetry and cookery are the three he names.[9] In due course, the theologian – and likewise, as it were, the composer, the poet and even the cook – is able to speak with her or his own voice. In theology, borrowed locutions, idioms, insights and theologoumena either fall away or are assimilated as theological thought unfolds. And it is almost impossible to discern exactly how and when this complex process of winnowing and thriving takes place. In any event, imitation is *but one* of a number of interconnected habits and practices marking the formation and development of a theologian's theology. In spots scattered throughout his primer, Griffiths draws attention to several of these habits and practices: reading theology and the acquisition of fluency in the canon of theological literature, the development and mastery of theological vocabulary, participation in dialogue and theological debate, learning the art of asking questions and framing theological problems, making conceptual distinctions and integrating experience and reason, to name but a few. Griffiths's little handbook points to the fact that to learn and to participate in Christian theology is always to engage in a discourse. Theology, in just this sense, is *discursive*; the theologian 'run(s) around with words (from Latin, *discurrere*)',[10] ever engaging in an ongoing conversation about God and all things in relation to God. Moreover, relatedly, and as I have argued elsewhere, theology is *curricular*, 'acquired as knowledge over a deliberate course of study and thus well-suited for the practices and good habits of pedagogy'.[11] Theologians, then, learn and advance in theology through reading, talking, debating and writing, and in the throes of trial and error, and over the course of intellectual progress earned through the study of building blocks of material. To be sure, Christian theology typically (though not necessarily) also arises from and is deeply connected to faith's actions and practices – prayer, contemplation, silence, worship, liturgics, witness, proclamation and so on. More than any other factor, however, the essentially discursive character of theology preps the soil from which theological thought emerges and grows.

What this entails for the study of Jüngel's theology – or the study of *any* theologian's theology, for that matter – is that the best approach for describing the origins and evolution of his thought is to consider the *world of discourse* in which he learned the ropes of Christian theology and to which he contributed throughout his career. The sheer genealogical narratives common in anglophone Jüngel lore will not do, for, demonstrably so, they lead to oversimplified interpretations of the formation and development of his thought. What is needed, rather, is a survey of, as I put it in the first chapter, what was 'in the air' in German theology during Jüngel's formative Berlin period and his long commorancy in Tübingen.

Along these lines, my task in the present chapter is relatively modest. To exhaustively redraw the landscape of mid-twentieth-century German theology is the stuff of a doctoral dissertation or scholarly monograph or textbook on modern Protestantism, not a guidebook on a particular theologian. Instead, I labour here, in the first instance, to identify the various points of debate and discussion in mid-twentieth-century German theology and philosophy which furnished for Jüngel his intellectual bearings, and, in the second, to make some suggestions along the way for how to understand the development of his thought in light of these connections. I have identified nine significant talking points which gave shape to the world of discourse in which Jüngel participated during his formative years and as his theology continued to mature. While undoubtedly I could name others here, these nine abridgements of key long-running conversations will suffice to give readers a good sense for how Jüngel's thought fits into and contributes to the story of Christian theology. All of the figures from theology and philosophy noted above make appearances beneath these nine headings. We encounter them, however, in the contexts of larger patterns of theological or philosophical discourse, rather than as intellectual influences who simply furnish Jüngel with this or that idea or concept. Space demands that I cover much ground quickly. For each of these talking points, I provide a brief summary and some comments on the significance of the topic at hand for the study of Jüngel's thought.

Subjectivity and objectivity in philosophy and theology since Descartes

As indicated, it is beyond the scope of this guidebook to attempt to epitomize the sweep of philosophical and theological thought since the European Enlightenment and then to pinpoint Jüngel's contribution within that broad trajectory. It is enough to remark here that Jüngel was thoroughly well versed in the various movements and counter-movements marking philosophy and theology during the last three centuries, especially the intellectual developments unfolding in the universities of continental Europe. Jüngel's writings bear witness to his encyclopedic knowledge of the Enlightenment and its ongoing legacy. He draws upon key texts and interacts with numerous prominent thinkers from this long, complex period of intellectual history, and his works include extensive engagements with seminal figures such as Descartes, Spinoza, Leibniz, Kant, Fichte, Schleiermacher, Hegel, Schelling, Kierkegaard, Feuerbach, Marx and Nietzsche. He also cites with some regularity luminaries from the modern history of German letters, including Goethe, Schiller, Hölderlin, Rilke and Thomas Mann. Readers should not be surprised to learn that I will refrain from invoking the language of 'influence' to describe Jüngel's intellectual relationship with any of these figures. While, to be sure, he might favour this thinker over that one, I reiterate that it is better to approach his work as contributing to an extensive nexus of discourse than to attempt to trace lines of direct intellectual lineage.

In this and the next section, let me focus briefly on two interrelated features of the legacy of the European Enlightenment concerning which Jüngel especially is interested. First, since at least Descartes, philosophy has gone to great lengths to address the epistemological dilemma of the distinction between the knowing subject and the known object. At the heart of this ongoing discussion, which has encompassed several discreet periods of modern and postmodern thought, are questions about the nature of human understanding, judgement and perception, and the formation and identity of the self. Jüngel particularly is concerned throughout his writings to probe the theological consequences of this dilemma and to map out for the sake of Christian theology the fate of the Cartesian '*cogito*' ('I think') in idealism, dialectical materialism and phenomenology, and in the hermeneutics which flourished in philosophy after the twentieth-century 'turn to language'. We should not be surprised that Jüngel, having cut his theological teeth during an era when the philosophies of Heidegger, Gadamer and Ricœur, and the theologies of Barth, Bultmann, Bonhoeffer, Fuchs and Ebeling, were in the air, gravitates towards a hermeneutical reading of the problem of subjectivity. But it would be a mistake to suggest, as some have done, that Jüngel simply marries Heidegger's radical critique of subjectivity and later turn toward the problem of language with Luther's *theologia crucis* or Barth's doctrine of revelation or some theologoumenon otherwise. Jüngel, rather, negotiates his own path through this morass, proposing along the way that the subject–object dilemma inevitably leads us to the heart of the Christian confession itself.

Two dimensions of Jüngel's approach to this problem are worth flagging in this guidebook. First, during his years in Berlin immediately following the completion of his doctoral dissertation, Jüngel turned his attention to the question of whether and in what sense *God* can be known as an object – a point of dissension marking the long-standing dispute between Bultmann and Barth and their respective heirs. Both theologians rejected the idea that God is known as an object in a scientifically neutral sense. For his part, Bultmann ever worried that claims to 'objective' theological knowledge invariably evince the objectification of God. Accordingly, God, understood as an object of *knowledge*, is perceived as unconditionally accessible to the knowing subject. To this 'scientific' mode of knowledge Bultmann contrasts faith, which bears a different kind of relation to its object. 'Where science is concerned', he writes, 'God is unknowable'.[12] By contrast, 'there can only be talk of God on the basis of *revelation*, and revelation can only be heard in *faith*'.[13] While Barth may have agreed with Bultmann in principle that theology must find a way around the Scylla of scientific objectivity, he feared that Bultmann did not do enough to escape the snare of the Charybdis of theological *subjectivity*. Barth, that is, perceived that Bultmann gave away the store to the self-constituting subject in his efforts to sever theological knowledge from epistemic objectification.

One of the items on Jüngel's agenda in the early study *God's Being Is in Becoming* is to offer a close reading – as he puts it in the subtitle to the volume, a 'paraphrase' – of Barth's solution to this problem as it unfolds in the *Church Dogmatics*. Jüngel argues that, for Barth, God grants genuine theological knowledge to creatures in the form of a very specific mode of objectivity. In the event of divine self-revelation, God 'commandeers' a creaturely object and makes use of it as a 'sacrament', through it communicating God's being in becoming as Father, Son and Holy Spirit. To Jüngel's mind, in so distinguishing between God's 'primary' objectivity (God's self-knowledge) and 'secondary' objectivity (God's self-disclosure through the vehicle of a creaturely object), Barth evades the dangers on both sides of the subject–object dilemma and, in doing so, actually draws closer to Bultmann's position than either theologian ever recognized.[14]

Later on, and in his study *God as the Mystery of the World*, Jüngel addresses a second dimension of the modern problem of subjectivity and objectivity. In a pivotal section titled 'The Certainty of Faith as the Deprivation of Security' (*Mystery*, 169–184), Jüngel addresses what he considers to be the real quandary at the heart of the Cartesian grounding of subjectivity in the *cogito*. By establishing the 'I think' as the foundation of reality, Jüngel argues, Descartes identifies human thought with human being: *cogito, ergo sum*. But this ontological decision, Jüngel warns, leads to an expression of egocentricity of a vicious and idolatrous kind: namely, the *ego* becomes ensnared in an unbroken cycle of self-actualization through thinking. Is it any wonder, he comments, that Descartes's 'I think' gives way to the 'I (morally) act' of the high Enlightenment, and later to the 'I will' of Nietzsche and the 'I work' of Marxism and industrial capitalism? 'The thinker', as Jüngel abridges it, 'has become the producer, the maker. And this has happened, not although but because he thinks. The world now is only the pure object of the human subject' (*Mystery*, 178).

Jüngel acknowledges in the section that his reading of this trajectory hardly is original to him, and the footnotes throughout the passage reveal that he considers himself part of a tradition of analysis that includes, most recently, Heidegger, dialectical theology and the New Hermeneutic. Furthermore, in *God as the Mystery of the World* and elsewhere, he incorporates into his own contribution many of the responses philosophy and theology have offered in response to the Cartesian attempt to secure the self in the *cogito*: a revisionary approach to the enterprise of metaphysics, a rejection of the idea of truth as sheerly the correspondence of knowledge and object, an emphasis on existence as ever unfolding beneath the shadow of death, attention to the temporal character of human existence, a stress on the individual's life-in-the-world and the need for authenticity and so on. Jüngel, however, reimagines both the problem and its recommended solutions in light of the message of the crucifixion and resurrection of Jesus Christ. In the coming of God to the world in the resurrected Crucified One, and in the interruptive 'word of the cross' (1 Cor 1:18), God breaks into the 'life-continuity' (*Lebenszusammenhang*) of the *homo faber*, the human person ensnared by the deadly false assurance that the world can be mastered through human thought, will and action, and that the self can be actualized through works. We will continue to encounter the various features of this reading of the human condition as we move forward in this guidebook.

To be sure, Jüngel's work is deeply connected to the philosophical and theological worlds of discourse on subjectivity, epistemology, metaphysics and hermeneutics, as briefly described here. But it is not the case that he simply assumes, adopts and/or joins together ideas floated about during antecedent generations of intellectual history. Rather, it might be best to describe his programme as a thoroughgoing *critique* of modernity from the perspective of the confession of the crucified and resurrected Jesus Christ.

It is along these lines that we briefly may consider here Jüngel's intellectual relationship to Heidegger. Three English-language doctoral dissertations[15] and a handful of shorter pieces[16] have stressed the importance of Heidegger for Jüngel's theology. Jüngel certainly was well versed in Heidegger's writings, and a number of Jüngel's own publications contain extensive engagements with the philosopher's thought. I am not convinced, though, that Jüngel merely borrows from or repeats Heidegger's ontology and critique of ontotheology, redressing Heideggerian existentialism in Christian garb. A better and more accurate way to frame this intellectual relationship is put forth by Arnold Neufeldt-Fast, who builds upon comments made by Jüngel himself in several reflective pieces to suggest that we ought to think of Heidegger as serving for Jüngel as 'the *Anstoß* – that is, both impulse and offence – for a recognition of the dangers of metaphysics, *and* as one who *provoked* Jüngel to think theology from its own ground, that is, "to think God," to *think* faith and the being of humanity without beginning with the self-grounding subject of metaphysics'.[17] Neufeldt-Fast goes on in his analysis to highlight some striking parallels between Heidegger's philosophy and Jüngel's theology – namely, both Heidegger and Jüngel are troubled by classical metaphysical and philosophical approaches to human being, to time and historicity and to truth. At the same time, and as Neufeldt-Fast shows, because of his theological commitments, Jüngel departs sharply from Heidegger once he goes on to articulate how human being exists in time when confronted by the liberating truth of the word of God. To put all this in another vein, it might be best to consider Jüngel as being somewhat in league with Heidegger in terms of the *diagnosis*, both of the problem assailing the human person in the modern world and of modern thought's general failure to appraise that problem properly. But he is able to offer a very different *solution* than Heidegger by working out a theological account of the human condition and of the God who addresses us in the word of the justifying gospel.

Historical-criticism of the Bible

We spend some time in Chapter 4, considering a mid-career essay by Jüngel on the problem of the historical Jesus ('The Dogmatic Significance of the Question of the Historical Jesus'). In that piece, Jüngel makes some intriguing observations on how the Cartesian distinction between subject and object funds the scientific approaches to biblical scholarship, often shorthanded as 'historical-criticism', which have flourished since the Enlightenment. In particular, Jüngel is concerned in the essay to probe the assumptions about epistemology and historical consciousness which buttress the enterprise of historical-critical exegesis. The guild of sceptical, critical, historical scholarship on the Bible, he asserts, suffers from 'an *inappropriate concept of time*'. Animated by the Cartesian supposition of the ego mastering the world through thought, the guild conceives 'time as a *period of time*, as a spatial *length of time*, with which one can and must measure *distances* from the presently existing "I" and its here and now – distance which either date the past by measuring from the here and now backwards or date the future by measuring forwards [*sic*]' (*Essays II*, 104). By contrast, Jüngel argues, 'the relation between God and humanity does not allow itself to be gauged as a length of time which can be measured through a movement' (*Essays II*, 105). Rather, the word of divine address is 'the event of an *adventus* [coming] in which the *measurable* difference between before and after becomes meaningless' (*Essays II*, 106).

Demonstrably, these comments from 'Dogmatic Significance' serve as a tidy summary of the way Jüngel understands the interconnections between history, scripture, the reader and time. Jüngel took his formal theological training during a period in which many scholars, especially those inspired by Barth and Bultmann, had grown sceptical of the presuppositions and methods of historical-criticism. His own work resides within this larger pattern of discourse marking German theology at mid-century. In league with like-minded exegetes, he resists characterizing scripture as an inert object of study, its meaning ascertainable only by way of scientific research. Indeed, for Jüngel, inquiry into scripture's meaning by way of historical, scientific analysis effectively neutralizes scripture's potency. For it is in the event of the proclamation of scripture – that is, when we *hear* scripture preached – that God interrupts the very course of existence ingredient to which is our attempt to master the world (scripture included) through objective thought. For Jüngel, when we are willing to hear scripture as a living word, rather than devote our energies to investigating it as an impotent source of historical data, we might find ourselves irrevocably changed by the experience.

Given all this, it is ironic that many of Jüngel's suppositions about scripture are themselves the yield of historical-critical research. For instance, from comments scattered about his writings we gather that he accepts numerous critical consensuses regarding the provenances of particular biblical texts. He is alert to the fact that the units of scripture differ from one another theologically and would rather dwell upon such differences than attempt to ignore or to harmonize them.[18] At all points, he pays due attention to those aspects of the 'world behind the text' which inform exegesis. And even the problem of the continuity and discontinuity between the historical Jesus and the Christ of faith (a recurring theme in his work) is the outcome of a classical historical-critical conundrum: namely, how to reconcile the phenomenon of early Christian proclamation with the new understanding of first-century Judaism and Christianity earned through patient scientific research. In all this, we discover that Jüngel's negotiations between historical-critical exegesis and positive Christian dogmatics are fairly typical of theology undertaken in the context of the German university in the centuries following the *Aufklärung*. On one hand, in his own exegetical work Jüngel capitalizes on the findings of scientific research into the biblical texts. On the other, due to his theological commitments he is unafraid to assail quite sharply some of the central tenets of critical biblical scholarship. To read Jüngel's work is to dwell within this tension.

Having said all of this, there is one additional – and rather critical – comment that must be raised here. When considering Jüngel's exegetical engagements with the biblical texts, it is remarkable to note how conspicuously he is not 'up' on current trends in biblical studies. As we encountered in the biographical sketch in Chapter 1, Jüngel earned his doctorate in New Testament, not in dogmatics or systematic theology. As we might expect, *Paulus und Jesus* exhibits a command of contemporaneous literature on the Gospels and Paul's letters. To be sure, Bultmann, Käsemann, Fuchs and Ebeling stand out from the rest of the pack. But Jüngel the doctoral student did succeed in mastering the (albeit) select field of scholarship into which the dissertation made a lasting contribution. Following the publication of *Paulus und Jesus*, however, Jüngel never substantively expanded his mastery of the field of New Testament research. Bultmann, the 'Old Marburgers' and a handful of exegetes from mid-century reappear in his writings with some frequency. Beyond that narrow bandwidth of thought, though, Jüngel fails to venture. Consequently, readers of Jüngel likely will wonder what might have been had he engaged with the New Perspective on Paul, the so-called third quest for the historical Jesus, newfound apocalyptic readings of the biblical texts and so on. For better or worse, Jüngel's exegesis of scripture remained conditioned almost exclusively by the intellectual and theological climate of his formative Berlin period.

The reception of Luther's thought in modern Protestantism

Jüngel cites Luther more than any other figure from the early modern period. His little pamphlet on Luther from 1978, rendered in English under the title *The Freedom of a Christian*,[19] originated as a plenary address from the Fifth World Congress on Luther Research, which took place in Lund, Sweden, in August of 1977. He wrote several other short pieces on the reformer's theology, including the important (though as-yet untranslated) early essay, '*Quae supra nos, nihil ad nos*', written for a Festschrift for Ebeling (available in *TE II*, 202–251). Beyond a doubt, Luther is important for Jüngel. But it will not do to baldly claim that Jüngel borrows this or that concept from Luther, or that he takes pains simply to repristinate certain aspects of Luther's thought: for instance, Luther's *theologia crucis* or account of the hiddenness of God or doctrine of justification. Rather, in his engagements with Luther, Jüngel contributes to a long-running trajectory of the reception of Luther's theology in German scholarship, among Protestants in particular. In order to grasp Jüngel's use of the reformer, some comments on this larger pattern of discourse are in order.

To mark the occasion of the quatercentenary of Luther's birth, publisher Hermann Böhlau launched the Weimar edition of Luther's works, better known by its academic shorthand, the *Weimarer Ausgabe*. The availability of a critical edition of the reformer's writings inspired fresh interest in Luther's theology and its significance in the first half of the twentieth century. The 1910s and 1920s witnessed the flourishing of the so-called Luther Renaissance, a movement of scholarship incited by Karl Holl's (1886–1926) groundbreaking research on Luther's theology. For Holl and his followers, critical engagement with the writings of Luther served as a stimulus for constructive exercises in theology, exegesis, hermeneutics and ethics. During its salad days, the Luther Renaissance advertised itself as a genuine alternative to the dialectical theology emerging at the same time and associated with Barth, Bultmann, Gogarten, Brunner and others. As with the dialectical theologians, the Luther scholars of the period promised theological answers to modern dilemmas such as historical consciousness, the decline of metaphysics and the problem of religion. But here Luther, rather than, say, Barth's 'new world within the Bible', was viewed as a wellspring of insight and authority. While the spirit of the Luther Renaissance barely survived the periods of Nazi hegemony and the Second World War due to the political tensions marking those times, the international network of scholars of the reformer's thought reorganized itself in the 1950s. Gerhard Ebeling, with whom Jüngel was associated for most of his career, was active in the guild of Luther researchers during its second heyday, and in 1964 published the book, *Luther: An Introduction to His Thought*,[20] widely held to be among the most significant examples of German Luther scholarship from the twentieth century.

It is generally acknowledged that in several significant respects, Holl and his immediate followers set the tone for research into Luther's thought in the mid- and late twentieth century, particularly in Germany. For our purposes here, it is important to note some of the suppositions the scholars of the Luther Renaissance emphasized in their work on the reformer. First and foremost, Holl and his colleagues and heirs understood the reformation as a theological *revolution* which occurred when Luther 'discovered' the gospel of God's justifying righteousness, itself long concealed during the medieval period by the Church's suffocating edifice of a Christianity of works (or so the revolutionary story goes). As a result of this focus on Luther's so-called tower experience, the scholars of the Luther Renaissance fixated on certain themes they saw as emerging in the reformer's vast literary deposit: namely, a forensic account of the doctrine of justification, the location of the genesis of the reformation discovery as the problem of the guilty conscience, the deployment of the distinction between law and gospel to categorize all instantiations of speech and the theology of the cross (*theologia crucis*) as the crisis of metaphysics and of philosophical and theological speculation. Beyond all this, Luther scholarship of this ilk identified the reformer's tower experience as a key episode in the unfolding of Germany's national mythology. As a result, Luther's politics and, as it were, the geography of the reformation received special interest in academic circles throughout Germany's century of national crisis, both for good and (often enough) for ill.

As indicated, Jüngel's intellectual and theological formation took place in the period when Luther research in the tradition of Holl was in its second ascendancy. He does not mention reading Luther in any meaningful way during his time in Naumburg and his first years in Berlin. During his 'illegal' semester in Zürich, however, he was exposed to Luther's theology and to the field of Luther research through his apprenticeship with Ebeling. 'It was through Ebeling', he writes, 'that I really came to know Luther's works' (*Leidenschaft*, 21). Jüngel's own published research on Luther bears many of the hallmarks of the Holl–Ebeling trajectory. He turns to Luther when working out his own insights on forensic justification, the plight of righteousness according to works, the law–gospel distinction, the *theologia crucis* and the decline of metaphysics. He pays little attention, though, to aspects of the reformer's thought further afield from this tight nexus of issues. Demonstrably so, his reading of Luther's contribution and of the reformation in general fits well within the revolutionary paradigm popularized by Holl and his colleagues earlier in the century. And, although Jüngel never advocates for a nationalistic reading of Luther, it is somewhat disappointing that he nowhere acknowledges the dangers accompanying the reception of Luther as a German folk hero.

In my comments on historical criticism, above, I proposed that Jüngel never really moved beyond the New Testament scholarship that was in the air during his critically formative Berlin period. I submit that the same is true generally regarding his work on Luther. Aside from a few dismissive remarks he makes on the 'New Finnish School of Luther Research' in *Justification*,[21] he never substantively engages or really even acknowledges alternative interpretations of the reformer's contribution from the broad and variegated field of Luther studies. What we discover in Jüngel's work, rather, appears as a continuation of the kind of Luther reception that dominated German university culture for most of the last century. And perhaps more than any other scholar outside of Ebeling, Jüngel seeks to integrate the insights of that tradition of German Luther research into the discourse of Christian dogmatics. David Yeago has argued that works of theology at the intersection of German Luther scholarship and dogmatics tend to showcase certain exaggerated structural features:[22] the law and gospel distinction as a totalizing hermeneutic for making and critiquing theological statements, the criteriological use of the doctrine of justification, the prioritization of economy over theology and so on. Readers of Jüngel quickly will discover that such characteristics are indeed conspicuous throughout his theological writings.

The rise of modern atheism and the disappearance of God under Stalinism

As I pointed out in the biographical sketch in Chapter 1, Jüngel's theology was profoundly and lastingly impacted by his experiences coming of age in the DDR during the post-war period and learning and initially teaching theology in East Berlin in the 1950s and 1960s. It was during these decades immediately following the war that state atheism descended upon the DDR. While citizens were not prohibited from practising traditional religions, Marxist-Leninist atheism was the official policy of the East German state from its establishment in 1949 to its dissolution fifty-one years later. Jüngel's experience of the church as a beacon of truth shining forth in the darkness of state atheism and the atheistic state lies in the background of his career-long interest in atheism as a theological problem. In fact, had Jüngel not endured his adolescence and young adulthood in the DDR, it is likely that we would be without some of the key texts from the canon of his writings. In particular, the argument of *God as the Mystery of the World* depends upon the 'dispute between theism and atheism' mentioned in the book's subtitle. And the other monographs and numerous essays take for granted that the reader is well versed in the story of modern atheism from its emergence in the form of philosophical atheism in the works of figures such as Feuerbach, Marx and Nietzsche to the flowering of state atheism in the mid-twentieth century. The world of discourse at the intersection of atheism and the Christian confession is a pivotal component of Jüngel's theological contribution.

Upon first glance, readers of Jüngel's theology in Britain and North America are likely to find his writings on atheism disorienting and even a bit off target. The first two decades of the twenty-first century have witnessed the rise of the militant 'new atheism' popularized in the anglophone world by public intellectuals such as Richard Dawkins, Christopher Hitchens and Sam Harris. The new atheism combines a wide-ranging critique of traditional religious beliefs with confidence in science's ability to solve the various problems besetting human civilization. By consequence, theistic responses to the new atheism generally seek to shore up the rational, epistemic and ethical warrants for religious belief, and to undercut what is viewed as a burgeoning *over*confidence in science and scientific method. Jüngel's response to atheism hardly squares with these current debates. He is uninterested in mounting an apologetic defence of religion on rational grounds. Moreover, although he contributed a number of short pieces to the ongoing discussion in the German academy about the *wissenschaftlich* – 'scientific' – study of theology in the modern research university alongside other fields, on the whole he seems content for theology to play the 'fool in the house of the sciences', as he memorably puts it in the title of a late-career essay.[23] For Jüngel, theology's principal task is to hear the word of God and reiterate it, and as such theology scarcely is obliged to engage, debate or collaborate with the sciences, unless such interaction befits the cause of Christian proclamation. He thus is highly allergic to the kind of militant apologetics funding today's dispute between religious philosophers and proponents of the new atheism.

Jüngel is keen to take atheism seriously on its own terms and to treat atheists with a high level respect, a disposition resulting not least from his experience with his brother, Rainer's atheism. 'My brother, who is a genuine atheist and not only older, but also stronger, than I am, would probably still threaten to give me a good hiding if I were to call him a defective human being,' he jests in one spot. But Jüngel immediately turns serious and theological: 'The proclamation of the justification of the godless can hardly thrive in the soil of such apologetic religious propaganda. Anyone who has to talk about the overcoming of godlessness by God will do better to take the atheist seriously as a particularly mature form of the *homo humanus*.'[24] All of this helps to explain the basic drift of Jüngel's approach to the challenge of atheism: namely, by taking the atheist as seriously and respectfully as possible, Jüngel endeavours to capitalize upon the genuine *insight* he discovers at the heart of the trajectory of classical atheism, using that insight to stimulate a self-critical posture in Christian dogmatics.

As I will demonstrate in my summary of *God as the Mystery of the World* in Chapter 3, this pathway into the problem of modern atheism sets up Jüngel's assertion of the advent of God in Jesus Christ as the world's mystery. To shorthand the argument for now: in Jüngel's reading, Christian theology must take atheism seriously insofar as it calls into question the metaphysical deity of classical theism. He enlists Fichte, Feuerbach and Nietzsche to show that the atheism which burgeoned in the eighteenth and nineteenth centuries assumed both the possibility of the self-grounding of human thought in the Cartesian *cogito* and the ontological prioritization of essence over existence. Indeed, Jüngel shows that these two assumptions are intertwined. The self-constituting 'I think' cannot tolerate the notion of a divine essence subsisting apart from the existence of God in the world. But this entails that since nothing is above or beyond us, the *cogito* can no longer ground its security in the metaphysical idea of God. Jüngel explains that his trio of atheists represents the successive steps from the establishment of the 'I think' to the death of the idea of God, metaphysically defined. Fichte recognized the imminent evaporation of the idea of God and suggested that God not be thought at all. Feuerbach countered that we must think God, but only the basis of human existence extended 'to the heights of divine essence' (*Mystery*, 151). Nietzsche went even further by asserting that our thought of God *just is* the elevation of human existence. There is no divine essence, only the 'superman' (*Übermensch*): 'God hath died; now do we desire – the superman to live.'[25] Again, what Jüngel works out in the units of *God as the Mystery of the World* subsequent to this summary of the atheistic rejection of metaphysical theism is an argument that cuts against *both* atheism *and* classical metaphysics. Or better: for Jüngel, the Christian confession of the death of Jesus Christ, the God-man, puts to death the metaphysical God at the heart of the modern dilemma of atheism. By sticking to its Christological confession, he contends, faith can conceive the challenge of atheism as a genuine opportunity to revise its own metaphysical assumptions.

A host of themes come together in Jüngel's career-spanning response to classical atheism, so understood. As we encountered already in the first section of this chapter, he proposes that the Christian confession upends Cartesian certainty by declaring that the attempt to ground reality in the *cogito* leads to idolatry of an abject sort. Also, from his early close readings of Barth's *Church Dogmatics* onward, Jüngel has asserted that the Christian doctrine of the trinity demands that we think of the existence and essence of God as a unity, a theme to which we will return in our analysis of *God's Being Is in Becoming* in Chapter 3. In addition, many of Jüngel's explorations in political theology are located here – namely, his approaches to the relationship between church and state[26] and to the challenge of secularization,[27] and his understanding of Christian worship as a *public* event of proclamation.[28]

Karl Barth's theology and its legacy

It is not easy to quantify the impact Karl Barth (1886–1968) had on mid-twentieth-century Protestant theology and on the theologians 'after Barth', among whom Jüngel often is ranked, and who often are credited with extending strings of theology which Barth originally unwound in the *Church Dogmatics*. Jüngel himself comments on the *quality* of Barth's impact: 'Barth's personal and literary influence profoundly changed the shape of Christian theology across confessional boundaries, significantly altered the direction of the Protestant church, and also left an unmistakable imprint on the political and cultural life of the twentieth century. Barth defied both the enduring and the passing currents of his time, even as he was conditioned by them.'[29] While Jüngel nowhere mentions reading Barth while a student at the Oberseminar in Naumburg, it is difficult to imagine him not encountering Barth as he advanced through the seminary curriculum. In any case, we know that Barth's theology was in the air in Berlin at the turn of the 1960s, thanks due in large part to the efforts of his friend Vogel. As mentioned earlier, it was Vogel who arranged for Jüngel to study with Barth during the 'illegal' semester in Switzerland in 1957–1958.

I have written at length elsewhere on the personal friendship and intellectual relationship between Barth and Jüngel.[30] By all accounts, the elderly Barth and the young Jüngel grew fond of each other during the latter's time abroad after an inauspicious first meeting during which Barth, as Jüngel put it later, regarded his German guest as a 'spy from the Bultmann school'. Jüngel quickly turned that first impression on its head in a session of Barth's seminar by adroitly interpreting a passage from the *Church Dogmatics* in defence of one of Bultmann's positions. Barth invited Jüngel 'to another dispute in the late evening over a bottle of wine',[31] the first of many conversations between the two during Jüngel's time in Switzerland. Barth would go on to sing Jüngel's praises in the official documentation he prepared for the Sprachenkonvikt. 'In my opinion, he is without a doubt one of a small number of students whose academic advancement is well warranted.' 'He has distinguished himself by a quick comprehension and an independent style of research', Barth writes, 'and is developing a challenging dissertation topic.'[32] Jüngel recalls that Barth even proposed that he remain in

Switzerland and become Barth's doctoral student. 'Barth wanted me to stay in Basel', Jüngel reports. 'He gave me a set of the *Church Dogmatics*, inscribing it, "To Eberhard Jüngel, on his way to God's beloved Eastern Zone." And then he asked if I did not want to stay in Switzerland after all.' Jüngel, however, was constrained by financial and political circumstances. 'I said to Barth, "I cannot stay"', Jüngel recalls, 'and explained to him that I had no money. But Barth replied, "I will rent you an apartment and pay the entire cost." While that was extraordinarily generous of him, when I explained that I was in Switzerland illegally and could get away with only one semester abroad, Barth understood immediately' (*Leidenschaft*, 25). Jüngel returned to Berlin, of course, and eventually chose Fuchs to supervise his dissertation in the field of New Testament studies. But he and Barth remained in contact until Barth's death in 1968. And Barth continued to laud Jüngel's emerging scholarship, in one place commenting that Jüngel is 'one among today's younger theologians who has studied me thoroughly and has the willingness and ability to do independently and fruitfully the further work which is needed today'.[33]

It is difficult, and even unnecessary, to attempt to pinpoint the significance of Barth for the theologians working in his wake. If I might dare draw an analogy from popular culture, it is not unlike searching for explicit lines of influence between, on one hand, Chuck Berry, the Beatles, Bob Dylan, the Rolling Stones, and so on, on the other, artists from subsequent generations of popular and rock music. Barth pioneered and broadcasted a new mode for thinking theologically, and his work, as it were, set the tone both for his contemporaries and for those who followed. As I have indicated, Jüngel frequently is identified as a theologian 'after Barth', that is, as one among a handful of scholars from the latter half of the twentieth century whose work carries on Barth's legacy. He moved up the academic ranks in Berlin during a time when Barth's work was heavily studied and vigorously debated. Moreover, Jüngel became part of an inner circle of younger theologians in whom the elderly Barth placed great hope. And certainly Jüngel remained committed throughout his career to exploring and engaging Barth's contribution. However, I propose that we do justice neither to Barth nor to Jüngel by insisting that the latter simply repeats the work of the former. In our investigations of *God's Being Is in Becoming* and the early essay 'Die Möglichkeit theologischer Anthropologie auf dem Grunde der Analogie', we witness how Barth served for Jüngel as both muse and goad, provoking him to strike his own course through the thicket of themes at the heart of both texts: namely, the doctrines of revelation and trinity, and the problem of analogy. We discover that Jüngel draws inspiration from Barth regarding these themes, even as he sharply diverges from Barth on certain points. The pattern holds elsewhere in Jüngel's engagements with Barth's Christology[34] and his understanding of human ethical action in response to divine revelation.[35]

I would be remiss if I did not mention one particularly thorny instance of this tension between inspiration and departure.[36] A number of anglophone studies on Jüngel assert or assume that he was utterly convinced by Barth's late turn towards credobaptism. According to such readings, Barth's argument in *CD* IV/4 is paradigmatic of Jüngel's own approach to the doctrine of baptism and, more generally, to sacramental theology. In the late 1960s, Jüngel wrote a handful of analytical essays on Barth's fragment on baptism. Careful scrutiny of these pieces reveals that Jüngel indeed found much to admire in *CD* IV/4, especially the sharp distinction Barth draws between divine and human action, and also his location of baptismal theology as an extension of the doctrine of reconciliation. But we discover, both in these texts and elsewhere in his writings on the sacraments, several significant differences between Jüngel's approach and what we find in Barth's fragment. Jüngel nowhere capitalizes on Barth's assertion that the baptisms with water and with the Spirit are fundamentally dissimilar. Moreover, in all of his other writings on sacramental theology, Jüngel stresses the tension between the agency of God and the *passivity* of the human recipient in the events of water baptism and the Lord's Supper. His emphasis on human passivity is far removed from Barth's thesis that water baptism 'is not itself … a mystery or sacrament' (*CD* IV/4, 102), but is, rather, exclusively a human *action*. And indeed, as Jüngel's theology of baptism and the Lord's Supper developed over time, he became increasingly comfortable with using 'sacrament' for these liturgical events, finally embracing the term outright. Likewise, as the trajectory of Jüngel's texts on sacramental theology moves forward, citations from Barth's writings all but disappear. All of this suggests, I think, that in regard to the sacraments, the extent of Jüngel's 'indebtedness' to the later Barth is much more complex than typically acknowledged. The similarities between their approaches must be understood in light of even greater dissimilarities.

Rudolf Bultmann – Demythologization and proclamation

If Barth's writings decisively shaped the discourse of the fields of systematic theology and Christian dogmatics at mid-century and during Jüngel's formative years, then the work of Rudolf Bultmann (1884–1976) had a similar impact in biblical studies and especially New Testament exegesis and theology. While Jüngel nowhere mentions the source of his first encounter with Bultmann's writings, we may reasonably guess that it was the mercurial Fuchs who introduced the young Jüngel to the work of his erstwhile Doktorvater. Whatever the case, we know with certainty that Jüngel read Bultmann extensively during his student years in Berlin. Like Barth, Bultmann was very much in the air at the time – an agent of both inspiration and irritation, depending on one's perspective. By all accounts, Jüngel found much to admire in Bultmann's work, especially as mediated through 'Old Marburgers' such as Fuchs, Ebeling and Käsemann. However, and possibly due to the fact that Jüngel switched disciplines from New Testament studies to Christian dogmatics almost immediately following the commencement of his teaching career, the impact of Bultmann on Jüngel's thought appears to orbit around a handful of concerns, as opposed to being comprehensive and diffuse. That is to say, it does not appear to be the case that Jüngel's work represents something like the extension of Bultmann's programme into the various regions of Christian teaching. I propose, rather, that Jüngel's use of Bultmann is somewhat restrained and that, as with his intellectual relationship to Barth, Jüngel's connection to Bultmann is marked by both points of inspiration and points of departure.

Worth mentioning for our purposes here are two interrelated aspects of Bultmann's thought which appear to have made some impression on Jüngel. The first is Bultmann's programme of 'demythologization', which encapsulates his approach to the texts of the New Testament. The concept of demythologization has suffered a rocky reception history in the anglophone world, due not least to commonly held misunderstandings of how Bultmann appropriated the category of 'myth' for use in New Testament exegesis. It widely is assumed that Bultmann's employment of myth to categorize certain passages of the New Testament implies a decision that such portions of scripture essentially are *untrue*. Accordingly, demythologization is viewed sheerly as the hermeneutical realization of modern science's assumption that myth is constitutive of the outdated worldview of prescientific cultures. We *de*-mythologize the New Testament simply by sifting out myth from fact. What Bultmann actually is up to, however, is much more delicate than this. On one hand, for Bultmann 'the theologian and the preacher owe their listeners intellectual clarity about what one can, and what one cannot accept as true' from the New Testament, and this entails jettisoning those episodes of the Christ narrative which a modern worldview cannot tolerate.[37] On the other, the goal of demythologization is to uncover the *truth* encapsulated in the mythical worldview underlying the New Testament texts. For Bultmann, early Christian myth holds an 'essentially soteriological function';[38] it *communicates* the Christian gospel, and thus is hardly simply outdated cosmological dross to be dumped aside for the sake of uncovering scripture's truth. New Testament myth, rather, as the original interpretation of the gospel, must be *reinterpreted* for the sake of proclaiming scripture's truth *today.*

This leads directly to the second feature of Bultmann's contribution with which Jüngel ever resonated: namely, for Bultmann, the work of theology and biblical exegesis is tied inextricably to the task of Christian *preaching*. As Bultmann's biographer puts it, 'the sermon, as proclamation of the word of God, belongs at the center of all theological activity'.[39] For it is in the sermon that the 'eschatological salvation-occurrence', which appeared in the world first in Jesus Christ, becomes accessible to the hearer. 'To make the eschatological salvation-occurrence and the forgiveness of sins a present reality requires a form of mediation that is structurally analogous to forgiveness itself. Since forgiveness occurs only in encounter, it can be promised only in the word and accepted only in faith.'[40] To phrase the same point differently and slightly more concretely, for Bultmann – and also for Jüngel – in preaching *something happens*. The preacher's task is to bring the ancient text and its liberating message to bear upon the horizon of the hearer. As such, the sermon is conceived as an event of connection and confrontation in the occurrence of which the hearer is awakened to the new possibilities for authentic human existence promised to those who believe. And again, because Bultmann understands the sermon as a nexus of existential possibilities, he views preaching as the end of all responsible theological and exegetical labour.

In a mid-career essay, Jüngel paraphrases Bultmann's programme of demythologization and acknowledges his basic agreement with the Marburg *Neutestamentler* on several points.[41] As I already have indicated, though, his proximity to Bultmann's thought reveals itself mainly in the areas of New Testament exegesis and his understanding of Christian preaching. Concepts and specific exegetical techniques associated with demythologization rarely present themselves in Jüngel's work elsewhere. Most notably, Bultmann seldom is foregrounded when Jüngel turns to address problems in Christian dogmatics located beneath the headings of the classical theological *loci*. All as such, I propose that while certainly we must appreciate Bultmann's place in Jüngel's intellectual and theological formation, it is best to refrain from overstating Bultmann's significance for Jüngel. And in any case, when considering the intellectual relationship between Bultmann and Jüngel, we must not neglect the role played by Bultmann's own students in mediating his legacy a generation further down. To that end we now turn to our next 'talking point', a pattern of theological discourse exclusively associated with a handful of Bultmann's erstwhile pupils.

The New Hermeneutic

So far in this chapter we have considered items of discussion which generally shaped the discourse of German Protestant theology during the two decades following the war. Demonstrably so, every young theologian working in Germany in the late 1950s and early 1960s would have thoroughly familiarized herself or himself with the problem of subjectivity and objectivity since the Enlightenment, with the promises and pitfalls of historical-critical exegesis, with the legacy of Luther, with the theological challenge of modern atheism and with the works of the masters of the fading generation, notably, Barth and Bultmann. With the so-called New Hermeneutic, however, we are moving very close to Jüngel's immediate orbit. Indeed, as I will propose in my survey of his doctoral dissertation, *Paulus und Jesus*, Jüngel's first book is, in many ways, the quintessential work of the long-bygone movement located at the intersection of exegesis and dogmatics.

The New Hermeneutic, sometimes alternately called the 'new' or 'second quest for the historical Jesus', is a programme for hermeneutical theology spearheaded by and chiefly associated with Jüngel's teachers Fuchs and Ebeling. In the background of the New Hermeneutic lies a problem which had pestered Protestant thought from the middle of the nineteenth century up to the First World War: namely, the question of the continuity and discontinuity between the man Jesus of Nazareth and the Christ confessed by Christian faith. During the long nineteenth century, scholars from a variety of disciplines in the European research universities came to prize the intellectual principle of 'historical consciousness'. In the guilds of religious studies and exegesis, this commitment took the form of scholarly preoccupation with the historical origins of the Christian religion and with the events of history 'behind' the texts of the New Testament. Direct interest in the historical Jesus and in the beginnings of Christianity waned, however, with the flowering of dialectical theology in the period following the war. Barth, Bultmann, Emil Brunner and others of the era did not place much confidence in the tools of critical historical research for discovering the 'true' Jesus. However, a generation later, and in the wake of a famous paper from 1953 by Käsemann, a small group of Bultmann's former pupils – Fuchs and Ebeling among them – renewed the quest for the historical Jesus. With Bultmann and Barth, the scholars of this second quest held that Christianity cannot be proven or disproven through the means of historical inquiry. Against Bultmann and Barth, though, they argued that faith should be directly interested in its origins. After all, Christians always have held that Jesus of Nazareth was a real man who, following the events of the first Easter, was declared the Lord Christ by the nascent church. Faith, that is, takes for granted continuity between the Christ it confesses and the man Jesus. To ignore the Jesus of history is to neglect this essential continuity.

Within the burgeoning movement, Fuchs and Ebeling in particular were convinced that the problem of the relationship between Jesus of Nazareth and the Christ of faith could be resolved by way of a *new* programme for *hermeneutics*. Heidegger's late-career musings on the ontological entailments of language were in the air at the time. Fuchs and Ebeling wrote with much confidence that the new turn in philosophy offered a means to overcome theological impasses. They proposed, for chief instance, that Jesus of Nazareth and the Christ of faith were linked by language. In his public ministry, the man Jesus preached interruptive 'speech-events' – the parables, the 'Son of Man' statements from the Gospels, the 'I am' claims found in Johannine literature and so on. Likewise, Christian proclamation – that is, preaching about the resurrected, ascended and reigning Christ – is an interruptive speech-event, presenting the lordship of Christ to the hearer of the sermon. Fuchs and Ebeling were colleagues in Tübingen in the mid-1950s, and from that point forward they produced a number of works, both in tandem and separately, but always with one voice, elaborating and defending the New Hermeneutic.

Working with Fuchs in Berlin on the relationship between Paul and Jesus, and during his studies also serving in Zürich as Ebeling's apprentice, Jüngel found himself in the thick of the small world of discourse surrounding the New Hermeneutic in its brief heyday. Since the dissertation tidily elaborates the central concerns of the movement, I will defer until the next chapter most of my commentary on Jüngel's contribution to the New Hermeneutic. But a handful of interrelated remarks seem especially pertinent to the present task of describing the unfolding of Jüngel's intellectual and theological formation. As mentioned at the beginning of this chapter and in dialogue with Paul Griffiths, theologians 'learn the ropes', so to speak, by imitation and reiteration. It should come as no surprise, then, that *Paulus und Jesus* and proximate texts resemble the works of Fuchs and Ebeling, both in content and in form. With his teachers, Jüngel assumes that the Jesus of Nazareth/Christ of faith relationship indeed is a problem to be resolved by work at the intersection of exegesis, hermeneutics, philosophy and dogmatics. Too, he proposes that the link between the Jesus of history and the Christ of Christian confession is proclamation, a thesis squarely in line with key statements from Fuchs and Ebeling. Even the language he uses in the dissertation and in the little cluster of texts on the same range of themes corresponds to the rhetoric employed by Fuchs, Ebeling and their New Hermeneutic associates. We discover, for instance, that Jüngel is fond of invoking the neologisms *Sprachereignis* (lit. 'speech event') and *Wortgeschehen* ('word event'). Both terms recur with some frequency in his writings, especially in those essays published between *Paulus und Jesus* and *God as the Mystery of the World*. The concepts essentially are interchangeable, and Jüngel alternates between them without comment or qualification. The terms derive from his teachers, with Fuchs favouring *Sprachereignis* and Ebeling *Wortgeschehen*.

It is beyond dispute that Fuchs, Ebeling and the hermeneutical programme they spearheaded are essential components of Jüngel's intellectual and theological formation. Early on, a number of Jüngel's publications fit well within the bailiwick of the New Hermeneutic, and these texts, as it were, exemplify a third-generation reception of Bultmann's legacy made possible by Jüngel's close proximity to several of Bultmann's pupils during his formative Berlin period. However, as Jüngel matures and his theology branches into new directions, the commitments and even the concepts of the New Hermeneutic gradually fall away. In Chapter 4 we will examine a mid-career essay – 'The Dogmatic Significance of the Question of the Historical Jesus' – in the course of which the sway of Fuchs and Ebeling re-emerges in a striking manner. As a rule, though, Jüngel's intellectual relationship with his teachers fades from the forefront as his thought unfolds.

The new spirit of ecumenism

The first decade of Jüngel's academic career coincided with a period of significant ecumenical headway between the historically divided churches. The Second Vatican Council, occurring between 1962 and 1965, marked a shift in posture on the part of the Catholic Church towards other churches and ecclesial bodies. *Unitatis redintegratio* (*UR*; in *DEC* II, 908–923; abridged in *Denzinger*, 910–914), the council's decree on ecumenism, set the tone for Catholic participation in ecumenical work and also inspired a new mode of ecumenical engagement – the bilateral dialogue. Within a few years following the close of the council, a number of official Catholic-Protestant dialogues were moving forward, and the Vatican Secretariat for Promoting Christian Unity had initiated an official dialogue with the Orthodox churches. For the rest of the century, the ecumenical movement would flourish with the burgeoning of sanctioned bilateral dialogues, during the courses of which 'competent experts' (*UR* 4; in *DEC* II, 911) – officially designated representatives from the dialoguing churches who possess expertise either in an academic discipline or in ecclesiastical politics and leadership; or, in some instances, in both – gathered over distinct 'phases' of work to debate and discuss matters of ecumenical dissensus. In a recent essay comparing the period of ecumenical ascendancy following the council to the frustrated mood marking ecumenism after the turn of the century,[42] theologian and ecumenist Michael Root invokes the idea of 'paradigm shift', coined by physicist Thomas Kuhn in his book *The Structure of Scientific Revolutions*,[43] to describe the now bygone era. Root contends that ecumenism and ecumenical theology have witnessed a shift from a 'revolutionary' to a 'normal' paradigm and that new forms of ecumenical engagement and new attitudes towards dissensus and unity must and will emerge as the present era advances. For our purposes here, it is significant that the flourishing of Jüngel's theology occurred concurrently with the modern ecumenical movement's revolutionary phase. The ecumenical work unfolding during the last half of the century comprised one of the worlds of discourse in which Jüngel participated and to which he contributed.

Of course, as we observed in the biographical sketch in Chapter 1, Jüngel's ecumenical participation and contribution came, as it were, from the side. Jüngel never was tapped to represent the Protestant or Lutheran cause in any of the bilateral dialogues. Instead, and as I already have suggested, his ecumenical work by and large is critical and even incendiary. Especially in his writings on justification, he appears suspicious of ecumenical achievements potentially won through doctrinal compromise. Jüngel's ecumenical posture aligns with the revolutionary interpretation of Luther's tower experience and of the reformation in general. If, as Jüngel certainly seems to presuppose, Luther 'rediscovered' Paul's precious theology of justification after centuries of its concealment, the doctrine cannot be used as a bargaining chip for the sake of ecumenical rapprochement. On the contrary, for Jüngel justification – rightly conceived – is the *condition* and *basis* for genuine unity between the churches.[44]

We return to Jüngel's ecumenical contribution on two occasions in Chapters 3 and 4. For now, I reiterate that his career evenly coincided with a pivotal period in the history of the modern ecumenical movement. Given this, it is surprising that his ecumenical work has received so little special attention from anglophone scholars of his theology. As I see it, the age of the bilateral dialogues is a significant component of Jüngel's theological and intellectual background, and his writings on ecumenical themes form a distinct canon within his oeuvre. It is my hope that drawing attention to this aspect of his thought will inspire further investigations into Jüngel's ecumenical theology.

Jüngel's contemporaries

This final section is not on a 'talking point', per se, though here we do continue our consideration of particular patterns of discourse which gave shape to Jüngel's theology. A few words are in order on Jüngel's collegial relationships with a handful of notable contemporaries. After all, an important component of theological existence is the trial and error that comes as ideas are tested in the gauntlet of peer-to-peer conversation and debate.

As I mentioned earlier, Jüngel often is identified as a theologian 'after Barth', usually alongside his Tübingen colleague Jürgen Moltmann (1926–) and Munich systematician Wolfhart Pannenberg (1928–2014). Both theologians are associated with the 'Theology of Hope', which flourished in Western Europe in the mid-1960s, and then in the anglophone world later in the decade and following the English-language publications of Moltmann's *Theology of Hope*[45] and the volume *Revelation and History*,[46] edited by Pannenberg and focused on his contribution to Christian eschatology. Moltmann and Pannenberg both charge that Barth and the other dialectical theologians failed to take the problem of *history* seriously enough. In dialogue with classical theological sources and Marxist political philosophy, Moltmann works out an approach to Christian thought, piety and social action oriented at all points to the hope made possible in the resurrection of Jesus, itself a foretaste of the eschatological resurrection awaiting us in the future. Pannenberg draws attention to the actions of God in history to which the biblical texts bear witness. His early work is notable not least due to his insistence that theology must take the Old Testament seriously as a record of divine revelation occurring in and as the history of ancient Israel. Moltmann and Pannenberg went on to have very different careers in Christian theology. Demonstrably so, Moltmann's work ever toed the line between classical dogmatics and political theology, and many of his writings continue to inspire liberation theologians active in the majority world and in Europe and North America. Pannenberg's numerous publications exemplify *wissenschaftlich* theology undertaken in the context of a major German research university. His crowning career achievement was a three-volume *Systematic Theology*,[47] which remains one of the most significant works of Christian thought produced in the decades since Barth's *Church Dogmatics*.

By all accounts, Jüngel maintained a friendly collegial relationship with Moltmann.[48] In 1972, and as Jüngel was in the midst of a long trajectory of research and reflection leading up to the publication of *God as the Mystery of the World*, Moltmann published *The Crucified God*,[49] in which he argues that the crucifixion of Jesus Christ indeed signifies the death of God, and that *just so* the event of the cross is the source of hope for a suffering world. The book's theme found Moltmann in the near vicinity of Jüngel's work from the same period, and the two carried on a dialogue of sorts in the footnotes of various publications. In *Mystery* Jüngel summarizes his assessment of the collegial back and forth, contending that, in *The Crucified God*, Moltmann 'surprisingly often says materially the same thing even to the same formulations', but 'is thinking in an entirely different direction formally' (*Mystery*, 220n 65). As their careers move forward, and their theological interests diverge, the cross-references largely (but not entirely) disappear from their respective publications. Again, though, the two remained friends for the duration.

Jüngel's personal and intellectual relationship with Pannenberg is another matter. In his book *Jesus – God and Man*,[50] Pannenberg proposes that theology's understanding of the person and work of Jesus Christ must proceed 'from below to above', beginning with a critical analysis of the life of Jesus and of the episodes of the so-called career of Christ, and from there moving towards the category of divine revelation. In many ways, this approach to Christology epitomizes Pannenberg's departure from Barth's programme, which prioritizes revelation over evidence supposedly available to us by way of historical investigation. In two subsequent works – *Theology and the Philosophy of Science*[51] and *Anthropology in Theological Perspective*[52] – Pannenberg extends his approach 'from below to above' to issues proximate to the intersection of theology and the natural sciences. Jüngel expresses his 'serious reservations' regarding Pannenberg's programme in one spot (*Mystery*, 17n 6), and in an essay from 1975 suggests that Pannenberg's work exhibits the hallmark hazards of natural theology.[53] The relationship between the two men, both personal and professional, remained cool as their respective careers unfolded.

The Second Vatican Council provided new opportunities for Protestant and Catholic theologians to forge collaborative relationships. During the first decade of his career, Jüngel partnered with Jesuit theologian Karl Rahner (1904–1984) to produce several projects, including a co-authored pamphlet on sacramental theology which juxtaposes Rahner's Transcendental Thomist and Jüngel's idiosyncratic Protestant perspectives.[54] We will observe in Chapter 4 that Jüngel later grew largely convinced by Rahner's 'rule' concerning the relationship between the immanent trinity and the economic trinity. Throughout his career, Jüngel maintained a friendship and close collegial relationship with Tübingen theologian Hans Küng (1928–). Küng wrote his doctoral dissertation on Barth's doctrine of justification, arguing that Barth's thought signals a potential ecumenical breakthrough.[55] In the 1970s he found himself embroiled in an intense public controversy over the doctrine of papal infallibility incited by his book *Infallible? An Inquiry*.[56] He eventually lost his *missio canonica*, the licence to teach as a Catholic theologian, due to his refusal to recant his published positions. Jüngel wrote a sympathetic review of Küng's book upon its publication[57] and remained a supportive colleague during the difficult decade that followed. We must also mention here that, throughout his career, Jüngel was on cordial terms with his near-contemporary Benedict XVI (1927–). Citations of Benedict's works occasionally appear in Jüngel's writings, especially in texts written around the publication of the *JDDJ*. And one of Jüngel's best pieces from his last active decade is a delightful essay critically engaging Benedict's encyclical *Deus caritas est*.[58]

Space prevents me from doing more than mentioning several other colleagues from Jüngel's long career: the liberation theologian Dorothee Sölle (1929–2003), whose work probed the significance of Christian talk about God 'after Auschwitz'; his Tübingen colleague Oswald Beyer (1939–), who wrote numerous works on Luther's theology; Michael Beintker of Münster (1947–); the Munich systematic theologian Trutz Rendtorff (1931–2016); and Catholic theologians Karl Cardinal Lehmann (1936–2018) and Walter Cardinal Kasper (1933–).

A final note here: readers new to Jüngel's writings may be surprised to discover his conspicuous lack of engagement with theological discussions centred outside of continental Europe. For instance, apart from a few citations scattered here and there, he appears altogether unaware of trends and key texts in contemporaneous anglophone theology: e.g. the Anglo-

American strain of 'death of God' theology (as expressed by, for example, Altizer, van Buren, Robinson and Caputo); the reception of Barth in Britain and North America; the 'post-liberalism' of Hans Frei, George Lindbeck and their students; the Scottish dogmatics of the Torrances; British and North American Evangelicalism and Evangelical theology; the 'third quest' for the historical Jesus; the New Perspective on Paul; and so on. As an adolescent in the DDR, Jüngel did not receive formal education in the English language. He is not fluent in English and has a reputation for expecting Anglophones to correspond and converse with him in German. Due to his lack of fluency, the contemporaneous discourse of modern theology from English-speaking regions essentially is inaccessible to him.

Conclusion

My purpose in this chapter has been to destabilize impressions of Jüngel's formation and contribution which emerge from, as I have dubbed the trend, sheer genealogical accounts of the origins of his thought. I suspect some readers would rather I simply list the usual suspects identified as Jüngel's primary influences and trace lines of direct intellectual and theological reiteration and recapitulation. I worry, however, that the reduction of Jüngel's thought to his pedigree is far too simplistic an approach and discourages us from taking his work seriously in its own right. To be sure, in order to sort out Jüngel's interests and commitments, we need to deal with figures such as Luther, Barth, Bultmann, Heidegger, Fuchs and Ebeling. But I have recommended here that, rather than identifying such forebears as dominant intellectual and theological influences from whom Jüngel derived various suppositions and concepts, it is better to situate these individuals within the larger patterns of discourse marking the mood of German theology during the period from the end of the war to the close of the century. With this broad impression of Jüngel's intellectual and theological formation and development in mind, we now turn to explore some of Jüngel's specific contributions to the discourse of Christian theology.

CHAPTER 3
READING JÜNGEL I – THE FOUR MAJOR MONOGRAPHS

In this and the following chapter, I offer field notes on some of Jüngel's most enduring and significant works. Since two of his four major monographs – *God's Being Is in Becoming* and *God as the Mystery of the World* – are widely considered to be classics of modern Christian thought, and since a third – *Justification* – addresses a topic of ongoing interest and dispute in systematic and ecumenical theology, I begin here with Jüngel's books and then turn, in Chapter 4, to a survey of select essays. In addition to the three monographs just named, I also include here extensive comments on *Paulus und Jesus*, to date available only in German. As I will make clear, the dissertation is an essential text for understanding its author's thought. I have not incorporated notes on short volumes and pamphlets such as *Death, The Freedom of a Christian, Reden für die Stadt* and *Christ, Justice, and Peace*. While these and other similar texts are important items in Jüngel's literary deposit, they do not warrant the careful exegesis and commentary I devote here to the four major monographs.

Readers do well to keep in mind that, at least as I have presented Jüngel's published works in this guidebook, in these monographs he is unfolding exercises in *irregular* dogmatics. None of these works counts as a comprehensive statement intended to summarize the entire body of Christian divinity. Rather, in these books we discover Jüngel using the resources of the dogmatic and philosophical traditions to address disputed issues in theology. Shortly for now: at the heart of Jüngel's analysis of the New Testament in *Paulus und Jesus* is the question of the relation between Jesus of Nazareth and the Christ of faith; *God's Being Is in Becoming* is a 'paraphrase' of some key sections of Barth's *Church Dogmatics* focusing the doctrines of God and election and their intersection; on the surface a study of, in turn, the 'thinkability', 'speakability' and 'humanity' of God, *God as the Mystery of the World* consists of a sprawling argument which ties together a number of themes Jüngel explored during the first two decades of his career, including the trinitarian being of God, the problem of theological language, analogy, the modern atheistic rejection of classical metaphysics, human existence in the face of death, and the cross and resurrection of Jesus Christ; finally, *Justification* is Jüngel's contribution to an acrimonious debate over the titular doctrine sparked by the *Joint Declaration on the Doctrine of Justification*, which was ratified by the Roman Catholic Church and the Lutheran World Federation (LWF) in 1999.

As indicated, I have designed the following comments to be used as field notes on the four major monographs. The sections here proceed by way of summary, paraphrase and commentary, and I attempt throughout the chapter to alert the reader to how these key texts contributed to the development of Jüngel's thought from beginning to end. At all points, my goal is to foster charitable readings of the primary sources and to provide essential contextual, lexical and theological instruction. Having said as much, I quickly will concede that there are legitimate ways to read and receive these texts other than what I present here. My own ever-evolving intellectual, theological, ecclesial and personal commitments cannot but impact how I have understood and responded to Jüngel's thought over the years. For just this reason, readers do well to recognize that the commentary in this chapter is itself an act of interpretation and should be engaged accordingly. At the very least, this disclaimer reinforces a point I have made elsewhere in this guide: namely, that nothing here can substitute for the close reading of Jüngel's works themselves.

Paulus und Jesus

Unlike the other monographs I introduce here, Jüngel's first book, *Paulus und Jesus: Eine Untersuchung zur Präzisierung der Frage nach dem Ursprung der Christologie*, has yet to be translated into English.[1] Anglophone readers committed to puzzling out *Paulus und Jesus* must inch through the German original, which not only exhibits Jüngel's penchant for neologisms and wordplays but also is marked by technical jargon, references to now-outdated scientific studies in New Testament exegesis and an abundance of untranslated citations from the Greek texts of the Gospels and Paul's letters. Such features remind us that we are dealing here with a doctoral dissertation, a specialized work originally prepared for and defended during a public *Rigorosum* before a small committee of feisty experts. While the book currently is in print in a seventh revised edition, it has undergone only minor alterations since its first appearance in 1962. I do not anticipate that it will ever get rendered into English, as it reflects an era of German New

Testament scholarship that is long obsolete. It is, nevertheless, a significant entry in the canon of Jüngel's writings. *Paulus und Jesus* reveals the issues in the discipline of New Testament theology and exegesis on which Jüngel cut his teeth while studying with Fuchs during the Berlin period. Moreover, the monograph unfolds an array of commitments at the intersection of exegesis, theology, hermeneutics and the philosophy of language to which Jüngel continued to return throughout his career and especially during his first decade as a professional theologian.

The overarching theme of *Paulus und Jesus*, which unfolds over three major chapters and two short but substantive excurses on history and eschatology, is the problem of the continuity between, on one hand, Jesus's parabolic discourses and claims to the title of 'Son of Man', and, on the other, the apostolic – in particular, Pauline – proclamation of justification. Jüngel, employing terminology and a rhetorical style of argumentation similar to what one encounters in the work of his *Doktorvater*,[2] proposes that Jesus's message of God's imminent reign and Paul's preaching of the gospel of justification can be grouped beneath the general hermeneutical category of 'speech-event' (*Sprachereignis*). He contends that Jesus's parables, the 'Son of Man' tradition in the Matthean and Markan witnesses and Paul's doctrine of justification were addressing speech-events in the occurrences of which what was spoken (the kingdom of God and God's justifying righteousness) *came* to the hearer *as* the event of speech. The young Jüngel establishes this thesis through rigorous exegesis of the biblical texts and thoroughgoing engagements with the works of the major figures in nineteenth- and twentieth-century New Testament scholarship.

The eschatology Jüngel advances in the book is essential to his argument here and also lays a foundation of sorts for how he addresses eschatological themes in subsequent writings. In *Paulus und Jesus* he suggests that a proper appreciation of Jesus's parables requires the interpreter to abandon a *chronological* perspective on the kingdom's temporality, that is, a conception of time in which the kingdom 'is assigned a place in the space of time which is *measured* by an "I" existing in time, such that the *nearness* of the kingdom is conceived as its *distance* from a temporally existing *subject*' (Jüngel, *P&J*, 140). Over against this chronological approach to the time of the kingdom, Jüngel proposes that the drawing near of the kingdom in Jesus's parables creates a 'distinction in time' (*P&J*, 206) between time as *chronos* and time as 'moved time', or 'time [as] set in motion by the end of time' (*P&J*, 141). In Jesus's parabolic discourses, this moved time interrupts the continuity of chronological time, bringing with it the eschatological presence of the kingdom.[3] It is thus in Jesus's word – the '*new* word' – that 'a new time is set against the old time' (*P&J*, 206).

This drawing together of eschatology and language is the linchpin of Jüngel's thesis and remains a central commitment animating his theology as it matures. In the dissertation, he uncovers an insight pertaining to his approach to theological language that abides with him as his thought advances: namely, Jüngel insists here that the eschatologically new word does not neatly divide up according to the Aristotelian distinction of form and content. As I soon will show, in *God as the Mystery of the World*, this distinction – and Jüngel's insistence that it is hardly fit for describing the structure of theological language – is a key ingredient of his dispute with what he there calls the 'Augustinian hermeneutics of signification'. But it is important for us to observe that the issue emerges all the way back in his argument in the dissertation. In *Paulus und Jesus* it is not Augustine that draws Jüngel's critical reproach, but rather Aristotle as mediated through Marburg New Testament scholar Adolf Jülicher, whose two-volume scientific study of the parables has divided scholars ever since it first appeared in print at the close of the nineteenth century. A sturdy foe of any allegorical or figural programme for the interpretation of Jesus's parabolic discourses, Jülicher argues that each of Jesus's parables neatly divides into an 'image-half' (*Bildhälfte*) and a 'thing-half' (*Sachhälfte*) that relate to one another at a third point of comparison (*tertium comparationis*).[4] Jüngel proposes in *Paulus und Jesus* that this approach to the parables turns them into mere 'literary constructions' (*P&J*, 136), the meanings of which are self-evident and effortlessly readable from the stories that constitute the parabolic 'image-halves'. As an alternative to Jülicher's interpretative method, Jüngel proposes that the kingdom of God arrives interruptedly in the event of the proclamation of the parables. He rejects the (here) Aristotelian and (elsewhere) Augustinian hermeneutical principle that the interpreter can 'separate the "content" of Jesus's proclamation from … the bare "form" of it'. On the contrary, 'the Kingdom comes in parable as parable (comes) to speech. The parables of Jesus bring to speech the Kingdom as parable' (*P&J*, 135).

Jüngel's resolution to this cluster of hermeneutical issues in turn gives rise to an idiosyncratic account of the person of Jesus Christ. It is demonstrable that Jüngel never truly departs from the Christological judgements he makes in the dissertation, even if later he mitigates the sharpness of his positions by softening his rhetoric and nuancing his claims. The portrayal of the Jesus of history that emerges in *Paulus und Jesus* corresponds to the theology of speech-events Jüngel employs to draw together the proclamation of Jesus and the preaching of Paul. Who *was* this man from Nazareth who wandered about Galilee and Jerusalem proclaiming the imminent arrival of the kingdom of God? In the book, Jüngel circumscribes his discussion of the identity of Jesus to the analysis of Jesus's message of God's impending reign. Jüngel does not at all appear to be interested in a 'first quest' type of inquiry into the historical Jesus, that is, in reconstructing a life of Jesus from those bits of the Gospel narratives deemed factual. Nor, for that matter, does he go to any lengths in *Paulus und Jesus* to situate the man Jesus of Nazareth within the tumultuous political, cultural and religious *Sitz im Leben* of first-century Palestinian Judaism. Rather, here Jüngel occupies himself almost exclusively with Jesus's proclamation of eschatological speech-events in his parables and 'Son of man' statements. Narrative details in the Gospels of Jesus's 'behaviour' – for instance, pericopes chronicling his miracles – are categorized as 'commentary on his proclamation' (*P&J*, 277). As Fuchs similarly puts it, 'as his conduct shows, Jesus clearly did not want to be understood apart from his proclamation, but rather in it'.[5] Jesus's actions pointed back to and affirmed the authenticity of his eschatological message and are of no interest otherwise. If the upshot of such a reading of the Gospels is to draw attention to the teaching and preaching of Jesus and to the kingdom of God present in Jesus's message, its handicap is its tendency to dislodge Jesus from *any* 'context' – from history, from ordinary patterns of human behaviour, from Israel and Judaism, from first-century Palestinian society and politics, from contemporaneous anxieties about the hegemony of Roman rule and so on. Consequently, and as Webster tidily puts it, Jesus is presented in *Paulus und Jesus* as 'such a meteoric figure that his occupancy of a determinate historical and social world seems merely accidental or occasional'.[6]

This impression obtains in Jüngel's comments in the dissertation on the so-called Christ of faith, that is, on the church's confession of the crucified and resurrected Jesus as Lord. Who *is* the living Lord the church worships and witnesses to as ever present and active? As ever, the mainspring of his argument is proclamation, which, in Jüngel's reading, establishes the link between the man Jesus of Nazareth and the Christ of the Christian faith. Jüngel proposes in *Paulus und Jesus* that the apostolic preaching of the soteriological significance and eschatological reign of Christ is, just like Jesus's own proclamation, a speech-event in the occurrence of which that which is spoken comes to speech.[7] That is to say,

Christ *is* present and active *as* preaching that conforms to the apostolic standard. On one hand, such a conception establishes the church's missionary proclamation as the *place* where Christ can be encountered in the world, in doing so resisting the liberal Protestant project of reducing the identity of Christ to Jesus's ethical teachings. At the same time, Jüngel risks enclosing Christ within proclamation. Reading *Paulus und Jesus*, one is struck by the ease with which Jüngel wields the categories of the New Hermeneutic for addressing Christological dilemmas. However, to my mind, in allowing such categories to guide and even dominate his decisions, he raises more questions than he answers. In particular, I continue to ponder the matter of *where* for Jüngel the resurrected and ascended Christ is located. While he does not substantively develop this theme in the dissertation, in the early pages of the text he provides an important clue that betrays his position: namely, his assertion that Jesus 'in the speech-event of the Pauline doctrine of justification ... comes to speech *anew*' (*P&J*, 5). Jesus, that is, who brought to speech the kingdom in his public proclamation, now himself comes to speech anew in the apostolic preaching. This at least appears to suggest that for the young Jüngel, Jesus Christ was resurrected and ascended into the apostolic kerygma and has no existence otherwise.[8]

There is one additional point worth mentioning here. Jüngel commences the 'Preface to the First Edition' of *Paulus und Jesus* by proposing that the topic at hand – namely, the relationship between Paul's doctrine of justification and the message of Jesus – is a matter of concern for both biblical studies and Christian theology. The book, he comments, 'gives an impression [which he does not dispute] of establishing a synthesis between the widely divergent disciplines of New Testament exegesis and dogmatics; a synthesis, moreover, between the thought of Rudolf Bultmann and that of Karl Barth' (*P&J*, v). Jüngel goes on in the book's 'Introduction' to sketch a summary of contemporaneous discussions among schools of thought from both disciplines concerning the historical and theological significance of the crucifixion and resurrection of Jesus and the early Christian message about him (*P&J*, 1–16). As I suggested in Chapter 2, Jüngel's intellectual relationships to Bultmann and to Barth (and to others, for that matter) constitute an extremely knotty aspect of his theological formation and development, and we should avoid drawing swift and unrefined conclusions about statements such as what we discover in the 'Preface' to the dissertation. We certainly should resist reading his somewhat brash comment on synthesizing Bultmann and Barth as something of a programmatic statement for the entirety of his career and written work. In any event, it is important to observe that while Bultmann abides in *Paulus und Jesus* as a key interlocutor, Barth becomes something of an afterthought following the 'Preface' and 'Introduction'. It is only later on – particularly in the next text I will introduce – that Barth becomes for Jüngel both a muse and sparring partner. *Paulus und Jesus* is an exercise in New Testament theology and exegesis, and it is Bultmann and his heirs who furnish Jüngel's presuppositions, inspire his approach and inform his discussion of the continuity and discontinuity between the Apostle Paul and Jesus of Nazareth. The dissertation is, in the end, a quintessential demonstration of the New Hermeneutic. It neatly bottles up what was in the air in critical exegesis of the New Testament among the 'Old Marburgers' and their students in the period following the war. Readers of Jüngel's corpus must keep this fact in mind and come to appreciate the extent to which *Paulus und Jesus* sheds light upon, or perhaps casts its shadow over, his subsequent contributions.

God's Being Is in Becoming

Following the defence and publication of *Paulus und Jesus*, the young Jüngel turned to the problem of analogy, producing two short pieces on Barth and on Parmenides and Heraclitus, the latter of which originated as his Habilitationsschrift, completed at the Sprachenkonvikt in 1962. While, as I have just noted, Barth hardly is Jüngel's focus in *Paulus und Jesus*, the period immediately subsequent to the dissertation foregrounds Barth as a key interlocutor for Jüngel's flourishing theology. Jüngel's second monograph, *God's Being Is in Becoming: The Trinitarian Being of God in the Theology of Karl Barth* (1965),[9] consists of a fine-grained analysis of portions of Barth's *Church Dogmatics*. The work is notoriously difficult to classify. While Jüngel lays claim to the genre of 'paraphrase', suggesting in his subtitle an interpretative reiteration of Barth's trinitarianism in the *Church Dogmatics*, the monograph is, in fact, something much more ambitious, namely, a dogmatic analysis of the intersecting themes of trinitarian theology, the doctrine of election, the relationship between history and eschatology and the problem of human language for God. While the study does indeed proceed by way of direct engagements with Barth's mature trinitarian theology, throughout the text we discover Jüngel judiciously using the *Church Dogmatics* to break open unexplored trajectories of thought. As such, the book puts on display both Jüngel's acumen as a close reader of theological literature and his ingenuity and self-assuredness in taking theology in new directions. It is no wonder, then, that the book abides as one of the signal publications of its author's literary output.

There is yet another reason why *God's Being Is in Becoming* continues to find readers today. For the past two decades or so, and particularly in anglophone circles, there has raged a sometimes acrimonious debate among Barth scholars concerning the relationship between Barth's pioneering interpretation of the doctrine of election and his trinitarian theology. On one hand, several scholars have argued that, for Barth, divine election – that is, God's determination to be God only as God for us – just *is* God's self-identification as Father, Son and Holy Spirit. God *is* not, as it were, prior to or apart from the event of election.[10] On the other hand, and in antithesis to the position just described, other scholars have contended that, in Barth's view, divine election does not somehow constitute the being of God. Rather, prior to and apart from the event of election, God *is*.[11] While at first glance it may appear that this debate is merely a point of neuralgia within the community of Barth scholarship, it is not too difficult to perceive that many significant issues of Christian doctrine emerge from this cluster of concerns. For those involved in the controversy, orthodoxy and the future of Christian theology are at stake.

God's Being Is in Becoming is an early key text expressing an interpretation of Barth in the vicinity of the first of the two positions outlined above. For many scholars on that side of the divide over Barth's theology, the book, which to this day is assigned as a text in courses on Barth in a number of theology programmes in the anglophone world, gave them their first taste of a serious engagement with Barth's trinitarianism that takes into account his trailblazing doctrine of election. By way of illustrating the significance of *God's Being Is in Becoming* for the one side of the ongoing controversy, we may cite Bruce L. McCormack, one of North America's leading theologians and a brilliant expositor of Barth's theology, especially of these issues at the intersection of the doctrines of God and divine election. In a letter written to Jüngel and published in a collection of personal notes presented to him on his seventieth birthday, McCormack remarks that 'no book has influenced my own reading of Barth's theology to the degree that (*God's Being Is in Becoming*) has'.[12] If I have a dog of my own in the fight over the relationship between trinity and election in Barth's thought, I will not reveal it in this survey of *God's Being Is in Becoming*. Rather, I bring up the dispute and the issues precipitating it as a way of introducing the heart of Jüngel's argument in the book.

As with most of Jüngel's major works, it takes some effort to discern the broad patterns of thought which emerge in *God's Being Is in Becoming*. In the comments that follow, I address what I consider to be the five most significant claims composing Jüngel's argument. In the course of the book, these claims entwine around each other and, at all points, are brought into the service of Jüngel's exegesis of the *Church Dogmatics*.

First, Jüngel argues in the book that *God's existence is identical to God's essence*. This assertion, to which he returns repeatedly throughout the text, is introduced already in the monograph's first few pages.[13] Responding to Protestant theologian Helmut Gollwitzer's doctrine of God, Jüngel suggests that his interlocutor posits 'a gap in a metaphysical background to the being of God which is indifferent to God's historical acts of revelation' (Jüngel, *Becoming*, 6). The source of Gollwitzer's 'gap', Jüngel demonstrates, is his definition of and strict differentiation between divine essence and divine will, and likewise between the essence and existence of God. Accordingly, God is *in God's essence* a being 'in-and-for-himself' who, as it were, *subsequently wills* to be God 'for-us'. Further, God's being 'for-us', which is 'fulfilled' in temporal history[14] through the events of Jesus Christ (*Becoming*, 98), is constitutive only of the divine will – God's existence – and not of the divine essence. Hence the 'gap': according to Gollwitzer according to Jüngel, the essence of God must be wholly distinguished from both the free decision of God to relate to an 'other' and the enacting of that decision in the economy of salvation. Gollwitzer thus appears to describe God's essence as God's sheer triune self-relatedness in abstraction from any real relation that God might have with creatures. Jüngel deems this a fatal move for theology, insofar as it 'reintroduces an abstract deity anterior to God's action in the economy of salvation, and so undermines the all-important fact that the one whom we encounter in salvation is God as God truly is'.[15]

Over against Gollwitzer and in dialogue with Barth, Jüngel asserts throughout *God's Being Is in Becoming* that the doctrine of the triune God must consist of the *identity* of God's existence with God's essence and thus also the identity of God's being *pro nobis* (for us) with God's being *in se* (the inner life of God). Put differently and invoking commonly employed trinitarian jargon, for Jüngel, God's free actions towards and in the *economy* of creation and redemption must in some way identically correspond to God's *immanent* life of triune relations.[16] There is no immanent divine being *in se* anterior to God's being *pro nobis*. Rather, according to Jüngel, God's being for us *just is* God's inner life; inversely, God's immanent being *just is* God's being for us.

Jüngel goes on to assert that the identity of divine essence and existence and, likewise, the identity both of God's being *in se* and *pro nobis* and of God's action *ad extra* and the immanent triune life is, ultimately, a *Christological* claim.[17] In order to develop this thesis, he points to Barth's strongly supralapsarian account of the doctrine of election. The theological term 'supralapsarian' means 'before the fall'; for Barth and also for Jüngel, God's determination to be God only as God *pro nobis* is a decision made before the fall of humanity occurred – indeed, it 'happened' (inasmuch as we can think of such things as 'happenings') even prior to creation, 'before the foundation of the world', as the Epistle to the Ephesians puts it, 'in the mystery of God's will … set forth in Christ' (Ephesians 1:4, 9). The Christology emerging in the text of *God's Being Is in Becoming* is coordinated according to two '*histories*' – the 'primal-historical' event of divine election and the 'temporal-historical' events associated with Jesus of Nazareth and in which the primal decision of God is enacted. In Jüngel's reading of Barth, these two histories are construed as identical. The events of the cross and resurrection of Jesus Christ are understood as the temporal actualizations of the primal-historical decision of election. For Jüngel, it is only by coordinating the two histories in this way that we can affirm that *God* is the one revealed on Good Friday and Easter Sunday.

The second central claim of *God's Being Is in Becoming* that I will highlight here builds upon the first one. Jüngel asserts that *the event of election is* God's *primal history*. According to Jüngel, the event of election is the primal-historical, free decision in which God determines both God's own self-relatedness and also the relation between God and humanity. Election thus is the event of the concrete identity between God's being *in se* and being *pro nobis*, and between God's essence and existence. This proposal deserves careful analysis. First, we must pause for a moment to consider Jüngel's claim that, in the event of election, God determines God's own self-*relatedness*. In characteristic opaqueness, Jüngel states, 'God relates himself to himself (in the primal decision of election) in that he determines himself to be the one who elects' (*Becoming*, 85). That is, God determines in the event of election to be God only as the one who, in Jesus Christ, decides to relate another – that is, to humanity. As Barth puts it, God 'does not will *to be Himself* in any other way than He is in this relationship' to humanity (Barth, *CD* II/1, 274; emphasis added). We can immediately see how such an construal of election counters Gollwitzer's separation of divine essence and existence, for it locates the being of God, and thus God's essence, in the event of God's free, wilful decision.

But in what sense does this decision of God 'to be the one who elects' constitute God's *self*-relatedness? Jüngel suggests that the free decision of God to be God only in relation to humanity entails that election is an act of *triune* self-differentiation: 'In that here one of the three modes of being is *determined* to be the God who elects, we have to understand God's primal decision as an *event* in the being of God which *differentiates* the modes of God's being' (*Becoming*, 86). This move effectively grounds the triunity of God in the event of election, as it is not the case, at least according to Jüngel, that the three triune persons exist, as it were, antecedently to election in perichoretic self-relatedness and *then* decide to be God only in relation to humanity. Rather, precisely *in deciding* to be God only in relation to humanity, God self-differentiates into the 'modes' of God's being. Jüngel offers what is, upon final analysis, a rather inchoate elaboration of this event of self-differentiation, first by addressing the trinitarian relation of the 'modes' of Father and Son:

> The eternal Son participates as subject in the election of the Father in that by his own free decision he *affirms* the *determination* which the Father wills for him, to be the God who elects the man Jesus and chooses oneness with him. The eternal Son *elects* his election by the Father. (*Becoming*, 88)

Father and Son are differentiated from one another insofar as election is a *two*fold event of divine self-determination: the Father determines to be the elector by choosing the Son to participate in election as one who elects; in turn, the Son determines, in perfect accord with the will of the Father, to be the elector by 'choosing oneness with' the man Jesus. The Father elects the Son; the Son 'elects his election by the Father'.

According to Jüngel, this twofold event of divine self-determination takes place 'in the freedom of the *Spirit*' (*Becoming*, 88). Jüngel unfortunately does not go on in *God's Being Is in Becoming* to explain in any detail the concrete identity of the Spirit, nor does he extensively elaborate the claim that the Spirit's role in God's triune self-determination is an act of *freedom*. Significantly, however, he does assert, again quoting Barth, that this 'freedom of the Spirit' is the 'unity' of the Father and the Son (*Becoming*, 15). We can conclude from this that Jüngel has in mind a particular reading of an Augustinian model of God's triunity, according to which the Spirit is hypostasized *as* the relation of Father and Son.[18] So elsewhere he favourably paraphrases one of Karl Rahner's theses: 'the hypostasis (of the Holy Spirit) *consists in* the fact that Father and Son affirm each other in love and realize themselves by this loving, reciprocal affirmation, such that each of them experiences himself by experiencing the other'.[19] As we have already seen, in *God's Being Is in Becoming* the loving reciprocity of Father and Son is expressed according to the idea of the divine will. That is, the twofold event of self-determination between Father and Son is a *free agreement* between them and just in this sense is the event of their unity. The person of the Holy Spirit *is* the freedom within which this inner-triune event of election takes place and thus appears as the hypostasis of the reciprocity between Father and Son.

It is critical to observe from this discussion that, for Jüngel, the being of God in no way is static, simple being, but rather is being-as-event, being in becoming (hence the monograph's title). It is precisely for this reason that Jüngel refers to election as a primal *history*. God is historical being insofar as, in the loving, willing act of election, God 'comes from' God, 'comes to' God and 'comes as' God.[20] This movement within God is a *primal* history insofar as it necessarily takes place, as it were, prior to the divine actions of creation and redemption, even as it directly corresponds *as movement* to God's saving self-presentation to the world in the events of Jesus of Nazareth.

Having wrestled with Jüngel's assertion that the event of election is *God's* primal history, we now turn to his claim in *God's Being Is in Becoming* that *election is* humanity's *primal history*. It is crucial that, for Jüngel, the movement in God in the event of election that constitutes God's primal history does not exclude but includes humanity. This astonishing insight, which emerges from Jüngel's reading of the *Church Dogmatics*, explains how God's being *in se* corresponds to God's being *pro nobis*. In the event of election, Jüngel argues, God lovingly decides to be God only as the one who turns to humanity. Moreover, in the triune person of the Son of God – the hypostasis of whom *includes* the humanity of the man Jesus Christ – God is both the one who elects *and* elect humanity (*Becoming*, 87). According to Jüngel, then, humanity is concretely present *to God* in the primal-historical event of election in the humanity of Jesus Christ. To put the matter another way, the humanity of the man Jesus is *held* in the person of the Son of God and is in this sense present before God in God's primal decision. As Jüngel comments elsewhere in an essay on Barth's Christology, 'the eternal Son of God holds a place for the earthly Son of Man. That is, God's gracious election holds a place for the man Jesus in the being of God from all eternity'.[21]

In *God's Being Is in Becoming*, Jüngel explains this inclusion of humanity in the event of election in the following way:

God's primal decision is ... the 'primal relationship' between God and humanity, in which God turns to humanity and so is *already* with humanity before humanity was created. The primal decision constitutes the primal relationship of God to humanity, and in this primal relationship there takes place 'primal history', in which, *before* humanity has been created, God already relates himself to us. God's being takes place as *historia praeveniens* [prevenient history]. In this *historia praeveniens* God determines himself to be ours as one of us ... The *historia praeveniens* in which and as which this divine self-determination takes place is Jesus Christ. (*Becoming*, 91)

If we follow the logic of the last three sentences, we see that, for Jüngel, this *historia praeveniens* is (1) the history and, as it were, location where and during which God's *being* occurs; (2) the event of God's decision to be God only 'ours as one of us'; and (3) Jesus Christ. It follows, then, that Jesus Christ – in particular his 'mode' (to stick with Jüngel's potentially problematic terminology) in this primal history (i.e., the person Son of God) – is determinative for *both* divine and human being. As the Son of God, Jesus Christ is the triune person in whom God's being *in se* and being *pro nobis* are identical. And, because God 'turns to' and just so is 'already with' humanity in the mode of Jesus Christ, the eternal being of the Son is the location of the pre-temporal, pre-creation being of humanity.

The fourth central claim from *God's Being Is in Becoming* we will examine here springs forth from what we have already considered: *the temporal history of Jesus of Nazareth is the fulfilment in time of God's eternal self-differentiating decision*. Recall that, over against Gollwitzer's doctrine of God, Jüngel posits a relation of identity between God's essence and existence, and likewise asserts that the 'what-being' of God can indeed be known from and in relation to God's 'that-being'.[22] Similarly, God's actions towards and in the economy of creation and redemption are identical to God's immanent being as Father, Son and Holy Spirit. These positions suggest a concrete, real relation between God's primal decision to be God only with and for humanity and those temporal-historical events in which God enacts this decision in the economy. Jüngel invokes the motif of 'fulfilment' to describe this real relation. He proposes that 'the temporal history of Jesus Christ is the *fulfillment in time* of God's eternal resolve' (*Becoming*, 98; emphasis added). We might also say, further, that God, having turned to humanity in the primal event of election, now in the temporal history of Jesus of

Nazareth turns to humanity in such a way that this movement – this 'turning to humanity' – is brought to completion.

All of this raises the question of *which* events constitute the temporal history that serves as the fulfilment of God's primal decision. In *God's Being Is in Becoming* and elsewhere in his writings, Jüngel consistently offers rather contracted answers to this question. By 'temporal history' Jüngel does not seem to have in mind the unfolding, coherent narrative of Jesus of Nazareth attested to in the New Testament – the so-called career of Christ: his conception, birth, public ministry and miracles, transfiguration, suffering and crucifixion, resurrection, post-resurrection appearances, ascension and so on. Nor does he ever appear to be too concerned to situate the biographical details of Jesus within the larger framework of the narrative of Israel and Israel's national and religious self-understanding. Rather, for Jüngel the 'temporal history' of Jesus that corresponds to the primal history of election seems to serve as a sort of shorthand for *only* Jesus's suffering and crucifixion.

Jüngel's rather narrow reading of the Jesus events informs his solution to the problem of the relation between the temporal-historical events of Jesus of Nazareth and the primal-historical event of election. For Jüngel, in the event of election God determines to be God only in relation to humanity, and this determination is fulfilled in temporal history precisely as Jesus Christ obediently 'hand(s) himself over to the opposition to God which characterizes human existence' and in doing so 'suffers' this opposition to God, 'even to death on the cross' (*Becoming*, 98). Because the primal-historical decision of election and its temporal-historical fulfilment are, in effect, *one* event (just as divine essence and will, God *in se* and *pro nobis*, and so on, are identical), the 'perishing', 'death' and 'passive obedience' of Jesus Christ are determinative for the being of God. In the event of election and its temporal-historical fulfilment, God brings mortality, death and the passivity of obedience into God's own being. 'Thus the Father, too, participates with the Son in the passion, and the divine unity of God's modes of being proves itself in the suffering of Jesus Christ. God's being *is* a being in the act of suffering, ... (and) even in death a being in *becoming*' (*Becoming*, 102).

Finally, in *God's Being Is in Becoming*, Jüngel proposes that *primal history and its temporal fulfilment are events of the word of God*. In our survey of *Paulus und Jesus*, we observed that, from early on, Jüngel is interested in exploring the importance of *language* for various problems in Christian dogmatics. In *God's Being Is in Becoming*, we discover that the theme of language continues to serve as a major source of Jüngel's theological focus.

For Jüngel, it is pivotal that the primal historical decision of election *and* the temporal-historical events of Jesus's suffering and crucifixion are a twofold movement of a *single divine word-event.* God's decision is God's *word.* Accordingly, Jüngel proposes in *God's Being Is in Becoming* that the event of election is an event of speech in which God says 'Yes' both to God and to humanity, and in speaking this 'Yes' differentiates God's own being and brings an 'other' into God's being in the humanity of Jesus. Likewise, the events of the 'temporal history' of Jesus Christ that correspond to the primal history of election are events of speech in which God, by saying 'Yes' to humanity in the context of the world, fulfils in time God's eternal self-differentiating 'Yes'. As Jüngel puts it:

> This *Yes* of God to himself constitutes his being as God the Father, God the Son and God the Holy Spirit … This 'Yes' of God to himself is the *mystery* of God's being and as such one cannot go behind it. For in God's saying 'Yes' to himself, God's being *corresponds* to itself as Father, as Son and as Holy Spirit. (*Becoming*, 111)

And later:

> God's grace is … the *reiteration in relation to something other* of the *Yes* to himself which constitutes God's being. In so far as this *Yes* in relation to something other than God calls this 'something other' into being, God's gracious *Yes* sets his being in relation to nothingness. But in so far as this *Yes* of grace frees the creation which has been called into being from the threat which comes through nothingness, God's gracious *Yes* exposes his being to that nothingness. (*Becoming*, 122; emphasis added)

From these two passages we make several observations concerning Jüngel's idea of the word of God as God's 'Yes': (1) God says 'Yes' to God, and this 'Yes' constitutes and determines God's being, such that 'one cannot go behind' this event of speech to discover some anterior or antecedent deity; (2) God's 'Yes' to God is *the* event of triune self-differentiation, for in this 'Yes' God 'corresponds' to God as Father, Son and Holy Spirit; (3) this *same* self-determinative 'Yes' is 'reiterated' to 'something other than' the being of God (that is, to humanity); (4) this 'Yes' reiterated *ad extra* constitutes the being of the other by 'calling the other into being' from nothingness and 'setting free' the other from the threat of nothingness (that is, it is a *creative* and *saving* 'Yes'); and (5) this 'Yes' reiterated *ad extra* 'sets' the being of God in 'relation' and even 'exposes' it to the nothingness from which the other is created and liberated.

God's being as Father, Son and Holy Spirit is the self-determinative and self-differentiating event of this 'Yes' spoken *ad intra*; God's being for us is the reiteration of this 'Yes' to 'something other', first also *ad intra* in the 'Yes' spoken to the humanity that is held in the hypostasis of the Son of God and then *ad extra* in the suffering and crucifixion of the man Jesus, in which events God's 'Yes' corresponds to concrete temporal history. As this 'Yes' for and to us, God's word creatively and savingly determines human being and creatively and savingly differentiates God from human being. This same 'Yes' spoken *ad extra* as the gospel – the 'apostolic "Yes"' – is that *human* speech through which God savingly 'shares' God's decision to be God only with humanity, and for this reason is that event of human speech that corresponds to the word of God. The triune God *just is* a 'concrete speech event'[23] – a 'doubly relational' (*Becoming*, 114ff.), 'verbal' (*Becoming*, 111) being who exists in an inexhaustible event of language constituted by a single word ('Yes') spoken at once *ad intra* and *ad extra*. In the humanity of Jesus Christ, humanity is, in a fundamental sense, the *passive recipient* of this 'Yes'. Likewise, the being of the justified human person also is fundamentally 'shaped' by the word (Jüngel, *Justification*, 199). Thus it is not language per se that constitutes the being of God and the being of the human person, but rather a very specific word, namely, the 'Yes' that is the word of God.

God as the Mystery of the World

Jüngel's 1977 monograph *God as the Mystery of the World: On the Foundation of the Theology of the Crucified One in the Dispute between Theism and Atheism* arguably is his most important work and is widely considered to be one of the great masterpieces of late twentieth-century theological literature. The book serves as a waystation of sorts in Jüngel's theological development, roughly summarizing and harmonizing the fifteen years' worth of work which had unfolded since the publication of *Paulus und Jesus*. We thus encounter in the book an author who already had logged many miles on the various pathways of thought he now hopes to map out for his readers. If the drawback here is a sense of déjà vu for those well versed in the antecedent publications, the utility of *God as the Mystery of the World* is that it can be handed to readers new to Jüngel's theology as a compendium of his interesting approach to a host of issues lying at the intersection of traditional theological categories (most notably: the doctrines of God and revelation, and Christology) and the concerns of contemporary heremeneutics and philosophy of language. It is, however, a notoriously demanding book, boasting a complex and occasionally opaque architecture, and an idiomatic style of theological rhetoric which does not quite tidy up in English. Indeed, while Jüngel's original German text is marked by humour, colourful allusions, puns and clever, even poetic, wordplays, much of this flair goes missing in translation. As a result, although *God as the Mystery of the World* is Jüngel's most ambitious theological statement, many anglophone readers new to his writing find it confounding and frustrating.

Jüngel commences his argument by commenting upon the problems of thinking and speaking about God in modernity, in doing so identifying those aspects of the theological tradition from which he desires to depart and setting the stage for his own countermove, which, we discover, is an approach to theological thought and speech that prioritizes the revelation of God's humanity in the crucifixion of Jesus Christ. Readers are advised to pay careful attention to the opening section of the book, 'The Definition of the Problem' (Jüngel, *Mystery*, 3–14), as it unfolds a feature of considerable importance for understanding the entirety of the volume. In the first subsection, Jüngel calls into question the legitimacy of, as he encapsulates it, the 'traditional hermeneutics of signification', which, according to his reading, is a theological gloss on the Aristotelian distinction of form and content. His argument here, which echoes many of the themes I already have addressed in this guide, goes something like this: the Latin theological tradition, following Augustine's neo-Platonic retrieval of Aristotle, supposes that reality consists of signs and things signified. A language, for chief instance, is a system of signs – words – organized according to flexible syntactical and grammatical rules such that its user is empowered with the capacity to grasp the reality that lies extrinsically to occurrences of speech. So far, Jüngel concedes, so good. But what happens when the 'thing' allegedly signified by human words is *God*? The hermeneutics of the sign, Jüngel contends, collapse whenever God is identified as the *res significata* (the thing signified by the sign), for otherwise it allows church and theology to speak of God, but only in such a way that God remains remote from the word, a thing absent to the speech that signifies God. Jüngel is worried, then, that the Latin theological tradition is committed to a hermeneutical programme according to which God cannot be encountered in speech and thought. God remains, as it were, ineffable and incogitable in human God-talk and God-thought.

For all intents and purposes, *God as the Mystery of the World* consists of an outright hermeneutical counterproposal to this tradition, so read. For Jüngel, precisely because the hermeneutics of signification posits a gap between the sign and the thing signified, it is unsuitable for the task assigned to it when employed for the purpose of theological speaking and thinking. Consequently, he argues in the course of the book that something altogether different and new happens in revelation, in *God's* word. Normal human discourse, marked as it is by the structural correspondences of sign and thing, knowledge and object, form and content, and so on, does not suffice as a vessel for communicating a word corresponding to God, and therefore must be broken, or interrupted, whenever God conscripts human language for the sake of revelation. God, that is, is the primal *speaker* in our God-talk, who, in speaking, explodes the limits and capacities of human language with new possibilities. God comes to speech in and as the superfluity of meaning occurring in the word about God, which, when heard in faith, is capable of speaking new life to the hearer. In just this sense, God, in Jüngel's idiom, is *more than necessary*.[24] God, in perfect freedom vis-à-vis worldly necessity, comes to the world in a word of sheer self- and life-giving love. So it is not the case that theology simply must discard the hermeneutics of the sign. Rather, Jüngel proposes that theology must juxtapose a hermeneutic of event with the Augustinian semiotics in order to demonstrate how the word of God behaves in comparison to the ordinary usages of the words of human language.

Jüngel weaves together his reading of this hermeneutical dilemma and its proposed solution with a critique of both classical and modern metaphysical doctrines of God. This segment of the book's argument unfolds in the course of the second chapter of the text ('Talk about the Death of God as an Expression of the Uncertainty of Modern Thinking about God', in *Mystery*, 43–104), and the trajectory of the analysis, though it at first appears to meander, is, in fact, crafted with delicate care. Jüngel begins by demonstrating that the so-called Death of God theology, a movement that had enjoyed a brief spell of salad days in the 1960s, emerged as a result of one of modern thought's central suppositions: namely, that the metaphysical tradition assigns to God a location 'over' the creaturely economy and, precisely so, on an ontological plane unreachable via any avenues of creaturely mediation. Nietzsche's madman, caricaturing one of modernity's responses to this metaphysical concept of deity, concludes that God has effectively been displaced, since a God located above   that is, *beyond* – the world would transcend all the categories and concepts of human thought and the words of human language. Interestingly, Jüngel wastes hardly a breath discussing the proponents and primary sources associated with the 'Death of God' theology, using, as it were, merely the movement's name and Nietzschean background as bare furniture for subsequent readings of, in turn, Bonhoeffer, Hegel and (briefly) Feuerbach. His analysis here works *because of*, rather than in spite of, the anachronistic arrangement of his interlocutors. According to Jüngel's exegesis, Bonhoeffer and Hegel read the modern problem of the death of God *Christologically*, asserting, albeit in very different ways, that, in the death of Jesus Christ, God has taken up into the being of God the absence of being. The consequence of this move for both theologians, Jüngel shows, is a non-religious (Bonhoeffer) or atheistic (Hegel) reorientation of theological thought and speech, for the death of God in the death of Jesus Christ is, by logic, the death of Western metaphysics – that is, of a philosophical, though frequently baptized, concept of God. It is Feuerbach who, oddly enough, becomes both a hero and a foil in Jüngel's tale precisely because he dared push back against his forebear Hegel by asserting that the entire edifice of Christian thought and practice collapses if it is defined as the identity of faith and unbelief, of God and death, of theology and its negation.

Contending that modern theology has not answered Feuerbach's legitimate protest against Hegel's Christological idea of the death of God sufficiently, Jüngel now turns to advance his own proposal, his demonstration of which composes three large chapters covering the final three-fourths of the book's pages. Contra Feuerbach and going beyond Hegel's insight, Jüngel urges that the thesis of the being of God as the unity of life and death in Jesus Christ provides Christian theology with a genuine opportunity to overturn metaphysical theism. Arguing that God's existence is identical to God's essence, he proposes that the death of Jesus Christ, in both its eternal decision and historical enactment, *is* God's self-differentiation as Father and Son in the power of the Holy Spirit. Consequently, it is God's identification with this dead man that forms the basis of theological thinking that corresponds to truth. If not, theology drifts into speculation and props up the transcendent God of the philosophers, reducing theological discourse to abject apophaticism (Chapter III, 'On the Possibility of Thinking God', in *Mystery*, 105–225). Moreover, theology's God-talk parallels theological God-thought, insofar as theology can speak of God and thus commence its unique mode of discourse only by narrating the story of God's decision to be God by and in God's identification with the crucified Christ. Such a story, when proclaimed, is the world's mystery, an interruptive event of language that confounds all creaturely values and notions of truth and beauty, precisely by introducing the impossible possibility of the Creator's unity with non-being. And the event of language enacted to tell this story is neither univocal nor equivocal speech, but rather a use of human language which presupposes both God's concrete difference from the world and God's immanent presence in the world. The language of faith, therefore, is analogical – though not in the sense of the *analogia entis*. Faith, rather, corresponds to an '*analogia adventus*' ('analogy of advent'), in the linguistic event of which the dissimilarity between God and the world is reimagined in light of God's intimate nearness to creatures (Chapter IV, 'On the Speakability of God', in *Mystery*, 226–298). And such a vision for a thoroughgoing *theological* theology entails a radical reorientation of traditional trinitarian concepts. For a doctrine of God that begins and ends with God's going forth and returning in the crucified and resurrected one must include God's intimate, ontological involvement with creaturely time – with history - and never otherwise (Chapter V, 'On the Humanity of God', in *Mystery*, 299–396).

I hardly can do justice here to the many nuances of Jüngel's argument and therefore will conclude these comments by making some general observations that readers might do well to keep in mind when tackling this difficult book for the first time. First, it is imperative to recognize that the heart of *God as the Mystery of the World*, as a piece of irregular dogmatics, is a hermeneutical response to what is, inevitably, a hermeneutical dilemma and to read the book just as such. As I already have suggested, the book is probably best approached as a grand summary of the nexus of hermeneutical proposals Jüngel had been developing since writing *Paulus und Jesus* in the early 1960s. In the main portion of *God as the Mystery of the World*, Jüngel persistently occupies himself with the problem of the relation of God's words and human words, always describing the former as the crisis of the latter in the event of revelation. For Jüngel, thought and speech of God are possible only on the basis of the new hermeneutical situation that emerges when God comes to the world in the word.

Second, we do well to note that, in German, the titles of the three final chapters are symmetrical, a rhetorical feature that falls away in translation: *Zur Denkbarkeit Gottes, Zur Sagbarkeit Gottes, Zur Menschlichkeit Gottes* (again, these chapters are translated in the English text as 'On the Possibility of Thinking God', 'On the Speakability of God' and 'On the Humanity of God'). However, Jüngel's argument hardly is linear. The argument, rather, unrolls not unlike the procedure of working around the spokes of a wheel in order to grasp the contours of the wheel's centre; in this instance, the humanity of God – including and especially the death of God – in Jesus Christ, the Crucified One. This being the case, I propose that it is not necessary to read these three chapters in their given order. On the contrary, the best strategy for new readers may be to begin the book's major portion, having worked through the introduction and chapter two, with the final chapter, 'On the Humanity of God', for there Jüngel both employs and modifies the tradition's trinitarian language for God in order to identify the implications of the incarnation for the doctrine of God. This material is helpful to have in mind when working through the earlier chapters on God's conceivability and utterability. In any case, I raise this rather unorthodox suggestion here in order to stress the caveat that the 'wheels within wheels' structure of Jüngel's argument in the book demands considerable flexibility and creativity on the part of his readers.

Third, and to reiterate a critically important point, since *God as the Mystery of the World* exemplifies irregular dogmatics, readers should not expect to find the book, especially in the long plateau of the argument, behaving as an exhaustive, organized summary of the Christian faith in the course of which every 'i' is dotted and 't' crossed. Nor is it advisable to go thumbing through the pages in search of 'Jüngel's doctrine of _____', as if the volume provided textbook definitions of various theologoumena. My point, sheerly put, is that quite a lot goes missing in *God as the Mystery of the World*. It is, as I have presented it, a text written to address a specific nexus of issues, and Jüngel is very selective in employing concepts and doctrinal materials towards a solution. Consequently, many alternative moves simply are not considered. We should indeed ask how Jüngel's account of God's *Denkbarkeit*, *Sagbarkeit* and *Menschlichkeit* may have appeared had he a more robust pneumatology, or ecclesiology, or doctrine of creation and so on. At the same time, we should not be too quick to let what is lacking distract us from what we actually find in the course of the analysis.

Finally, it is worth briefly considering the extent to which Jüngel ventures into uncharted territory in *God as the Mystery of the World*. In an early review of the German original, American theologian Garrett Green reads *God as the Mystery of the World* through the lens of the remarks Jüngel made fifteen years earlier in the 'Preface to the First Edition' of *Paulus und Jesus*, wherein, as we already have seen, Jüngel proposes that his dissertation is 'an attempt to synthesize the ideas of Rudolf Bultmann and Karl Barth'. Green suggests that Jüngel remained committed to this effort well into his theological career, and that *God as the Mystery of the World* perhaps best is viewed as an extension into 'fundamental theology' of an internecine conflict between Bultmannians and Barthians. For Green, Jüngel 'apparently sees himself as heir to the tradition of dialectical theology, remaining loyal to the fundamental unity of its cofounders while moving decisively beyond the partisan squabbles between their disciples'.[25] In Green's reading of the text, though, it is just here that Jüngel disappoints. For Jüngel, he argues, does not actually solve anything, but rather merely recasts the terms of the debate 'in a framework derived chiefly from the Bultmann school and particularly from the architects of the "new hermeneutic"'.[26]

I cite Green at length here mainly because his review highlights (albeit perhaps a bit too critically) the fact that one encounters in *God as the Mystery of the World* the echoes of many of the noisy debates and discussions sounding in German theology during the first two decades of Jüngel's career. To switch metaphors, Green rightly detects that the monograph plays in a Bultmannian key, while featuring refrains reminiscent of Barth's mature programme for Christian dogmatics. The problems Jüngel goes to great lengths to resolve in the book – the subject–object dilemma, the capacities and limitations of language for Christian talk about God, the tension between *Historie* and *Geschichte*, the identity of the man Jesus of Nazareth and his relationship to the Christ proclaimed by faith, the putative failure of the metaphysical tradition, the crisis of enlightened modernity and the challenge to faith of modern atheism, and the perceived need to revise Protestantism's hermeneutical commitments for the sake of a Christianity come of age – are common themes also in the writings of Bultmann and the 'Old Marburgers'. Likewise, the conceptual tools Jüngel employs in hopes of resolving these issues – the event character of language, a Heideggerian analysis of *Dasein*, a categorical use of the law–gospel distinction, an exclusively forensic description of the event of justification and so on – can be found in liberal doses in works by Bultmann, Käsemann, Fuchs and Ebeling. At the same time, the trinitarian language for God that pervades *God as the Mystery of the World* recalls Barth rather than Bultmann, and it is here that the cross-currency between the two camps of dialectical theology becomes most lucid and interesting.

In Chapter 2, I attempted to dissuade readers from conceiving Jüngel's theological contribution as a concoction of two or more of his influences. If I have reservations concerning Green's comments on *God as the Mystery of the World*, they lay here. As I have shown in this section, the book surely is more than the yield of an in-house fracas between the Bultmannian and

Barthian camps of the dialectical theology which first emerged in German Protestantism between the wars. Still, while Jüngel's opus does not reduce to that long-running conflict, it is not at all difficult to discern strong lines of continuity between the book and the world of discourse marking theology and biblical studies during Jüngel's theology maturity in Berlin. Demonstrably so, Jüngel does not stray too far in *God as the Mystery of the World* from that world of discourse. It is only later, mainly as Jüngel addresses third article issues (namely, the church and the sacraments) and becomes embroiled in the late twentieth-century ecumenical dialogues, that he truly begins to take his basic theological commitments into new directions.

In summary, I recommend that it might be best to view the book as, in at least two senses, a capstone text. For readers of Jüngel's works, *God as the Mystery of the World* assimilates the different strands of textual exegesis and constructive dogmatics from its author's first two decades into a single comprehensive statement. For readers of German theology in the modern period, the book neatly encapsulates one of several options for Christian thought 'come of age' during a century marked by both advancement and tumult.

Justification

Jüngel's book *Justification – The Heart of the Christian Faith*, his only major publication to appear after *God as the Mystery of the World*, summarizes his approach to a theme of perennial interest in Christian dogmatics and ecumenical theology. For students of Jüngel's thought, it is key item in the canon, serving as a compendium of his basic theological commitments and boasting all the remarkable literary and rhetorical traits found in its author's best work. At the same time, the book is something of a relic. It was written as a contribution to, as Jüngel puts it, a contemporaneous 'quarrel' about the centrality of the doctrine of justification in Protestant theology (Jüngel, *Justification*, xxxiii), a controversy incited by the publicity surrounding the preparation and eventual publication of the *Joint Declaration on the Doctrine of Justification (JDDJ)* by the Roman Catholic Church and the Lutheran World Federation (LWF). Jüngel played the roles of gadfly and firebrand during this pivotal episode in the history of the modern ecumenical movement, effectively leading a public revolt of Protestant theologians against the *JDDJ* before eventually lending his support to the document. *Justification*, which he produced in the midst of the melee, offers an exposition of the doctrine under dispute, commencing with some methodological considerations and then unfolding an account of justification from the plight of sin to the solution of the gospel. There is a polemical undercurrent to the work, no doubt sparked by the immediate circumstances. Readers unfamiliar with this background are advised to consult secondary sources on the developments in Catholic-Lutheran ecumenism leading up to the signing of the *JDDJ* in 1999.[27]

For the sake of introducing the book to readers of this guide, the following comments, as it were, frame the monograph according to three trajectories: Jüngel's own ongoing interest in extending hermeneutical discussions to various topics of Christian dogmatics, the aforementioned climate of ecumenical theology and the bilateral dialogues at the end of the twentieth century, and the peculiar brand of Lutheran thought Jüngel advances in the volume's argument.

First, some remarks on the location of *Justification* within the context of Jüngel's theological oeuvre. The first German edition of the book appeared in 1998,[28] about halfway through Jüngel's seventh decade and thirty-six years after the publication of *Paulus und Jesus*. It is Jüngel's final theological monograph, and, following its appearance, he produced only a handful of short pieces on various topics. As such, *Justification* brings to a close the last major productive phase of Jüngel's career. After *Justification* there unfolds a decade-long coda marked by minor contributions. Given this placement, readers should not be surprised to discover in the book the summary and reiteration of many things said previously during the preceding period.

The heart of *Justification* consists of a rich theological account of how the event of justification occurs in the course of the Christian life. Jüngel presupposes that both the justification of the sinner and theology's reflection upon it as a salvific phenomenon originate in the gracious word-event, received in faith as the addressing speech of the gospel, that communicates God's identification with the humanity – especially the suffering and death – of Jesus Christ. The plight, solution and repercussions of the event of justification are situated accordingly. Jüngel describes sin – the problem resolved by the act of God's justifying grace – as the false, relationless and deadly existence which is directly consequential to the insatiable human drive to justify and actualize the self through thinking, willing and working. And yet, so he argues, God solves this fundamental human predicament precisely by interrupting the course of the 'deadly sham existence' of sin (*Justification*, 1) in order to bring to speech a relationship that is itself the abyss of mystery: namely, God's relationship to the world and to the sinner in the form of *God's own* humanity. Righteousness, the gift made possible *only* by and in the interruptive event of the word of the gospel, is conceived as relational peace, God's reparation of the relationships – to God, to others, to the self and to the world – which are twisted and, inevitably, deadly whenever God's word and work are eclipsed by humanity's compulsion towards self-actualization. Ethics, the outflow of the justifying work of God into the Christian life, are possible only when the priority of God's action and speech is recognized as the foundation and condition of all human moral actions.

From this short prospectus, we see that Jüngel's account in *Justification* of the justifying event and its entailments incorporates many of the issues occupying his attention from *Paulus und Jesus* forward. While the locution 'word-event' does not recur here, as ever Jüngel appeals to the idea of the interruptive action of the word of God to describe how justification impacts the word's hearer. The *addressing* function of language[29] and, likewise, the fundamental *passivity* of the human recipient of the justifying word[30] are key components of Jüngel's argument in the book. The economic action of God *pro nobis* gives shape to the account of the triune relations, much in the same way as what we find in *God's Being Is in Becoming*.[31] Furthermore, both divine being and human being are defined relationally throughout the monograph; indeed, the entire drama of justification is couched in relational terms, with the plight of sin defined as relationlessness leading to death and justifying righteousness as a renewal of life's fundamental relationships for the sake of human participation in the richly relational life of the triune God. To establish this reading of the event of justification, Jüngel enlists a familiar band of conversation partners, as citations from Barth, Bultmann, Ebeling, Käsemann, Schleiermacher and especially Luther abound. In short, the concerns, moves and conclusions we encounter in *Justification* hardly are surprising given the trajectory of Jüngel's theological career. The monograph tidily extends and expands his agenda for hermeneutical theology to the *articulus statis et cadentis ecclesiae*.

Second, *Justification* reflects an ecumenical sensibility which marked a dwindling era in the history of the modern ecumenical movement. As mentioned earlier, ecumenist Michael Root, borrowing a metaphor from physicist Thomas Kuhn, recently has suggested that ecumenism and ecumenical theology now have shifted from a 'revolutionary' phase to a 'normal' one, and that new modes of ecumenical engagement must and will emerge to match the cautious ecumenical mood of the present unfolding century.[32] In a similar vein, in his survey of the first four decades of Catholic involvement in dialogical ecumenism, Walter Cardinal Kasper observes that today's climate is marked by what he calls a 'new sobriety'.[33] Although, on one hand, recent decades have witnessed an increase in ecumenical and interfaith participation by local church ministers and laypersons, the present period, asserts Cardinal Kasper, likewise is characterized by widespread suspicion that the dialogical method of ecumenical convergence cannot actually achieve the movement's desired goal of full visible unity between the churches.[34] A subplot of the era dominated by the bilateral dialogues contributed to the present atmosphere of weariness concerning dialogical engagement. From the 1970s to the 1990s, a debate evolved among ecumenists over the possible existence of an ecumenical *Grunddifferenz* – a difference between confessions so fundamental in nature that it may be identified as the root cause of all other divergences.[35] While the bilateral dialogues were forging ahead during this period, a number of ecumenists, many of whom represented their respective churches and confessions in the dialogues, were questioning whether the dialogical approach to Christian differences indeed could uncover the true source(s) of division. Not surprisingly, the search for an ecumenical basic difference yielded no conclusive results while contributing to a sharp decline in enthusiasm for dialogical ecumenism. Root's 'normal ecumenism' and Cardinal Kasper's 'new sobriety' are attempts to encapsulate the ecumenical mood on this side of the shift in ecumenism which transpired towards the end of the last century.

For our purposes here, it is essential to see that Jüngel was writing *Justification* during a time in which dialogical ecumenism was losing steam even as it was on the threshold of earning what is perhaps its signature achievement – the *JDDJ*. The book is exhibitive of the earlier, waning era. Unlike many of his preceding publications, in *Justification* Jüngel emphasizes the territorial claims of the different Christian confessions and especially is concerned with the centuries-old border dispute between Protestants and Catholics over issues pertaining to soteriology. His prose throughout the text is sharp and polemical, his ambition in the volume to clarify a Protestant doctrine of justification *over against* traditional Catholic claims regarding works and grace. And yet, in spite of the combativeness and prophetic urgency occasionally marking the tone of the book, Jüngel is hardly a crusty, hidebound confessionalist here, even though some readers may initially mistake him for one. Rather, he writes from the vantage point of a committed ecumenist firmly convinced that historical Christian dissensuses will resolve themselves only through arduous theological labour. Indeed, if Tridentine Catholic teaching on salvation is one 'other' over against which Jüngel situates his polemic in *Justification*, so also is a leisurely brand of Protestant ecumenism that all too quickly concedes long-standing theological and confessional commitments for the sake of agreements between churches supposedly established on the basis of dialogue and documented in the ecumenical literature. For Jüngel, the *JDDJ*, appearing as it did as the culmination of a nearly thirty-year trajectory of bilateral dialogue between Catholics and Lutherans, should inspire celebration only if the positions of both sides are presented in the document unambiguously. He worries, however, that essential components of the Protestant doctrine of justification are sidestepped in the effort to reach a common understanding. In *Justification* he attempts to fill in what has gone missing by systematically presenting his own version of the Protestant view.

Third and finally, and dovetailing with the preceding comments on the context of the monograph in the history of the modern ecumenical movement, a few brief remarks are in order concerning how Jüngel's uneasy identity as a Lutheran theologian manifests itself in *Justification*. Of all the texts in the canon of his writings, it is in *Justification* that numerous quintessentially Lutheran theological concerns bubble to the surface. As such, the monograph sheds light on his idiosyncratic approach to theology undertaken in a Lutheran key while also demanding of readers some reflection upon its author's own commitments.

One entryway into this matter is to recall an observation I made in the course of the biographical sketch in Chapter 1: namely, that, both in *Justification* and elsewhere, Jüngel writes as an independent scholar of Christian theology and not as an official proxy either of the global network of member churches comprising the LWF or of any other organized Lutheran church body. Liberated from restraints potentially imposed upon him by an official appointment on an ecumenical working group, Jüngel is, as it were, free to follow his nose in organizing and executing his analysis of the doctrine of justification. To be sure, many of the hallmarks of classical Lutheran dogmatics emerge in the course of the volume: a central if not fully criteriological function assigned to justification; a heavy investment in the dialectic of law and gospel, with an emphasis on the importance of correctly distinguishing between them; and an underscoring of the forensic character of the event of justification, with the attendant caveat that any discussion of human participation in God's justifying grace must be qualified in reference to salvation's juridical setting; and so on. And yet, the monograph hardly is 'textbook' in its procedures and conclusions, and for this reason readers interested in a systematic summary of Lutheran teaching on justification will come away from the book disappointed. *Justification*, rather, presents Jüngel at his idiosyncratic best here, riffing on the concepts, categories, locutions and formulas of historic Lutheran dogmatics in order to advance his own agenda for reading the doctrine.

Along these lines, it is interesting to consider once again the roster of interlocutors Jüngel enlists for rejoinder in the book. Luther is invoked far more frequently than anyone else, an abundance of engagement that certainly is appropriate considering the decisive role the reformer played in the formulation of the early Protestant doctrine of justification. However, apart from some occasional citations of *Confessio Augustana* and Melanchthon's *Apologia*, the Lutheran confessional writings catalogued in the *Book of Concord* are absent from Jüngel's exposition. Moreover, his reception of Luther's texts and the history and theology of subsequent Lutheranism betrays an almost exclusive reliance upon the work of Ebeling. He does not draw upon the support of any of the other great twentieth-century statesmen of the Lutheran tradition, such as Werner Elert, Paul Althaus and Edmund Schlink. Nor does he appear at all to be interested in the insights of near-contemporary ecumenically minded Lutherans: say, of Peter Brunner, Regin Prenter, Gustaf Wingren and Oswald Beyer. Apart from a brief aside, Jüngel does not engage the then-controversial 'New Finnish' interpretation of Luther spearheaded by Tuomo Mannermaa, nor does he devote space to the burgeoning 'New Perspective on Paul'. And *Justification* does not exhibit any functional awareness on the part of its author of developments in anglophone Lutheran theology: for instance, of contemporaneous works by Carl Braaten, Gerhard Forde and Robert Jenson.

It is, then, a somewhat myopic vision for Lutheran theology that emerges in the book. To put it another way, recalling language used already in this section, *Justification* reflects the perspectival and rhetorical idiosyncrasies of its author. As such, perhaps the principal value of the book as a literary artefact resides in the fact that it reveals how Jüngel, at a particular juncture of his career and with the help of conceptual tools furnished by his unique take on Protestant theology at the intersection of hermeneutics and classical dogmatics, addressed a then-hot ecumenical bone of contention.

CHAPTER 4
READING JÜNGEL II – ELEVEN ESSENTIAL THEOLOGICAL ESSAYS

Some of Jüngel's best and most provocative contributions to modern Christian thought come in the form of the theological essay. He composed hundreds of essays over the course of his career, publishing the pieces as book chapters or as articles in peer-review journals. While the four monographs display his dexterity in unfolding complex arguments over many pages, Jüngel's theological essays exhibit his skill at presenting particular themes in short, rhetorically charged expositions. It is in his essays that readers are most likely to encounter the proclamatory or prophetic character of Jüngel's theology and to witness his commitment to the integration of dogmatics and the tasks of Christian preaching.

Jüngel's essays reveal an astonishing breadth of engagement with issues at the heart of Christian theology. In just the eleven essays we survey, we observe Jüngel addressing the relationship between God and the world, the problems of analogy and natural theology, the continuity and discontinuity between the historical Jesus and the Christ of faith, the phenomenon of theological language, the doctrine of the trinity, history and eschatology, ecclesiology, ecumenism, the role of the doctrine of justification in theology, the church's public acts of worship and sacramental theology. In these essays alone he enlists a legion of interlocutors. Aristotle, Augustine, Thomas, Luther, Melanchthon, Kant, Hegel, Schleiermacher, Steffens, Nietzsche, Barth, Przywara, Heidegger, Bultmann, Fuchs, Rahner, Balthasar, Schmaus, Lévinas, Käsemann, Ebeling, Gadamer, Pannenberg, Pesch and Kasper each receives critical treatment in the pieces introduced here; numerous other names pop up in the footnotes. At the very least, such observations, however cursory, should help to dispel the impression that Jüngel fixates only on a handful of pet theological issues, and that his thought, whether as a whole or on any given topic, easily reduces to a mixture of a handful of influences. To be sure, as a rule Jüngel's essays resound in a common theological register, exhibit his idiosyncratic style and wordsmanship and feature engagements with, from out of the multitude of cited sources, a shortlist of key dialogue partners. The essays also display some of the shortcomings of Jüngel's programme for Christian theology, as I indicate in several of the sections that follow. And yet, it is in this portion of his oeuvre that the full range and significance of his contribution is most conspicuous.

It hardly is possible within the limits of this guide to introduce or even to identify each of Jüngel's signature short pieces. Instead, I have curated a small roster of essays – seven available in English; four as yet untranslated – I consider to be essential for a serious study of Jüngel's theology. For the most part, the pieces surveyed here mark, as it were, 'turning points' in Jüngel's thought, either by introducing new themes and problems for exposition or by summarizing long pathways of research and contemplation. As such, these eleven essays pinpoint important waystations on Jüngel's theological journey. I have arranged my comments in chronological order to reflect the developmental significance of the essays at hand, and readers who explore this material in the order provided will get a good sense of the itinerary of his thought from beginning to end. On the other hand, readers need not take the essays themselves in chronological turn. To appreciate the breadth of Jüngel's programme, I might recommend beginning with 'My Theology', and from that staging point proceed to 'Possibility and Actuality', 'The New' and 'Metaphorical Truth'. From these four essays readers will gain a basic grasp of Jüngel's approach to the nature, structure and tasks of Christian theology. The other eight essays covered here perhaps are best read roughly in creedal order, beginning with pieces on the doctrine of God ('"Economic" and "Imminent" Trinity' and 'Die Möglichkeit') and from there moving to Christology ('Effectiveness' and 'Dogmatic Significance'), justification ('Klarheit'), ecclesiology ('*Credere*'), ecumenism ('The Church as Sacrament?') and sacramental theology ('Sakrament und Repräsentation').

The following sections will unfold by way of paraphrase and commentary on the eleven essays. While I have endeavoured to keep critical comments in the background, perceptive readers will rather easily discern my own disposition towards these texts and their author's theology. Even the selection of essays for this chapter evinces a particular approach to Jüngel and his thought. Other scholars of Jüngel's theology undoubtedly would go about this very differently, and a few experts will be put off by the fact that I left aside this or that essay. To acknowledge just a few of the gems I found it necessary, but particularly painful, to omit: 'Die Freiheit der Theologie' (1967; in *TE II*, 11–36); 'Vom Tod des lebendigen Gottes' (1968; in *TE I*, 105–125);

'God – as a Word of Our Language'[1] (1969; his inaugural lecture at Zürich); *'Quae supra nos, nihil ad nos'* (1972; in *TE II*, 202–251); 'Theologie in der Spannung zwischen Wissenschaft und Bekenntnis' (1973; in *TE II*, 37–51); 'Das Dilemma der natürlichen Theologie und die Wahrheit ihres Problems' (1975; in *TE II*, 158–177): 'The Truth of Life',[2] (1976); 'Anthropomorphism' (1982; in *Essays I*, 72–94); 'The Sacrifice of Jesus as Sacrament and Example' (1982; in *Essays II*, 163–190); 'Einheit der Kirche – Konkret' (1983; in *TE III*, 335–345); 'Zum Wesen des Friedens' (1983; in *TE V*, 1–39); 'The Revelation of the Hiddenness of God' (1984; in *Essays II*, 120–144); 'Der Gottesdienst als Fest der Freiheit' (1984; in *TE IV*, 330–350); 'On Becoming Truly Human' (1985; in *Essays II*, 216–240); 'The Christian Understanding of Suffering'[3] (1988); 'The Last judgment as an Act of Grace'[4] (1990); 'Zum Wesen des Christentums' (1994; in *TE IV*, 1–23); 'Ganzheitsbegriffe' (1997; in *TE V*, 40–53); and *'Caritas fide formata'*[5] (2006). I submit, though, that the eleven essays covered here are very well suited to introduce the reader to Jüngel's theological contribution.

'Die Möglichkeit theologischer Anthropologie auf dem Grunde der Analogie' (1962)

Soon after completing his doctoral dissertation, Jüngel composed this examination of the problem of analogy, which also happens to be his first critical engagement with Barth's theology. In the essay (in *Barth*, 210–232), the literal rendering in English of which is 'The Possibility of Theological Anthropology on the Basis of Analogy: An Examination of Karl Barth's Understanding of Analogy', Jüngel draws together several prominent themes from the *Church Dogmatics* in order to trace Barth's rejection of the *analogia entis* (analogy of being) in favour of an *analogia fidei* (analogy of faith). He especially is keen to counter the reading of this nest of issues put forth by Hans Urs von Balthasar in his celebrated introduction to Barth's theology from 1951.[6] Balthasar had suggested that Barth's theology represents a genuine opportunity for ecumenical rapprochement between Roman Catholics and Protestants. For although Barth early on claimed to reject outright the *analogia entis* as the 'invention of antichrist' (Barth, *CD* I/1, xiii), as the *Church Dogmatics* matures he affirms that nature and human reason are ingredient to revealed theology. That is, Barth was becoming convinced, at least according to Balthasar, that revelation reconciles nature and grace, and reason and faith. Consequently, Balthasar contends, 'Barth's way of understanding God's revelation in Christ includes the analogy of being within the analogy of faith; and … the way the Catholic authors we have been citing understand the christocentricity of God's plan for the world allows the analogy of being to gain its density and concreteness only within the wider analogy of faith.'[7]

In our essay, Jüngel argues that, for Barth, the *analogia entis* and the *analogia fidei* are mutually exclusive categories, entailing 'as unrelenting a contradiction as the opposition between δικαιοσύνη ἐκ νόμου [righteousness from the law] and δικαιοσύνη ἐκ πίστεως [righteousness from faith]' (Jüngel, *Barth*, 211). For Jüngel, the key to understanding Barth on this point is to recognize that, in Barth's view, 'the being of the man Jesus is the ontological and epistemological ground of analogy' (*Barth*, 212), for in Jesus Christ God reveals what it means to be human and also what it means to be God. Faith in Jesus Christ involves the acknowledgement that in him alone divinity and humanity correspond, and this correspondence is the basis for authentic Christian thought and speech about God and humanity. Likewise, for Barth we cannot achieve genuine knowledge of God through rational reflection on nature, for such theological knowledge becomes possible only in the event of God's self-revelation in Jesus Christ. To fail to recognize Barth's commitment on this point, Jüngel urges, is to miss the heart of the *Church Dogmatics*. Moreover, in Jüngel's interpretation of Barth, there is no softening of the opposition between the *analogia entis* and the *analogia fidei* as Barth moves forward through the doctrines of God (*CD* II) and creation (*CD* III), and into the doctrine of reconciliation (Barth had just published *CD* IV/1 when Jüngel composed the essay). Rather, because of Barth's overriding concern to articulate the event of Jesus Christ, his rejection of the *analogia entis* obtains from beginning to end.

In clarifying what he contends is Barth's true position on the *analogia entis*, 'Die Möglichkeit' articulates Jüngel's own burgeoning contribution to the doctrine of analogy, a theme which first drew his interest when preparing his *Habilitationsschrift* on the origins of analogy in the metaphysical tradition and which would remain a matter of his attention throughout the 1960s and 1970s, culminating with the study *God as the Mystery of the World*. It is in *Mystery* that Jüngel advances an *analogy of advent* as a form of the *analogia fidei*. 'Die Möglichkeit' lays the groundwork for the analogy of advent in dialogue with Barth, chiefly by mapping out the trinitarian and anthropological coordinates of the correspondence between God and humanity. To paraphrase an extremely thorny passage, God relates to humanity, Jüngel argues, in that God says 'Yes' to humanity with the very same 'Yes' that constitutes God's inner-triune life. (1) God says 'Yes' to God, insofar as the Father 'affirms the Son in the Spirit'. (2) God says the same 'Yes' to humanity firstly insofar as God says 'Yes' to the humanity of Jesus Christ. (3) God says 'Yes' to humanity in the second instance insofar as God determines that humanity will be God's covenant partner. (4) God says 'Yes' to humanity thirdly insofar as God creates humanity to fulfil this covenant destiny (*Barth*, 225). For Jüngel it is critical that this 'Yes' is a phenomenon of *speech* (a *Sprachphänomen*): 'God speaks; humanity corresponds' in faith (*Barth*, 226). An *analogia entis*, by contrast, would be a *natural* phenomenon, accessible to reason apart from faith. Finally and relatedly, tacit here and explicit later is Jüngel's insistence that this 'Yes' is a *word of address* which *comes* to the world – and to the hearer – in the event of God's self-disclosure. Hence the eventual use of *adventus* as the ruling metaphor for Jüngel's approach to the *analogia fidei*.

Jüngel revisited Barth's approach to analogy in a celebrated essay on Barth's theological development, arguing, once more against Balthasar, that Barth's turn from dialectic to analogy owed much to a dispute from the mid-1920s with Erik Peterson, his erstwhile colleague from Göttingen (the essay titled 'Von der Dialektik zur Analogie: Die Schule Kierkegaards und der Einspruch Petersons'; in *Barth*, 127–179). For his part, Barth deemed 'Die Möglichkeit' worthy of lofty praise. 'I have just reread with close attention your essay on analogy', he wrote to Jüngel in November of 1962, 'and must not delay letting you know how pleased I am with this fine work. You undoubtedly express better than I could have done myself what I have thought and think on this subject'. For Barth, Jüngel's analysis effectively had put the matter to rest: 'The discussion has now passed a turning point and it certainly cannot go back again.'[8] Furthermore, as a result of his enthusiastic reception of 'Die Möglichkeit' and *God's Being Is in Becoming*, which appeared three years following the publication of our essay, Barth came to regard Jüngel as 'one among today's younger theologians who has studied me thoroughly and has the willingness and ability to do independently and fruitfully the further work which is needed today', as he puts the matter in an invitation to Jüngel to attend a celebration of his eightieth birthday in May of 1966.[9]

'Die Möglichkeit', then, is for several reasons a highly significant text for the study of Jüngel's theology. Only his second published journal essay, the piece inaugurates his career-long engagement with Barth's thought and is the staging point for his trajectory of research into the problem of analogy.

'The World as Possibility and Actuality' (1969)

At the end of the 1960s, we find Jüngel turning his attention to the exposition of the doctrine of justification, a theme he will go on to revisit in numerous texts from throughout the duration of his career. 'The World as Possibility and Actuality' (in *Essays I*, 95–123) spells out a key ingredient of his approach to this topic, for it is here that Jüngel endeavours to describe 'the ontology of the doctrine of justification', as he puts it in the subtitle. Jüngel proposes in the essay that the Christian confession of the God who justifies requires that we depart from classical metaphysical concepts of being. The language he uses to advance this discussion – namely, the distinction he draws between possibility and actuality – reappears in subsequent writings on a host of theological topics.

Following a brief preamble on the nature of theological and philosophical language, Jüngel states rather abruptly the situation against which intends to dispatch a corrective volley. 'From the beginnings of metaphysics', he writes, 'actuality has been given ontological priority over possibility. In this way, possibility was pushed out of place by actuality. Being was and is identified with actuality' (*Essays I*, 97). Jüngel identifies Aristotle as the forebear of the tradition in need of revision, and in the second section of the essay he offers his own short summary of Aristotle's conception of the prioritization of actuality over possibility. The philosopher 'does not think of the ontological priority of actuality over possibility simply as an ontic precedence of the actual over the possible', Jüngel qualifies. 'Rather, the priority of actuality consists in the fact that the possible is defined as the possible by reference to actuality' (*Essays I*, 98). At the heart of this determination, Jüngel argues, is Aristotle's idea of God as the 'unmoved prime mover'. Conceived as such, 'God is free of all possibility, he is the act for whose sake the world exists and out of love for whom the world is what it is. The world is moved by love for this perfect act.' By consequence, Jüngel concludes, Aristotle's God 'does not love' (*Essays I*, 100) and is the very opposite of the God of Jesus Christ, who loves the world in freedom.

Aristotle's prioritization of actuality 'determined not only philosophy and life in the world which it advocates, but also Christian theology, in a way which still affects us and which, indeed, is hardly ever questioned today' (*Essays I*, 101). Jüngel lists a short roster of fellow iconoclasts, naming Luther, Barth, Gogarten, Ebeling, Fuchs and Moltmann as theologians who dared challenge the hegemonic Aristotelian tradition (*Essays I*, 102). After a brief nod to the eschatological implications of the discussion at hand, he turns in the long fourth and fifth sections of the essay to unfold his own counter to Aristotle. In the first of these two sections, Jüngel offers an epitome of the doctrine of justification, arguing that Luther, who Jüngel considers to be foundational for the task of articulating the doctrine, called into question 'the Aristotelian thesis that a person becomes righteous by doing right' (*Essays I*, 104). On the contrary, for Luther 'we only come to *act* righteously once we *become* and *are* righteous', and this entails that we abandon the Aristotelian prioritization of actuality. To put it another way, in the event of justification the unjust person is *changed*, or *made righteous*, apart from her or his actions. The message of justification, therefore, is good news especially to *sinners*. For sin, as Jüngel defines it, is a state of relational 'nothingness' between the sinner and God which cannot be overcome by any *human* acts of atonement. It is, rather, only in the *divine* actions of Good Friday and Easter Sunday that new relational possibilities between God and humanity arise. 'Jesus's resurrection from the dead', Jüngel contends, 'promises that we shall be made anew out of the nothingness of relationlessness, remade *ex nihilo*, if through faith in the creative Word of God we allow ourselves to participate in the love of God which occurs as the death of Jesus Christ' (*Essays I*, 108).

Jüngel uses the final section of the essay to probe the ontological significance of the doctrine of justification he has just described. The tension between the 'radical nothingness of Good Friday' (*Essays I*, 110) and the sheer newness of Easter Sunday raises the question of God's relation to the world and its actualities. Jüngel maps out this tension by appealing to the category of the *im*possible. 'God and the world', he proposes, 'are not distinguished in such a way that the world is identified with the possible and God with the impossible. Rather, distinguishing the possible from the impossible is a matter for God – whereas the world, denying the fact that it is created, constantly identifies the possible with the impossible, thereby as it were making the impossible an actual state of affairs' (*Essay I*, 111). That is to say, because the world is mired in sin and nothingness, it can only understand the cross and the empty tomb as impossibilities. God, rather, alone 'is to be conceived as the one who makes the possible to be possible and the impossible to be impossible. As the one who does this, as the one who distinguishes the possible from the impossible, God distinguishes himself from the world ... God *is* and his being is in becoming' (*Essays I*, 112).

As the section unrolls, Jüngel intertwines three themes – history, language and promise – to explain how the distinction between God and the world corresponds to the prioritization of possibility over actuality. The world indeed has a history, he contends, but this history 'is constituted, not by the distinction of the actual from the not-yet-actual, but by the distinction between the possible and the impossible, by the Word of God' (*Essays I*, 113). The impossible possibilities of God 'grant' time to the justified sinner, releasing her or him from the tyranny of time conceived as the sheer unfolding of past, present and future. To be sure, the possibilities of God lay ahead of us in the future. However, 'future possibility must *address* actuality if it is to be more than pure abstraction from the actual. The indispensable *concretion* of the possible is the *event of the word*. In this event, that which God's love makes possible from outside, and not from a future which arises out of the past, is the ultimate concern of the world's actuality' (*Essays I*, 117). It is the word of God, then, as a particular event of language of address, which interrupts the time of the world, bringing with it new possibilities. In the word, the God who loves in perfect freedom comes to the world, even while, again, distinguishing God from the world. And the form the interruptive word of God takes is *promise*, the 'Yes' of divine righteous spoken to and on behalf of the *un*righteous. This 'Yes', however, always is anteceded by the 'No' of divine judgement. 'When justification takes place', Jüngel urges, 'there also occurs a divine "No" which reduces the sinner's actuality to nothingness, a "No" which is for the sake of the creative divine "Yes"' (*Essays I*, 114).

Nearly three decades later, and in the context of an acrimonious ecumenical dispute, Jüngel will restate these very themes in the more comprehensive and elegant presentation that we find in the book *Justification*. The present essay, then, is an essential text insofar as it marks the genesis of his idiosyncratic approach to the doctrine of justification.

'The Relationship between "Economic" and "Immanent" Trinity' (1975)

Readers familiar with the story of modern Christian theology will know the key text and theological 'rule' in the background of this short but significant essay from the mid-1970s.[10] Several years earlier, Jesuit theologian Karl Rahner had published a path-breaking study on the doctrine of the trinity,[11] his purpose for which was to inspire an advance in the doctrine of God for the sake of shifting trinitarian theology from the domain of abstract speculation to concrete belief and piety. The book traverses across several prominent points of classical trinitarian dogma in order to establish a master axiom for the doctrine of God: 'The "economic" trinity is the "immanent" trinity and the "immanent" trinity is the "economic" trinity.'[12] The essence of 'Rahner's Rule', as this controversial axiom frequently is shorthanded, is that God's actions in creating, redeeming and reconciling the world (that is, the 'economic' trinity) reveal who God really is in God's inner life (the 'immanent' trinity). Or, to invert the formula: there is no abstract, aloof deity dwelling in inaccessible glory *apart from* the creative, redemptive and reconciling actions of God in the economy of salvation. To put it yet another way: in order to know who God really is and what God really is like, we must take into account the self-revelation of God in creation, redemption and reconciliation.

In 'The Relationship between "Economic" and "Immanent" Trinity', Jüngel paraphrases Rahner's argument and draws out the significance of Rahner's Rule for the future of trinitarian theology. He begins the essay with some remarks on the importance of the doctrine of the trinity for the life of faith. 'Belief in God as the Three-in-One', he insists, 'marks the whole of Christian existence and is indispensable in Christian worship of God, Christian piety, Christian morality, and the theology that elucidates Christian truth.'[13] The doctrine demands abstract formulation, even as it speaks of a fundamental and concrete truth of the faith. On this basis, Jüngel champions Rahner's work on the trinity as a conceptually sophisticated doctrine of God that helps us think concretely about the mystery of the triune God. The five short sections that make up the heart of the essay unfold Jüngel's paraphrase of Rahner's book. Jüngel is drawn to Rahner's namesake rule because, as he sees it, it 'provides the new foundation of trinitarian teaching in the sense that it enables us to establish the trinitarian concept of God through a theology of the Crucified and thus responds to the exegetical problem better than was possible in classical teaching about the Trinity.'[14] For Jüngel, the basis of Christian talk of God is the self-revelation of God in the death and resurrection of Jesus Christ, not speculative reflection or philosophy. The force of Rahner's identification of the economic trinity and the immanent trinity is, as Jüngel reads it, to ground trinitarian doctrine in the cross. Such a move runs counter to the metaphysical tradition, which distinguishes economic from immanent in such a way so as to protect the inner life of God from change and suffering. Rahner's Rule, by contrast, allows us to speak of change and suffering as essential to the being of God.

Jüngel observes that 'trinitarian dogma grew out of christological dogma, and trinitarian development of doctrine progressed in the wake of christological development'. From this historical sequence he concludes that 'Christian faith, which knows no salvation outside Christ, can neither say who Jesus Christ is without understanding him as God, nor understand who God is without declaring his identity with Jesus'. This identification between God and Jesus Christ points to the essential *mystery* of the faith. In an evocative paragraph, Jüngel elaborates:

> Mystery is here not to be regarded as a 'mysterious affair' withheld from understanding, something which would cease to be a mystery if an explanation were forthcoming. A mystery is not an enigma. The Trinity is a mystery, not because we know nothing about it, but because God himself here meets us. It is not a mystery to be kept shrouded in secrecy; it is an openly announced mystery (cf. 1 Tim 3:16), which may in no case be concealed (1 Cor 9:16). The mystery of the Trinity does not become less mysterious through growth in understanding, but becomes ever more mysterious. As such it is communicable. Its soteriological power lies in its communicability. The mystery of the Trinity involves the truth of the faith which makes us free (Jn 8:32). Man's certainty of salvation reposes on this mystery. The mystery of the Trinity is the mystery of salvation.[15]

Note that Jüngel's concept of mystery keeps us squarely on the path of revealed theology. We do not enter into the mystery of the faith by considering, on the basis of finite, creaturely things, what God *is not* (the *via negativa*), nor do we, as it were, ascend the ladder of finite, creaturely things in order to eventually reach, by way of speculation, the mysterious infinite (the way of natural theology, at least as Jüngel reads it). Rather, the mystery of the faith – that is, the place where we encounter the splendour and majesty of God – *is* the mystery of salvation, revealed in the death and resurrection of Jesus. As such, for Jüngel we plunge ever deeper into the abyss of the triune God as the mystery of the world by fixing our attention on the self-revelation of God in Jesus Christ. *Quae supra nos, nihil ad nos*, he titles an earlier essay (in Jüngel, *TE II*, 202–251), borrowing an old Socratic dictum: 'That which is above us is nothing to us.'

Jüngel draws his paraphrase of Rahner to a close in the important seventh section of the essay by offering a sharp, concise summary of an approach to trinitarian theology which captures the essence of Rahner's insight. Interestingly, many of his proposals in this section mirror statements which had emerged earlier in *God's Being Is in Becoming*, his paraphrase of Barth's trinitarian theology. Two features in the conclusion, however, are unique to the shorter piece. First, Jüngel suggests that we can map the unity of the economic and immanent trinity by attending to theme of divine *advent* or, we might say, divine *processions*.[16] He drafts three theses on the coming of God, each of which corresponds to one of the triune persons: 'God proceeds *from* God' points to the 'unoriginated origin' of divine being and revelation in God the Father; 'God proceeds *to* God' abridges the narrative of the unfolding of divine being and revelation 'within the horizon of time' in the mission of God the Son; and 'God proceeds *as* God' emphasizes that the coming of God from God and God to God happens in the person of the Holy Spirit, who constitutes the identity-in-distinction, or original-and-reiteration, marking the inner life of God. Taken together, these divine processions qualify the being of God as 'the mutual distinction and relationship of Father, Son and Spirit.'[17]

Second, and directly consequent to this theology of the advent of God, Jüngel refuses to conceive the life of God as static, unmoved being. Rather, the processions of God from God, to God and as God unleash the 'freedom and unmerited grace of God' to creatures. Perhaps better: the inner life of God overflows to creatures, precisely because the inner life of God just *is* the processions which include God's creating, redeeming and reconciling the world. Jüngel therefore concludes the essay by qualifying that the relationship between the economic and immanent trinity is one of *identity-in-distinction*. To suggest a sheer identification between the economic and immanent trinity would restrict the being of God to creaturely experience. On the contrary, for Jüngel the doctrine of the trinity is faith's confession that God shares with creatures the very love which constitutes God's inner life as Father, Son and Spirit.[18] God's being-in-becoming is thus the mystery of the world.

'The Effectiveness of Christ Withdrawn' (1978)

One of the undercurrents of *God as the Mystery of the World* is the twofold theme of the presence and absence of God. Jüngel wrestles with the question of how we encounter, experience and know God if God is not to be conceived as an 'object' in the Cartesian epistemological sense, that is, as a thing in the world available to us via the senses in the same way that, say, a tree or a person or even the world itself is. One of Jüngel's key claims in the monograph is that the Christian doctrine of the word of God provides the conceptual tools necessary for resolving this dilemma. 'In the word', he writes, 'God *is* present as the absent one' (Jüngel, *Mystery*, 182). When we hear God speaking to us in the word, God is intimately present to us – nearer, indeed, than we ever can be to ourselves. However, unlike the objects which are close to us at hand and therefore apprehendable by our senses, God transcends worldly things and never can be objectified by experience, thought and language. As such, God is absent from us even as God is present to us. For Jüngel, only the word of God preserves this mysterious, analogical structure of God's presence and absence.

In the essay 'The Effectiveness of Christ Withdrawn: On the Process of Historical Understanding as an Introduction to Christology' (in *Essays I*, 214–231), which was published just after the appearance of the first German edition of *God as the Mystery of the World*, Jüngel examines a special instance of this twofold theme. At the outset of the piece, he explains that his chief concern is to address 'the question which every Christology has to answer: *Who is Jesus Christ?*' (*Essays I*, 214). But he suggests that the question itself immediately bumps up against the problem of history. For Jesus Christ is not with us as our contemporary but speaks to us from out of a bygone past. Once again, then, we observe Jüngel turning to the cluster of issues surrounding the historical Jesus. However, 'The effectiveness of Christ Withdrawn' introduces a new framework for addressing this problem by capitalizing upon the twin themes of presence and absence. In what sense, he asks, can the Christian faith claim that Jesus Christ is effective in the present, when, as someone who has died, he necessarily is absent from us, ever withdrawing further into the past?

Jüngel perceives that what is at stake in this question is the specific theological problem that 'a truth which is considered *divine*, a so-called *eternal truth* [is to] be grasped in the form of an *historical event*, and thus must be understood wholly within the temporality of history' (*Essays I*, 216). He argues that we must tackle this dilemma by considering the hermeneutical implications of historical consciousness. He introduces two terms which, to his mind, help to qualify how we relate to the past: '*positive* effective history' and '*private* effective history'. The first term, which Jüngel borrows from the philosopher Hans-Georg Gadamer, refers generally to the 'sense that we feel the effects of a past event long afterwards'.[19] But to Gadamer's rather basic hermeneutical conception Jüngel adds the more subtle second term, which encapsulates the idea that 'sometimes a piece of the past (a person, situation or event) is effective *only as* it recedes further and further into the distance of history, whether for good or ill. In such a case, it is the *withdrawal* that has effects' (*Essays I*, 223).

As the essay unfolds, Jüngel insists that the crucified – viz., *dead* – Jesus continues to be effective in the present in the sense of private effective history. His argument unfolds in two steps. First, Jüngel introduces to his analysis of the historical Jesus the distinction between possibility and actuality, which by this point had become a recurring motif in his writings. In 'The Effectiveness of Christ Withdrawn' he proposes that the historical truth of the death of Jesus must 'exceed the actuality of a "brute fact"' (*Essays I*, 224), since otherwise the dead Jesus simply would recede further and further into the past in such a way that he would cease to be effective in the present. Jüngel instead suggests that 'the actual is more than simply actual, more than naked facticity'. The actual contains 'possibilities which do not pass away with the actuality of the brute fact … It is the possibilities which actuality brings with it and leaves behind which make a fact occurring in time into something like an event' (*Essays I*, 225). Accordingly, for Jüngel the death of Jesus was no mere actuality in the sense of a brute fact, but rather, in the event of its actuality, opened up possibilities that continue to be effective in the present.

Having established as much, Jüngel next briefly takes the argument down an entirely different path by offering a novel interpretation of the genre of the New Testament Gospels (*Essays I*, 227–229). He proposes that the Evangelists were not at all interested in constructing uninterrupted factual biographies of Jesus, but rather in portraying the *whole* of Jesus's existence without delineating the full details of his earthly life. Furthermore, for Jüngel, the point of the Gospels is to demonstrate that Jesus was (to his contemporaries and to readers of the Gospels in the past) and is (to readers in the present) *salvifically effective*. The Evangelists supply narrative details lending support to the salvific effectiveness of Jesus, even though such details do not necessarily count as *reports* of actual events of the life of Jesus. For instance:

> In Mk 2.5 the sins of the paralytic are forgiven; but even though Mark records no other healing which is combined with the forgiveness of sins, this does not mean that Mark 2.5 is about a unique event. Rather in this one particular story, Mark seeks to bring out something which is characteristic of all Jesus's healings. Jesus's healing activity is in itself that which forgives sins. (*Essays I*, 228)

The pericope therefore is *true* without necessarily being *factual*. The Evangelist, that is, conveys the salvific effectiveness of Jesus's healings through a story that, in all likelihood, does not actually correspond to 'a unique event' that took place during Jesus's public ministry. Moreover, this interplay between narrative and history, Jüngel submits, is generally true of the Gospel pericopes. To put it a different way, the Gospel pericopes serve as *synechdoces*, in which the 'single event(s) stand for the whole' (*Essays I*, 228). And this folds back upon the distinction between actuality and possibility, since the point of the Gospels never was simply to restate the actual events of Jesus but to open up new possibilities for the hearers of the Christian message.

This understanding of the New Testament Gospels corresponds to the overarching thesis of the essay that Jesus is effective in the sense of private effective history. Jüngel contends that 'the *death* of Jesus evoked *faith* in Jesus Christ, and the *absence* of Jesus gave rise to the New Testament as a testimony to his presence'. The Gospels tell the story of one who has passed away – indeed, of one who ever is receding into the past – but do so in such a way that readers in every age can experience his effectiveness, that is, the possibilities inaugurated by his death and which transcend worldly actualities. Accordingly, he concludes, 'Jesus's effectiveness consists in his *death*, in his *withdrawal*' (*Essays I*, 231).

Taken on its own, such an approach to negotiating the tension between Jesus's death and his ongoing importance raises a concern of no small Christological significance. Upon reading the essay we may reasonably wonder whether Jüngel has left Jesus for dead. For Jüngel here, the Jesus to whom faith is related has *passed into history* and is meaningful for faith just as such. How, though, does such a position square with the classical Christian confession of Christ the prophet, priest and king – a living, active *subject* who remains significant for and present to us precisely insofar as he ever lives and acts on our behalf? By taking such an odd approach to Christology in order to avoid the problem of objectification, Jüngel leaves dangling the question of Christ's active subjectivity. Having said as much, we do well to bear in mind that clarifying the subjective agency of Christ transcends the task and scope of the essay at hand. It is worth recalling, too, that, outside of his work in the classroom, Jüngel never attempted a regular dogmatics of the person and work of Jesus Christ. Had he done so, we might have expected him to frame any talk of the withdrawal and absence of Jesus within a discussion of the advent (surely an antonym of 'withdrawal' and, as we have seen, a major motif in Jüngel's writings), presence and active subjectivity of Christ. Elsewhere I have endeavoured to locate this essay along some of the broader contours of Jüngel's Christology, in doing so expressing the fear that his emphasis on Jesus's death and withdrawal yields more questions than answers.[20] My suggestion here is that readers approach this fascinating piece for what it is – namely, a concise exercise in irregular dogmatics focused on the question of the suitability of hermeneutical (Gadamerian) categories for addressing the problem of the historical Jesus. Whether the essay is of any use beyond the study of Jüngel's thought may depend upon the extent to which one agrees with him that the problem of the relation between the Jesus of history and the Christ of faith is genuinely unsettling, and, if so, that the category of withdrawal is well-suited to resolve it. In any case, for students of Jüngel's work the piece offers a window into how he used a contemporaneous discussion to shed new light on an old problem.

'The Church as Sacrament?' (1983)

As I have suggested, even though Jüngel never served in an official capacity on any ecumenical dialogue commission, he made a number of signal *theological* contributions to the modern quest for unity between the churches. In particular, in several short pieces and the major monograph *Justification*, he addresses issues at stake in the bilateral dialogues between the Lutheran churches and the Roman Catholic Church.[21] 'The Church as Sacrament?' (in *Essays I*, 189–213), which originated as a paper given at an ecumenical congress on Luther's ecclesiology (*Essays I*, 189n 1), is an early and rather provocative piece from Jüngel's ecumenical output.

Jüngel seized upon the occasion of the congress to address, in dialogue with Luther, the problem of the church's sacramentality. The larger context behind Jüngel's contribution to this particular discussion is the aforementioned controversy over *Grunddifferenzen*, or 'basic differences', which erupted during the late 1970s and early 1980s in a number of dialogues and in ecumenical theology more generally. Jüngel summarizes this controversy at the outset of the essay. On the basis of the substantial progress made in the decade following the Second Vatican Council towards a common understanding of the doctrine of justification,[22] some members of the various Roman Catholic-Protestant bilateral dialogues grew hopeful that consensuses could be reached on other church-dividing doctrines. But the sense of anticipation proved to be 'a brief flame, quickly extinguished' (*Essays I*, 189), as the second wave of dialogues and working groups were largely unsuccessful in overcoming the divisions which have separated the churches since the time of the reformation. During this period of increasing ecumenical frustration and disappointment, a number of ecumenists advised that a basic difference, or a series of basic differences, lay beneath the ongoing dissensuses between the churches. Especially prominent among such proposals was the idea that 'the evident stagnation of the process of ecumenical understanding between the Roman Catholic church and the churches of the reformation is rooted in a different understanding of the church which has not so far been overcome' (*Essays I*, 189).[23] In particular, the Roman Catholic and Protestant churches remain divided on the basis of a fundamentally different way of understanding the instrumentality of the church in the mediation of salvation. At the heart of this basic difference is the question of whether or not the church is a sacrament. Jüngel's essay on this question should thus be read as a thoroughgoing Protestant contribution to the ecclesiological form of the ecumenical discussion of basic differences.

Jüngel declares that his objective in the essay is 'to make some proposals about how we might *correctly* define the relation between church and sacrament' (*Essays I*, 191). He argues that both Roman Catholic and Protestant theologians have approached this relation from faulty understandings of the concept of sacrament.[24] Throughout his writings Jüngel insists that sacramental theology must begin with the biblical idea that Jesus Christ is the sacrament of God for the world. This commitment especially is clear in 'The Church as Sacrament?' and helps to explain the suggestive question mark in the essay's title. The true '"sacrament of unity" … is not the church but Christ himself', he writes, since 'in the New Testament, *sacramentum* is nothing other than the eschatological mystery of the saving divine decree in favor of sinners which was enacted in the history of Jesus Christ'. This New Testament definition of *sacramentum*, he goes on to explain, is the 'criterion from which alone we [must] orient our handling of the question of the sacramental character of the being and activity of the church' (*Essays I*, 191).

On the basis of this Christological approach to understanding the nature of the sacraments, in the second section of the text Jüngel counters the characteristically Roman Catholic claim that the church is the '*fundamental* sacrament' (*Ursakrament*) by appealing to Luther's exposition of the Lord's Supper. He asserts that the Catholic position on the church's fundamental sacramentality is 'a bold usurpation – an apparently typical Catholic identification of the church with its Lord' (*Essays I*, 193), since it suggests that the sacramentality of the church is of a kind with the sacramentality of Jesus Christ. On the other hand, citing support from Luther, Melanchthon, Zwingli, Karlstadt, Schleiermacher and Barth, he observes that Protestant theologians historically have been hesitant to use sacramental terminology for describing the church and its practices. Jüngel praises Luther for combining 'a desire to use the notion of "sacrament" in an exclusively Christological way with a high regard for what ought to be called a sacrament'. Luther, Jüngel argues, emphasized the Lord's Supper in his writings because he conceived the sacrament as 'the *self-presentation of Jesus Christ* in bread and wine, enacted through the creative power of his word of promise, which provokes and strengthens faith'. For Luther, then, 'the decisive point is that in the sacrament, *the gracious God himself is the one who acts*' (*Essays I*, 195). Consequently, in the event of the Lord's Supper, the human person is the fundamentally passive recipient of Christ's gracious self-presentation through the word added to the element. And it is just this insight, Jüngel argues, that goes against 'the Roman Catholic understanding of sacramentality as symbolic representation' (*Essays I*, 198), that is, the idea that the church, through its liturgical actions, repeats, extends and thus makes effectual the salvific being and action of Jesus Christ.[25]

'The Church as Sacrament?' is significant for bringing together in a single essay the main components of Jüngel's evolving perspectives on the themes of ecclesiology and sacramental theology. In the essay he capitalizes upon the contemporaneous debate surrounding ecumenical basic differences in order to draw together insights on the church and sacraments earned during the first two decades of his career. The essay likewise anticipates how he will continue to explore these themes as his theology matures. Later we consider capstone texts on ecclesiology and sacramental theology published after the turn of the millennium. Those pieces articulate clear and well-formed expressions of several positions surfacing in 'The Church as Sacrament?' The location of the present essay at the halfway point of Jüngel's constructive work on these important third article themes makes the essay essential reading for those interested in understanding his contribution.

'"My Theology" – A Short Summary' (1985)

Earlier on I recommended this delightful essay (in *Essays II*, 1–19) as the staging point for a journey through Jüngel's writings. He composed it on the occasion of his fiftieth year and for an edited collection of 'theological sketches' contributed by leading theologians from the last quarter of the twentieth century.[26] The piece serves as a compendium of Jüngel's contribution to modern Christian thought, giving us a window into how he understood his own vocation and theology at mid-career. 'My Theology' is not a memoir – that is, Jüngel is not occupied here with the task of chronicling his career from inception to the present in terms of university positions and key publications. It is interesting, even surprising, that in this 'summary' of his theology he does not mention any of his previous writings. Nor does he spend any time in the essay mapping out the contemporaneous scene in Christian theology in order to show how he fits or does not fit into any particular camp. Instead, the piece unfolds 'in the form of a theological "confession"' (*Essays II*, 4) and contains nine numbered passages introduced by statements of faith identifying aspects of theological existence. 'I believe', Jüngel confesses, 'therefore I speak, I listen, I am astonished, I think, I differentiate, I hope, I act, I am, and I suffer'.

Jüngel spends a few paragraphs in the opening section clearing his throat. 'As soon as I begin to talk of "my theology"', he comments, 'I am at a loss for words.' The problem is the juxtaposition of the possessive pronoun 'my' with the noun 'theology', an alignment which 'seems doubly presumptuous', as it expresses both 'a great overestimation of the theologian' and 'a wholly inappropriate underestimation of what theology is' (*Essays II*, 1). Theology hardly is something that the theologian can possess, Jüngel argues. On the contrary, the truth of theology must take possession of the theologian. 'Truth is neither a private nor collective possession. One cannot *have* it at all. If one is given it to deal with, it is in such a way that it grasps us and we, so to speak, belong to its kingdom (Jn 16:13). Without being grasped by the truth which is to be thought and spelled out, I cannot truly be a theologian.' For Jüngel, then, theology is never truly *ours*, but is like 'a talent entrusted to us' and over which we have temporary custodianship and responsibility (*Essays II*, 2). We exercise the gift of theology in and for the sake of the community of the faithful. Theology is 'an expression of my very personal participation in the will and capacity of all believers to understand'. As Jüngel sees it, then, theology exists in the tension between private contemplation and public stewardship. And it is precisely in this context that the personal dimension of Christian theology emerges. Accordingly, theology 'is in part theological biography', insofar as 'the courage to make use of one's own understanding corresponds to the freedom to express alongside others one's own experience of liberating truth, not so much in the way one expresses oneself but rather in that characteristic manner in which *I* pursue theology' (*Essays II*, 3).

What is especially noteworthy about the 'theological confession' composing the long second section of the essay is how Jüngel coordinates the nine aspects of theological existence with specific *tasks* of Christian theology. The confession 'I believe, therefore I speak' points to theology's responsibility to the truth of the gospel, which believers encounter in an 'incomparably new experience (that) fundamentally ruptures the series of worldly experiences, yet which is related to them, as an experience of God which as such is an experience with experience' (*Essays II*, 5). The task of theology, accordingly, is 'thoughtful, responsible talk of the God who liberates in his truth.' The confession 'I believe, therefore I listen' expresses Jüngel's commitment to a theology of the word of God. God 'comes to speech as the one who has come to the world in the person of the man Jesus' (*Essays II*, 6), and comes to speech ever anew in the proclamation of the gospel, which awakens faith in the one who hears and receives it. The theologian who listens for and to this word does so by attending to the witnesses of the Old and New Testaments. For Jüngel, 'theology is the exposition of the Holy Scriptures' (*Essays II*, 7), or it is nothing at all.

As we have observed throughout this guide, Jüngel recurrently stresses the notion that faith is an encounter with *mystery* – to be precise, with God as the mystery of the world. In 'My Theology' he proposes that the confession 'I believe, therefore I am astonished' captures theology's proper response to the mystery that is God. The confession points first to the doctrine of the trinity, which declares that God is 'eternal being and yet full of becoming'. Once again, here we discover Jüngel refusing to draw any final distinction between the eternal being of God and the actions of God in redeeming and reconciling the world. Faith believes 'the mystery of even greater selflessness in the midst of such great trinitarian self-relatedness … God from eternity and thus in and of himself is God for us' (*Essays II*, 7–8). Jüngel reminds his readers, though, that the confession of the triune God is mysterious not in the sense of a riddle or a secret which would cease to be mysterious once it is solved or revealed. Rather, 'the mystery allows itself to be known without ceasing to be a mystery … the more deeply one understands the mystery, the more mysterious it becomes'. Everything here hinges on the Christian confession of the incarnate, crucified and resurrected Lord. God is the mystery of the world insofar as God hides *sub contrario* – beneath God's opposite, becoming 'identifiable as history in space and time' (*Essays II*, 8) in the man Jesus of Nazareth. The *task* of a theology which follows God's mysterious self-revelation in the person of the Crucified One is to *remain* astonished, that is, to plunge ever deeper in the mystery of God as the unity of life and death on behalf of life.

'I believe, therefore I think.' Jüngel insists that theology takes shape according to the Anselmian pattern of *fides quarens intellectum*, faith seeking understanding. Reason does not establish or set the conditions for faith, but follows after faith's encounter with the revelation of divine mystery. For Jüngel, theology's proper ordering of faith and reason ensures that Christian thinking never reduces to 'objectivizing or instrumental thought' (*Essays II*, 10). On the contrary, theology discharged according to the pattern of *fides quarens intellectum* leads us *as pilgrims* into the depths of the mystery of God. The starting point for such thinking is the cross of Jesus Christ, the confession of which is, as Paul puts it, 'foolishness to those who are perishing' (1 Cor 1:18). The task of theology is to follow the message of the cross to wherever it leads, courageously revising traditional doctrines, categories and concepts whenever the confession of the gospel demands it. Jüngel is aware that such a vision for theology may have drastic consequences for the classical understanding of metaphysics and the being of God. 'All traditional divine attributes', he warns, 'will need to be critically and, if necessary, re-thought ... out of the event of (God's) advent' (*Essays II*, 11). What is on offer here, then, is a proposal for the methods, aims and tasks of theology following from the analogy of advent. In the coming of God to the world in the humanity of the crucified and resurrected Lord, there emerges 'that analogy which expresses in the midst of so great a difference an even greater similarity between God and the world. God comes nearer to the world than the world is able to be near to itself'. The theology that follows after the mystery of God's advent concerns itself with modes of the language of faith, such as narrative and metaphor, which encapsulate the *addressing* character of the gospel. We do well to note here a tacit connection drawn between theology and preaching. 'Thinking God means', Jüngel writes, 'to marshal the language of God in such a way that it concerns us absolutely, addressing us equally concerning God and ourselves' (*Essays II*, 12). When theology ceases to correspond to the structure of God's advent, it loses its homiletical edge.

'I believe', Jüngel confesses, 'therefore I differentiate. Faith is an act of original differentiation'. The theme of differentiation is found throughout Jüngel's writings and serves as a structural device that guides his analyses of a number of theological topics. In this portion of the essay he summarizes some key theological distinctions – namely, between God and the world, law and gospel, person and work, and activity and passivity. Following Luther, Jüngel suggests that things go awry in theology when the first of these distinctions – the differentiation between Creator and creature – gets blurred. Faith, he writes, is a continual making of distinctions, a persistent critique of the idol-producing confusion and mixing of the creature with its creator, and of the ensuing confusion and mixing of what is wholesomely distinguished within the created world. Accordingly, the thinking which follows faith is originally differentiating and eminently critical thinking.[27]

For Jüngel, this emphasis on differentiation rules out, among other things, natural theology, which, as he sees it, fails to properly distinguish between Creator and creature, and, in turn, encourages the misinterpretation of both God and the natural world.

Jüngel turns to eschatology with the confession 'I believe, therefore I hope.' 'The believer is certain that the final future which determines world history in its totality and each individual life-history within it, is a future already decided in the cross and resurrection of Jesus Christ' (*Essays II*, 15). Since hope in the eschatological consummation of all creation pervades and animates the life of faith, it too is ingredient to Christian theology. As far as theology's tasks are concerned, Jüngel proposes that Christian hope ought to stimulate theological interest in aesthetics. The communion among Christians makes 'the object of hope perceptible, without as it were allowing the dots of such eschatological visions to be connected to form a picture' (*Essays II*, 16). If I am reading Jüngel correctly here, he is recommending that the proper object of theological aesthetics is the refraction of eschatological beauty through the church's sacraments – specifically through the event of communion, or the Lord's Supper. Unfortunately, he does not elaborate this suggestive point in 'My Theology'. But elsewhere he hints at an aesthetical interpretation of the Lord's Supper by emphasizing the anticipation of the consummation which occurs whenever Christians celebrate the table.[28] In any case, it is interesting to note here the intertwining of eschatology, sacramental theology and theological aesthetics – a connection that warrants further consideration.

Jüngel moves quickly through the final three themes of his theological confession: 'I believe, therefore I act, I am, and I suffer.' The first of these aspects points to the political responsibility of the church and of each Christian. The theological basis for this responsibility is a fundamental differentiation: 'One must again strictly distinguish between the unambiguous character of heavenly government, in which the love that makes like unambiguous rules, and the ambivalence of all earthly – and thus also of all political – actions.' The political *task* of theology is to arouse and support believers as they act in and for the world by 'differentiating between God's activity and [human actions]' (*Essays II*, 16). Jüngel turns to ecclesiology with the confession 'I believe, therefore I am.' In a characteristically brief but dense assertion, he draws a link between the doctrine of God and ecclesiology by means of a social model of the trinity. 'The foundation of faith is the foundation of all being: the triune God who reveals himself in Jesus Christ as the community of reciprocal otherness. But such being can only be represented communally. Faith is therefore an eminently societal event.' The corresponding ecclesiological task of theology is twofold. First, 'theology watches over the purity of (the) divine service of representation as it takes place in liturgical celebration and in daily life in the world'. Theology thus operates responsibly as 'church theology' when it recognizes and exercises its duty to safeguard the church's *public* and *missional* expressions (*Essays II*, 17). Second and relatedly, the task of theology is 'to bring out the validity of the truth of faith in an *ecumenical* manner'. The theologian, Jüngel commends, must resist at all costs the fragmentation of the Christian church, 'which divides itself into communities of faith quarrelling with each other' (*Essays II*, 18). Theology, rather, is meant to be an instrument of the unity of the church.

Finally, the confession 'I believe, therefore I suffer' recalls Luther's preface to Volume One of the *Wittenberg Edition*, where he lists *tentatio* – suffering – as one of the three criteria for the study of theology, alongside *oratio* (prayer) and *meditatio* (meditation).[29] With Luther, Jüngel argues that theology 'as a whole becomes a theology of testing: *tentatio facit theologum*' (*Essays II*, 19), for the theologian lives and works in the tension 'between the definiteness of the revelation of God in the gospel, and the dreadful hiddenness of God's rule over the world, between the being of God which has been revealed and his deeply concealed action, between the revealed God and his hidden work' (*Essays II*, 18). The task of theology as *tentatio*, though, is never to bring undue attention to the personal suffering of the theologian, but always to proclaim the suffering *of God* in the crucifixion of Jesus Christ. In this way, Jüngel's *theologia crucis* – theology of the cross – highlights the overlapping interests between Christian theology and preaching.

'My Theology' offers a tidy, interesting compendium of Jüngel's thought, bringing together in a few pages many of the salient themes which mark his theological contribution. Moreover, the essay provides a wealth of wisdom for maturing theologians from a top scholar writing in the midst of his prime.

'The Dogmatic Significance of the Question of the Historical Jesus' (1988)

Jüngel revisits the problem of the continuity between Jesus of Nazareth and the Christ of Christian faith in this sprawling essay (in *Essays II*, 82–119) from the midpoint of his career. As the title indicates, his aim is to identify the significance for Christian dogmatics of critical research into the Jesus of history. 'Dogmatic Significance' is both quintessentially Jüngel and emblematic of his ongoing investment in the second quest for the historical Jesus. At the same time, the essay is conspicuously out of step with currents in New Testament theology and exegesis contemporaneous to its appearance at the end of the 1980s. The guild of biblical studies had moved far beyond the New Hermeneutic by this point, and the third quest just had recently emerged with the founding of the Westar Institute and the organization of the Jesus Seminar in 1985. The essay at hand does not reveal whether Jüngel was even aware of these changes of scholarly paradigm. On the contrary, apart from an interesting engagement in the middle of the piece with Jewish philosopher Emmanuel Lévinas, all of the authorities Jüngel enlists in the essay – namely, Barth, Bultmann and Ebeling – hark back to a bygone era of deliberation over the Jesus of history. Reading 'Dogmatic Significance' against this context, it is remarkable that Jüngel here pursues the second quest with such confidence and determination, and likewise indifference to concurrent academic debates.

Albert Schweitzer's famous monograph from 1906, *The Quest of The Historical Jesus*[30] – a book which effectively brought to an end the first phase of modern critical Jesus research – haunts Jüngel's argument in 'Dogmatic Significance', even if Schweitzer never appears in the footnotes. In various 'lives of Jesus' written between 1850 and 1900, critical scholars from the European universities had sought to make Jesus of Nazareth more palatable to modern readers by questioning the authenticity of New Testament passages asserting the supernatural character of Jesus's person and work. Schweitzer calls into question both the methods and conclusions of this era of Jesus scholarship before going on in the book to offer his own interpretation of Jesus and his ongoing significance. For Schweitzer, the New Testament must be read against the backdrop of contemporaneous Jewish apocalypticism. Jesus's own self-understanding emerged from this context and subsequently informed the 'thoroughgoing eschatology' that marked incipient Christianity.

In 'Dogmatic Significance', Jüngel invokes the idea of interruption – a metaphor which, as we have seen, pops up throughout his writings – to express the apocalyptic character of the life and activities of Jesus the Nazarene. First, he makes the observation that much of what Jesus did during his public ministry went against the grain of the ordinary and acceptable:

> The most general thing that could be said about the self-understanding of the historical Jesus and about his impact on his contemporaries is this: he represents an *elemental interruption* of the continuity of life in his world. In various aspects the synoptic traditions present Jesus in his earthly history as one who falls, as it were, outside the brackets of that which tends to be held appropriate and normal. (*Essays II*, 89)

Jesus's astonishing behaviour and public nonconformity mirrors his eschatological message. Jüngel proposes in the essay that the 'individual logia of Jesus', particularly his parables of the kingdom, are interruptive events of speech in the very proclamation of which the kingdom of God invades the world, assailing the status quo (*Essays II*, 89). He explains:

> The historical Jesus saw the coherence of the reality of the present world to be called into question by the coming kingdom of God, especially by the kingdom which through his own activity is immediately related to the present ... The nearness of the kingdom of God proclaimed by Jesus so changes the reality of the world, that it would seem that what is demanded is not a development of the continuity of reality but rather its reversal ... Something comes to the world which absolutely does not belong to it, but which can only be experienced as an *intrusion upon* or *interruption of* the coherence of the world. (*Essay II*, 89–90)

Jüngel goes on to argue that this radically interruptive structure of the relation between, on one hand, Jesus and his proclamation, and, on the other, the 'coherence of the world' demands we rethink some assumptions about history shared by those in search of the historical Jesus. The guild of historical scholarship, he alleges, suffers from 'an *inappropriate concept of time* of which both sides [of the contemporary debate over the historical Jesus] make use'. Accordingly, 'history' is conceived 'as a *period of time*, as a spatial *length of time*, with which one can and must measure *distances* from the presently existing "I" and its here and now – distance which either date the past by measuring from the here and now backwards or date the future by measuring forwards [sic]' (Essays II, 104). But God and Jesus and the kingdom cannot be measured in terms of temporal distance:

> The relation between God and humanity does not allow itself to be gauged as a length of time which can be measured through a movement … the relation between the 'now' in which God exists and the 'now' in which humanity exists cannot be measured as a distance. God's 'now' and our 'here and how' are *incommensurable.* (Essays II, 105–106)

By tying together Christology and eschatology in this way, Jüngel hopes to sidestep the modern historicist profile of Jesus of Nazareth as merely a fringe dweller; an itinerant Jewish teacher whose fanatical message challenged the piety and politics of his immediate contemporaries, and who unwittingly bequeathed to posterity a namesake religion when, upon his execution, his followers re-clothed his biography and teachings in supernatural garb. By contrast, Jüngel's Jesus of Nazareth inaugurates the kingdom by speaking an apocalyptic word from God, a word which truly changes the reality of the world by bringing to speech light and life in the midst of the world's darkness and death. But if the upshot of Jüngel's unabashedly second quest approach to the problem of the historical Jesus is the recovery of the interventive, apocalyptic – indeed, *supernatural* – character of Jesus's speech, its shortcoming is a tendency to depict Jesus of Nazareth as, in the vivid commentary of Webster, 'an eschatological, erratic, intrusive figure, distant from Israel, cutting across the grain of human time and space'.[31]

'Dogmatic Significance' is essential reading for those endeavouring to grasp Jüngel's theological contribution. The essay ties together the beginning and midpoint of his career and reintroduces themes and locutions persisting across his oeuvre. At the same time, the piece presents an approach to the issues at hand that is neither fashionable any longer nor perhaps even tenable. And it recalls nagging questions concerning Jüngel's understanding of the person and work of Jesus Christ.[32]

'The Emergence of the New' (1988)

While 'Dogmatic Significance' explores the implications for eschatology of the quest for the historical Jesus, 'The Emergence of the New' (Essays II, 35–58), published the same year, addresses the relationship between God and history in more general terms. Jüngel carefully negotiates the distinction between old and new to construe the temporal character of God's self-revelation and actions. I confess to the reader my fondness for this particular essay. To my mind, it is one of Jüngel's very best short pieces, containing all the hallmarks of his mature theological writing – incisive analysis of the issues at hand, lively engagement with a range of interlocutors and a compressed constructive section at the heart of the essay that somehow epitomizes in just a few pages the essence Jüngel's programme for Christian dogmatics. To boot, the piece boasts a surprise ending in the form of an evocative final paragraph in which Jüngel signposts a pathway for research and reflection, a pathway which, for whatever reason, he never returned to explore.

The essay begins with an interesting engagement with the thought of physicist Thomas Kuhn, whose contribution to the field of philosophy of science we briefly have encountered at two points, above, in our surveys of Jüngel's participation in ecumenical theology. As mentioned, Kuhn's important and controversial 1962 monograph, *The Structure of Scientific Revolution*,[33] set forth a new understanding of the nature of scientific progress and discovery. As a rule, Kuhn proposes, 'normal' science advances by way knowledge accrued according to established frameworks for experimentation and abstraction. New scientific insight, however, frequently occurs unexpectedly and episodically, emerging when the ordinary course of progress is disturbed. The interruption of normal science by the emergence of discovery marks a 'paradigm shift', a genuine revolution in scientific thought in the event of which a new way of thinking about a given topic displaces the old, now outmoded paradigm. For Kuhn, the new paradigm can be neither explained nor extrapolated from the old, but rather emerges as an altogether different pattern for scientific knowledge.

In our essay, Jüngel proposes that Kuhn's new model for scientific change is significant also for *theological* change. In the first two sections he considers some of the similarities between the two disciplines. To be sure, Jüngel argues, there is something like an 'ordinary' course of theological knowledge, especially insofar as theology has its own setting as a 'science' (*Wissenschaft*) in the modern research university. And yet, Jüngel observes, 'the history of theological knowledge also contains … "intellectual revolutions" in which there occurs fundamental paradigm shift' (*Essays II*, 39–40). He lists, out of chronological turn, the reformation, Augustine, Thomas, nominalism, historical criticism, Schleiermacher, dialectical theology, the counter-reformation, Ignatius Loyola and Vatican II as examples of paradigm shifts in the history of theology. Jüngel notes, though, that none of these revolutions occurred as a complete break with antecedent 'traditions' of theological thought. In particular, theological revolutions are 'only theologically fruitful when they occur within a paradigm which embraces every theological paradigm … This ancient and comprehensive paradigm we simply call – in rather schematized way – the biblical paradigm' (*Essays II*, 41).

Jüngel turns to the narratives and oracles of the prophets of Israel in order to craft a phenomenology of sorts of the 'new' knowledge of God he envisions in the essay. In Jüngel's reading, the prophets considered themselves to be charged with delivering disruptive words of divine address to the Israelites. These *new* words – which are, indeed, new *actions* – of God towards God's chosen people are not altogether unrelated to the old words and actions which constitute the history of Israel prior to the crises of the eighth to sixth centuries BCE. And yet, 'there is definitely no continuation of the history of the earlier event; rather the new word of God which constitutes and yet stands over against all history, relates itself to that history'. Jüngel qualifies the relation between the new word and history with the help of familiar terminology. 'The new word of God', he contends, '*seeks* in past history parables, analogies, correspondences. The new is thus that from which an analogy is drawn, through which what has goes before is made into the analogate' (*Essays II*, 46). What the narratives and oracles of the prophets show, then, is that the new and old words/actions of God relate to each other analogically – though as the *reversal* of the structure of the *analogia entis*: as 'the analogy of a becoming familiar which arises from utter strangeness, an analogy which is in this respect … the analogy of greater likeness in the midst of such a great dissimilarity between new and old' (*Essays II*, 47).

The third section is one of the most exhilarating passages in all of Jüngel's writings. At first glance a shift in the exposition from the Old Testament to the New Testament, the section is, in fact, a short compendium of Christian theology in five movements and in light of the proposals already set forth in the paper in dialogue with Kuhn and the prophets. Jüngel declares his thesis in the header paragraph: 'faith owes its very existence to the new which is unique, never to be surpassed, and never to become antiquated, namely, the new which has taken place in the person of Jesus Christ' (*Essays II*, 49). In the first subsection, Jüngel discusses the relationship between the old and new covenants, which he understands according to the distinction between law and gospel. In the short unit, he shows how this aspect of the analogy between old and new bears significant implications for the understanding of the human person. In particular, in light of the emergence of the new, the human person is defined in Christ and apart from works. In the second subsection, Jüngel turns directly to the question of time, unfolding a brief theological account of the distinction between the fleetingness of chronological time and the inexhaustible newness of Jesus Christ. 'In the person of Jesus Christ', he writes, 'something new has come on the scene which can never again be surpassed, which can never become obsolete, but rather will remain new for all time' (*Essays II*, 53). The third subsection extends this discussion to a compact eschatology in which Jüngel argues that the eschaton – the time *of God*, which never grows old – relates to the sequence of past, present and future as a disruptive event that determines and judges everything taking place in time. In the fourth subsection, Jüngel works out a brief trinitarian account of God's creative actions. Here he argues that it is in particular the work of the Holy Spirit to make all things new by 'unit[ing] the beginning to the end' (*Essays II*, 57).

The fifth subsection extends Jüngel's commentary on the newly creative work of the Holy Spirit before making an abrupt final turn. The suggestive paragraph with which Jüngel closes the essay is worth quoting at length:

> I do not want to conclude this discussion of the new without expressly giving something like a formal theological apology for the old. As a precautionary after-thought it needs to be said that it would be appropriate to reflect once more on the category of the old with equal thoroughness and detail from the perspective of the new ... In this essay I have spoken of the old almost without exception as an *antithetical concept* to the new ... But the old has another side to it ... The old is not necessarily *hopeless*, for it also belongs to the *good order of creation* in which each day has its evening, each human life may and should become old. Old age has its proper dignity. For God himself ... in the person of the heavenly Father is also the essence of the old ... the one from whom not only the eternal Son of God whom we have come to know in the person of Jesus Christ has his origin, but from whom also *everything* originates, and to whom not only the creative, renewing power of the Holy Spirit returns, but to whom also *everything* returns, so that through participation in the mystery of the trinitarian God everything is as it was of old, *with this ancient God* without whom everything simply is and remains utterly new. (*Essays II*, 58)

Three things of note stand out in this astonishing passage. First, we see that Jüngel does not express an interest in the old for its own sake but calls for a theological appraisal of the old 'from the perspective of the new'. Jüngel is clear in the earlier sections of the essay that Christian theology must prioritize the category of the new over the category of the old. But on the basis of its understanding of the new, theology can and should reflect upon the old. Second, note that Jüngel proposes that the old 'belongs to the good order of creation'. To be sure, certain New Testament passages indicate that a new creation springs forth in the world as dawn breaks on Easter Sunday. But Scripture also says much about *original* or *first* creation and about God's work of sustaining and governing creation and the creatures God has made. Jüngel's comments here suggest that theology must coordinate these two dimensions of the doctrine of creation, that is, the first and new events of creation. Third, we observe that Jüngel sketches the trinitarian coordinates of the distinction between old and new. The long final sentence with which he concludes the essay is highly evocative. For Jüngel, the Christian confession of God as Father, Son and Spirit requires us to give due acknowledgement to old *and* new, for insofar as we participate in the triune life of God, we live and move and have our being (Acts 17:28) in One who is *ever ancient* in the person of the Father and *ever new* in the persons of the Son and the Spirit. In our eternal presence before the triune God, the 'total and perfect possession at one time of unlimited life', as Boethius famously puts it,[34] old and new will become one.

Jüngel never returned to expand upon these comments. He published one other essay on the theological problem of the new,[35] and the later piece lacks a 'formal theological apology for the old'. The final paragraph from 'The Emergence of the New', then, stands as a signpost of a theological path not taken. But even these inchoate remarks offer some clues for how theology might do justice to the old while appreciating the sheer novelty of the new thing emerging in the world in the resurrection of the Crucified One.

'Um Gottes willen – Klarheit!' (1997)

'For God's sake – clarity!', Jüngel demands in this choleric essay from 1997, which he published in the prestigious journal *Zeitschrift für Theologie und Kirche*[36] during a critical moment in the modern ecumenical movement just before the ratification and publication of the *Joint Declaration on the Doctrine of Justification* (*JDDJ*). The essay is a study in theological *protest*. Jüngel zeroes in on what he considers to be a serious methodological flaw in the *JDDJ* and, using his former Tübingen colleague Walter Kasper as a foil, argues that the document in fact fails to achieve the unity between Catholics and Lutherans it claims to have established. I have argued on several occasions in this guidebook that Jüngel is best seen as an ecumenical provocateur. The uniqueness of his ecumenical contribution comes to the fore in 'Klarheit!' Although he never was selected to officially represent the Lutheran World Federation (LWF) in any of the phases of the international Catholic-Lutheran dialogue leading up to the *JDDJ*, his own theological commitments compel him to voice strenuous objections to the dialogue committee's work. And his remarks in this essay and in several other pieces from the same period actually sparked a revolt against the agreement among like-minded theologians.

In many ways, 'Klarheit!' is bound together with the book *Justification*, which we considered in the previous chapter. But some brief comments on the essay are in order here, as the piece sheds light upon a particular aspect of Jüngel's doctrine of justification and underscores the public dimension of his theological work.

One point of neuralgia which had emerged during the years leading up to the signing of the *JDDJ* by the LWF and the Roman Catholic Church in 1999 is the question of the function and location of the doctrine of justification in Christian theological discourse.[37] Several statements from Luther indicate that he considered the doctrine to possess an elevated status in relation to other regions of Christian teaching. 'The article of justification,' he remarks in one place, 'is the master and prince, the lord, the ruler, and the judge over all kinds of doctrines; it preserves and governs all church doctrine and raises up our conscience before God. Without this article, the world is utter death and darkness' (*WA* 39.1, 205). Justification, that is, takes its proper place as the *articulus stantis et cadentis ecclesiae* – the article by which the church stands or falls, as a later paraphrase of Luther puts it. In certain strands of Lutheran dogmatics, Luther's assertions about the primacy of justification in theological discourse have given way to an interesting *methodological* phenomenon. Here, the doctrine of justification is conceived as *the* criterion for all other dogmatic decisions. For Lutheran theologians of this ilk, justification, we might say, bears a *criteriological responsibility* across the theological system. The doctrine of justification plays a determinative role in the articulation of other doctrines, such that to address, say, Lutheran ecclesiology is to work out the entailments of justification for the understanding of the church. And we can follow these same lateral lines in the other direction as well: a failure in ecclesiology, or in the doctrine of God, or in eschatology, and so on, unmasks an error in the doctrine of justification. We might say that in such a vision of Lutheran teaching, justification becomes the article by which *theology* stands or falls. Getting justification right is crucial for making and judging all other theological claims.

In 'Klarheit!', Jüngel argues that the *JDDJ* fails to reflect the criteriological position of justification in relation to other doctrines, which he holds to be a cardinal principle of Lutheran theology. The document does indeed state that justification 'is more than just one part of Christian doctrine. It stands in an essential relation to all truths of faith, which are to be seen as internally related to each other. It is an indispensable criterion which constantly serves to orient all the teaching and practice of our churches to Christ' (*JDDJ* 18). Jüngel charges, however, that the phraseology of this clause represents a softening of language as the drafting of the document unfolded from 1995 to late 1997. The first German text of the *JDDJ* sought to articulate the criteriological function of justification with the ambiguous phrase '*als Kriterium*' (lit. 'as criterion'). Rome demanded a revision for the sake of clarity, and the word '*unverzichtbares*' – 'indispensable' – was added to the clause. Kasper took to the press to declare a victory, explaining in an article in the 12 August 1997 edition of *Katholische Nachrichten-Agentur*[38] that the addition of '*unverzichtbares*' satisfied Lutheran claims concerning justification's criteriological function while also preserving the Catholic contention that justification is *but one* criterion within a nexus of indispensable criteria.[39]

Jüngel counters in 'Klarheit!' that, ironically, Kasper unleashes a 'theological fog' in his very effort to clarify the revised draft's statement that justification is 'an indispensable criterion'.[40] He argues, first, that the phrase itself is tautological, as, by good logic, a criterion of some position is indispensable for that position. But he then suggests, further, that the Catholic concession that justification is indispensable relativizes the other criteria supposedly set alongside it. That is to say, in Jüngel's reading, Kasper's assertion that justification is 'indispensable' renders all other criteria 'dispensable' – a logical absurdity, since a criterion is indispensable and not otherwise. As Jüngel sees it, then, there can be only one criterion for Christian doctrine and, by good logic, that one criterion simply is indispensable. Appealing to Luther, Ebeling and Lutheran theologian Gerhard Gloege, Jüngel argues in the remaining portions of the essay that, for Lutherans, there can be no compromise on the point that the doctrine of justification is the one criterion, the 'hermeneutical category … which determines all of our thinking, speaking, and acting'.[41] Moreover, church unity emerges from agreement on this score or else not at all, for if justification indeed holds a criteriological function over all Christian thought, speech and action, the doctrine necessarily determines what is at stake in every ecumenical engagement. Since the *JDDJ* relativizes the criteriological role of justification, Jüngel opines, it represents an unmitigated ecumenical failure.

Readers are justified in wondering whether the criteriological function Jüngel assigns to the doctrine of justification in 'Klarheit!' and proximate texts obtains in his other works. After all, if Jüngel truly holds that the doctrine of justification defines and judges all other regions of Christian teaching, we should expect to see evidence of this structural and methodological commitment in his writings on a variety of topics. Now, tracing the breadcrumbs across his oeuvre from beginning to end exceeds the purpose and scope of this guidebook. But I will offer here my own appraisal, which, such as it is, results from many years wrestling with the texts. To my mind, Jüngel's writings elsewhere *do not* exhibit a criteriological deployment of the doctrine of justification. While, to be sure, justification recurs as a theme in many of Jüngel's works, outside of *Justification*, 'Klarheit!' and a handful of similar texts, he never seems especially interested to work out the interconnections between the doctrine of justification and whatever other topics happen to be at hand. Indeed, as Jüngel is ever up to writing *irregular* dogmatics, he rarely draws attention to the lateral and vertical structural features giving shape to systematic treatments of Christian doctrine.

Whatever the actual case elsewhere in his writings, Jüngel's call in 'Klarheit!' for Protestants to accept without compromise the criteriological function of the doctrine of justification managed to provoke quite a stir among his peers in the world of German theology and biblical studies. In the 27 January 1998 edition of the *Frankfurter Allgemeine Zeitung*, there appeared a petition signed by 141 German Protestant university professors urging pastors to reject the *JDDJ*.[42] 'The doctrine, structure and practice of the church are to be determined and judged by the doctrine of justification', the petition states.[43] From this basis, the document goes on to list seven areas in which, according to the signatories, the *JDDJ* fails to achieve consensus. While Jüngel is cited in the petition as the instigator of the revolt, he did not sign the final version of the statement. 'I could not identify with the letter of protest from my colleagues', he writes in the 'Preface to the Third Edition' of *Justification*, 'even though I agreed with it in many respects and a significant portion of the phraseology had been suggested by me. This was because some of the statements appeared to me to be expressions of confessional sterility' (*Justification*, xxvi). Meanwhile, heated debate over the declaration continued for another year, and in July 1999 and in an effort to assuage some of the concerns expressed during the fracas, the joint commission issued an 'Official Common Statement' and an 'Annex'. To this day, the *JDDJ* remains a source of controversy and frustration for some, especially for Lutherans persuaded by the positions Jüngel outlines in 'Klarheit!' and in other texts nearby.

'Sakrament und Repräsentation' (2001)

While Jüngel is known in the anglophone world mainly for his work in the areas of the doctrine of God, trinitarian theology, the thought of Karl Barth and justification by faith alone, some of his best short pieces address third article themes. He published a handful of essays and a small volume of lectures on sacramental theology, all of which, as I have shown elsewhere,[44] exhibit an astonishing degree of sophistication and novelty. 'Sakrament und Repräsentation' (in *TE V*, 274–287) is a late, mature statement on the sacraments drawing insights from earlier research while taking the exposition of the topic into new directions.

The opening section of the essay consists of a vintage statement from Jüngel on the problem of God's relation to world – a problem essential to the task of offering, as he puts it, a 'phenomenological description' of that which can be called a sacrament (*TE V*, 276–277). The discussion here trades upon an insight at the heart of Jüngel's sacramental theology: namely, his observation that the Latin word *sacramentum* comes from the Vulgate translation of the Greek μυστήριον – *mystery*. Jüngel's gloss on the New Testament use of μυστήριον is pivotal: mystery 'indicates at all times an event which itself cannot in any way be deduced from some connection to worldly being' (*TE V*, 275). The dialectic of possibility and actuality plays into Jüngel's hand here. He proposes that the *mysterium incarnationis* – that is, the mystery of the incarnation – 'concerns the coming to the world of God, which neither proceeds from the actuality of the world nor can be explained from its possibilities. The *mysterium incarnationis* brings its own possibilities with it, which are always, as *potentia aliena*, the opposite of the possibilities of the world'. He then asserts that '*every* sacramental event occurs in this same way, in that the arrival of divine grace, which cannot be explained from the context of the reality of the world, manifests itself in such events'. For Jüngel this does not mean that, in the sacrament, God remains sheerly absent from the world. Rather, God 'does not merely come close to the world, but comes even closer to the world than the world is capable of being to itself' (*TE V*, 276).

Jüngel argues that the category of *interruption* enables theology to describe the presence and absence of God in the sacraments phenomenologically. The definition he gives to interruption in the essay is worth considering in its entirety:

> That which deserves to be designated as *sacramental* is always an *elementary interruption* of the worldly continuity of life. Moreover it is decisive that this interruption is a *revolution*. The world cannot interrupt itself in order to grant God entrance. Were this possible, then the world would also be able to pardon itself. But this is out of the question. The world, rather, *is* interrupt*ed*. The human sinner, who is perpetually occupied with himself, cannot interrupt himself in order to be blessed by grace. He or she *is* interrupt*ed*. And this is an event that profoundly calls into question all previous forms of self-understanding. The event of elementary interruption is always a crisis for the actuality that is interrupted. Accordingly, the world is no longer the same as it was heretofore. (*TE V*, 277)

Note that Jüngel couches the discussion of sacramental interruption in the language of the justification of the sinner. Accordingly, the reason why the continuity of the world must be interrupted in order for God to arrive sacramentally is that, to paraphrase the passage, the sinner is ensnared in perpetual self-occupation. A radical break, indeed a 'crisis', is necessary for overcoming this sinful compulsion that characterizes the actuality of the world. And this break occurs in the event of justification, as he later puts it, in 'an indicative of grace which interrupts the rule of the continuous and determinative imperative of our world' (*TE V*, 280). The law enslaves the sinner to the deadly lie that human self-actualization is possible through works. The interruptive and gracious indicative of the gospel liberates the sinner from the yoke of the law by demonstrating that true humanity begins only *outside* the self and in the very event of the word of God. For Jüngel, this interruptive structure of the event of justification obtains in the sacraments.

And yet, Jüngel goes on to say, the true mystery of the sacraments is that in them '*certain chosen* worldly entities are taken up in the event of worship in order to make the coming of God communicable in a worldly sense' (*TE V*, 278). In the interruptive events of the sacraments, *elements* of the world – bread and wine (in the Lord's Supper) and water (in Christian baptism) – participate in God's communicative agency.[45] To be precise, when the word of God is added to the bread and wine and water, what results is a *verbum visibile* – a visible word (*TE V*, 279). This way of describing the sacrament derives from Augustine and is common stock in Catholic and Protestant sacramental theologies. But to the idea of 'visible words' Jüngel adds an important Christological gloss: namely, he reminds us that (1) the word of God added to the element in the sacrament *is* Jesus Christ and (2) only Jesus Christ can properly be called the mystery of God for the world:

> Jesus Christ must be regarded as the *primal sacrament* in whom the *gracious primal decision* of God in favor of sinful man and his world has become *revealed* and *made effective*, and this same primal decision promises to become *revealed* and to be *made effective* anew by the power of the Holy Spirit in the representing and presenting actions [of the church]. This occurs in the event of the spoken *word* of the name of Jesus Christ and in the visible form of this word in the sacraments. (*TE V*, 281)

For Jüngel, the sacraments of baptism and the Lord's Supper are visible words in the events of which the one word, Jesus Christ, comes to the world.

Jüngel devotes the second half of the essay to the problem of divine and human agency in the sacraments. He begins by recalling the close connection between the sacraments and the passivity of the person in the event of justification. 'The sacramental event', he writes, 'is intended to present the human person, who is incorporated into the sacramental event by virtue of his faith, with the saving presence of God. In this respect (the sacrament) makes the human person a *recipient*' (*TE V*, 282–283). At the same time, Jüngel continues, the human participant in the sacrament *acts* in this event. Jüngel elsewhere summarizes the dilemma as follows: 'It must ... be explained how two elements correspond to one another (in the concept of sacrament): on the one hand, the exclusion of every human activity that could be understood as achievement or merit; and, on the other hand, the sacramental action as it corresponds to the gospel.'[46]

In 'Sakrament und Repräsentation', Jüngel suggests that a solution to this problem is found in the claim, itself a matter of broad ecumenical consensus, that 'Jesus Christ is not only the sacramental gift, but is also and above all else the sacramental giver'. To put this in other language: 'Jesus Christ is the *primary actor* in the action of the sacrament; he is the *actual agent* in the sacramental event.' Consequently, 'in the action of baptism (Jesus Christ) is the subject of the baptizing; in the action of the Eucharist his self-imaging and self-communication occurs in, with, and under wine and bread' (*TE V*, 283). Baptism and the Lord's Supper are properly called sacraments precisely because Jesus Christ, the unique sacrament of God, works in and through worldly elements and human actions.

But how should we understand the *human* actions through which Jesus Christ acts to grant his own sacramental presence? Jüngel suggests that we think of these human actions as *representative* actions – hence the essay's title. In the actions of baptism and the Lord's Supper, the church *re*presents what occurred historically and definitively in the life, death and resurrection of Jesus Christ. As such, the church's actions 'do not exist for themselves, but act exclusively to serve that which is represented ... and to ascribe to what is represented its proper significance'. The church, that is, does not *produce* anything, but rather *reenacts* what occurred once and for all in the gospel events. 'The sacrament works *in nobis* that which has already *extra nos*', Jüngel writes. 'And it makes effective the event that has already occurred as it represents it: *significando causant*' (*TE V*, 284). This, however, does not necessitate, as it does in certain versions of Catholic sacramental theology, that the representative actions of the church somehow *complete* the saving actions which occurred in the history of Jesus Christ. Even if we should grant that the work of Jesus Christ is, in some sense, an *opus perficiendum*, that is, a work to be completed, we must maintain, in harmony with *Sacrosanctum concilium*, the *Constitution on the sacred liturgy* of the Second Vatican Council (*DEC* II, 820–843; abridged in *Denzinger*, 846–859), that it is Jesus Christ himself that completes his work through the church's liturgical actions (*TE V*, 285).

It is Schleiermacher who provides Jüngel with the categorical distinction necessary for explaining the analogy between the primary action of Jesus Christ and the representative actions of the church in such a way that Christ remains the singular actor in the sacraments. In Jüngel's reading, Schleiermacher differentiates between the 'effective' action which is carried out in the normal course of working life and the 'representative' or 'performative' action which is carried out only in events of worship.[47] Jüngel elsewhere elaborates this distinction as it pertains to the Lord's Supper:

As Schleiermacher put it, the action of the community at the Lord's Supper is an activity of performance and thus to be distinguished from activities that produce or effect something. Activity of performance has nothing to do with the kind of production-oriented activities to which our everyday world forces us. Activity of performance is free of drudgery and toil. Activity of performance is activity of the Sabbath, by which we are unburdened of ourselves. That is precisely what happens whenever we perform the representation in the Lord's Supper of the action of Jesus Christ: we are unburdened of ourselves and so become able to help to carry the burdens of others.[48]

For Jüngel, representative action is human agency conceived in light of the event of justification. In contrast to the toilsome 'production-oriented activities' marking the work week, the performative actions taking place in worship are 'Sabbath' actions which liberate the human person from the compulsion to actualize the self through works. And this is the case precisely because Jesus Christ himself is present and active in baptism and the Lord's Supper in such a way that the corresponding human actions arise from the passivity of reception. Indeed, and as Jüngel puts it as the essay draws to a close, the only genuine human action in baptism and the Lord's Supper is *faith*, which is the passive human reception of God's saving action (*TE V*, 286).

'Credere in ecclesiam' (2002)

Our final waystation on this journey through some of Jüngel's most significant theological essays is this splendid late piece on the doctrine of the church. In 'Credere in ecclesiam',[49] Jüngel epitomizes his approach to ecclesiology by riffing on the essential 'marks of the church' from the Niceno-Constantinopolitan Creed – unity, holiness, catholicity and apostolicity. The piece is divided into two main portions, the first of which revolves around a technical discussion of the use of the verb *credere* in Latin versions of the Creed. Jüngel observes that the Latin text, which is the source of vernacular liturgical renderings of the Creed in Europe and the Americas, 'deviates from the Greek original in several respects, including the replacement of the plural πιστεύομεν with the singular *credo*, and the omission of the εἰς (*in*) before the statement about the church. The Latin thus reads: *Credo … unam sanctam catholicam et apostolicam ecclesiam.*'[50] As a result of this change, the Latin essentially declares *credere ecclesiam* – to believe *the church* – rather than *credere in ecclesiam* – to believe *in* the church.

As the title of the essay suggests, Jüngel finds this distinction critically important for ecclesiology and proposes that faith consists of believing *in* the church. The point of his argument is likely to be lost on many anglophone readers, since most modern English versions of the Creed drawing from the Latin text retain the construction 'I/we believe *in* one, holy, catholic, and apostolic church', whereas the German omits the preposition in the clause. Perhaps the best way to summarize the nuance is to invoke the classical theological distinction between *fides quae* – the content of faith; i.e., that which is believed – and *fides qua* – the faith with which we believe. *Credere ecclesiam* corresponds to *fides quae* – that is, the church is the object of the knowledge of faith. *Credere in ecclesiam*, on the other hand, points to the *fides qua* – 'because of the faith with which I confess, I believe in the church'.[51] For Jüngel, following Luther, the church can never be just an object of knowledge, for then its attributes – its unity, holiness, catholicity and apostolicity – would be evident to reason. On the contrary, 'it is necessary *to believe* that the church is one, holy, and catholic'.[52] The church, that is, is an *article of faith* alongside the other articles confessed in the Creed.

Still in the first unit of the text, Jüngel takes this technical discussion of *credere* a step further by invoking the related theme of the classical Protestant distinction between the *ecclesia visibilis* and the *ecclesia invisibilis* – the visible and invisible church. Belief in the church as an object of knowledge – *credere ecclesiam* – would entail that the church's essence and attributes are visible in the church's institutions, tradition(s), practices and offices. Citing a key paragraph from the *Catechism of the Catholic Church*, Jüngel shows that the Catholic dogma of the Church seeks to combine an understanding of the Church as an object of *faith*, rather than knowledge, with the idea of the Church's essential visibility.[53] Over against this, Jüngel offers a distinctively Protestant understanding of the church 'as a community of believers constituted by Word and sacrament, which *participates*, as the body of Christ, in the life of the triune God, and which *represents* and *presents* that life in an earthly and historical form by the power of God's Spirit'. By 'earthly and historical form', Jüngel does not have in mind the church's institutional structures. Rather, 'the church presents and represents the triune life of God in a twofold earthly and historical form: in service to God (in liturgical worship), on one hand, and in service to the world (in "holy and acceptable … spiritual worship" [Rom 12:1], carried out in everyday life), on the other'. The church is *hidden* in this twofold form: 'It is invisible (in service to God and service to the world) in such a way that it can yet be identified, so that we can say that the hidden church (*ecclesia abscondita*) is present here and now'.[54]

Commenting on the distinction between the *ecclesia visibilis* and the *ecclesia invisibilis*, Webster writes:

Properly defined, the concept of the invisibility of the church is a standing denial of any easy identification of divine and human work. Talk of the church's invisibility secures the all-important point that 'only as *creatura verbi divini* is the Church an object of faith, because God's action in establishing and disclosing the true relationship between the creator and his creation that makes faith possible can be confessed as the content of faith.' Yet when this necessary gesture takes over, and is allowed to become the only constitutive movement for ecclesiology, other problems quickly emerge, and a picture of the church is promoted in which the human Christian community is unstable, liminal, and so incapable of sustaining a coherent historical and social trajectory.[55]

To my mind, Jüngel's deployment of the distinction in '*Credere in ecclesiam*' exhibits both the possibilities and the shortfalls that Webster identifies in these remarks. On one hand, the assertion that the church exists in the world only as the *ecclesia abscondita* entails that 'the church cannot constitute itself, it cannot produce itself any more than it can create and sustain itself, since it is *God's own work* … It is the *creature of God's word*, through which God makes possible communion between Godself and sinful humanity: *ecclesia enim creatura est Euangelii* [the church is the creature of the gospel]'.[56] On the other hand, because Jüngel's emphasis falls so decisively upon differentiating the creative word of God and the church as the creature of the word, and because he invokes the distinction between the *ecclesia visibilis* and the *ecclesia invisibilis* to subordinate the church to the word, we discover in the essay Jüngel struggling to define and describe the human community of the church as concretely connected to, as Webster puts it, 'a coherent historical and social trajectory'. Jüngel is well aware of the dilemma – in one place in the essay he acknowledges the danger of 'ecclesiological Docetism' – invoking the early Christological heresy to express the temptation to render the visible church 'inessential, or to deny it with vigorous hostility, or to regard it as a necessary evil'.[57] But the entire account of ecclesiology we find in the essay raises the question of whether Jüngel succeeds in overcoming this challenge.

The issues at stake here rise to the surface in the second unit of the essay on the attributes of the church. While the Creed itself summarizes the Christian confession of the church as belief in 'One, Holy, Catholic, and Apostolic Church', Jüngel marshals the marks in the following order: apostolicity, catholicity, holiness and unity. Apostolicity takes precedence over the other three marks because, as Jüngel sees it, the way we conceive the church's essential catholicity, holiness and unity depends upon our understanding of the Creed's confession of an 'Apostolic Church'. The mark of apostolicity, then, is *foundational*, at least theologically and ecumenically so, as getting apostolicity right sets ecclesiology on a true course and makes possible genuine Christian unity. Jüngel's summarizes apostolicity as follows:

> *Credo in ...* apostolicam *ecclesiam*: By the *apostolicity* of the church we are to understand the faithfulness of the church to the mission and task (expressed in an original way in the primitive Christian apostolate) of proclaiming the gospel in thought, word, and deed. And since the successor of the apostles is the New Testament canon (and not the bishop) ... the church exists in *apostolic succession* because and to the extent that it thinks, speaks, and acts according to the scriptures. The church existing in apostolic succession is the church existing in the power of the Holy Spirit and to this extent led into all truth. To be sure, the church is not maintained by virtue of its own decree, but only by virtue of the power of the truth of the gospel which overcomes the church's errors ... The claim of infallibility associated with the apostolicity of the church consists of the promise communicated to the church that God himself will receive the church in truth. God, however, receives the church in the truth only insofar as he accentuates the truth of the gospel and affirms and receives the church as an earthly space for this truth. Every speech and action of the visible church that exists under the conditions of the world is therefore always to be measured by the truth of the gospel.[58]

Two terms rising to the surface in this description are 'apostolic succession' and 'infallibility', as both concepts are at the heart of ongoing ecumenical dissensuses between Protestants and Catholics over the nature of church *authority*. Jüngel's comments nicely summarize the common Protestant position that the authority of *scripture* stands over against authority exercised through the church's offices and officers. Apostolic succession – that is, the continuity between the church in any age and the incipient church of the original apostles – is measured here according to the faithfulness of today's church (in its teaching and preaching) to the canon of scripture, rather than in terms of office and episcopacy. Likewise, the benchmark of the church's infallibility is the truth of the gospel, the proclamation of the good news of Jesus Christ 'in thought, word, and deed' and in harmony with scripture. Note that Jüngel insists that it is *God* who ensures that the church conforms to this standard. But this is because it is God who inspires and illuminates scripture, and who, by the power of the Holy Spirit, leads the church into all truth. The force of this compressed statement on apostolicity, then, is that God alone, through God's word, is the church's supreme and final authority – (tacitly) not the bishop.

Jüngel's prioritization of apostolicity, defined according to the reformation principles of *sola Scriptura* (scripture alone) and *solo verbo* (word alone), sets the tone for his interpretation of the other three marks of the church. The church's essential *catholicity*, he asserts, 'is the universal extensity of its unity by virtue of which the one and only church exists in all the world and … testifies to the world of the gracious dominion of Jesus Christ over the entire world'. The emphasis here on the extension of the church into the world through the preaching of the gospel leads Jüngel to stress the public and political character of the church's witness, for biblical proclamation serves as the medium through which the church challenges the state to recognize that it is called to be 'the secular image of the coming kingdom of God'.[59] The church is essentially *holy*, Jüngel goes on to say, 'because and to the extent that its sins are forgiven'. The discussion of holiness in the essay is couched in terms of a quintessentially Lutheran account of justification. The forgiveness of sins transpires when the sinner passively receives the alien righteousness of God in the preaching of scripture according to the proper differentiation of law and gospel. Hence, the principles of scripture alone and word alone are never too far out of reach here, even in Jüngel's suggestive (if rather brief) comments on the 'triple diaconate' through which, as he sees it, the church extends its holiness abroad.[60]

The church's *unity* is *essentially* the fundamental attribute among the marks. However, Jüngel's definition of apostolicity determines how he understands church unity. Accordingly, true ecumenism emerges not on the basis of *visible* unity marked by a common episcopal structure of offices but from the *invisible* unity made possible through the justifying grace of the gospel. Moreover, the invisible and thus essential unity of the church *includes difference*, for the church in its essence reflects the being of the triune God, who, as Father, Son and Holy Spirit, is a 'communion of reciprocal otherness'.[61] For Jüngel, this trinitarian basis for ecclesiology and ecumenism is critical for negotiating the relationships between the divided churches. He wraps up the essay with some comments and questions on the status of the Lutheran-Catholic dialogue, which, perhaps more than any other bilateral discussion, exhibits the tension between visible and invisible models for Christian ecumenism.

CONCLUSION
JÜNGEL'S THEOLOGY – ACHIEVEMENTS, CHALLENGES AND PROSPECTS

The foregoing chapters have found me somewhat reserved regarding evaluative comments on Jüngel's theological programme. But a few modest proposals along such lines are in order here at the end of this *Guide for the Perplexed*. Let me conclude, then, by offering some suggestions on the achievements, challenges and prospects of Jüngel's contribution to the story of Christian theology.

As I have presented Jüngel and his work in this guidebook, one of the enduring marks of his theological legacy is his confidence in *the freedom of Christian theology*. Jüngel's early intellectual and theological maturity transpired against the backdrop of the Soviet tyranny which descended upon Eastern Europe following the war. As a student in East Germany in the late 1950s and then as an instructor of ordinands 'behind the wall' at the Sprachenkonvikt, Jüngel came to prize the word of the gospel as a message of liberating truth which cannot be kept under wraps by the world's darkness. Consequently, his theological writings feature a prophetic edge missing in more pedestrian programmes of Christian divinity emerging during the past half-century. The prophetic character of Jüngel's work directly corresponds to his conviction that theology is *bound* to serve a word that is not fettered, and that, precisely for this reason, theology is utterly *free* to go about its business with courage and great joy. That Jüngel managed from the beginning of his career to its end to give witness to this vision of theology is no small accomplishment.

Jüngel, too, reminds us of *the abiding significance of the reformation*. His career neatly paralleled the phase of the modern ecumenical movement inspired by the Second Vatican Council and marked by bilateral dialogues between long-divided churches. Jüngel by no means discouraged ecumenical engagements on the part of Protestants with the Catholic 'other'. From the margins of the ecumenical movement, though, he ever demanded that Protestants take their *doctrine* seriously – especially, as we have seen, the doctrine of justification, which Jüngel considered to be the heart of the reformation's enduring witness. Jüngel's ecumenical achievement, we might say, is his sustained assertion that doctrinal precision must never fall away for the sake of ecumenical gains. For Jüngel, the future of Christianity in the spirit of the reformation depends upon such a commitment.

As I have presented his work here, Jüngel hardly is interested in repristinating the thought of his theological and intellectual forebears. Jüngel's programme, rather, exhibits a pattern of *retrieval without recapitulation*. That is to say, his best work offers a paradigm for how to use theological resources to move contemporaneous discussions forward. For a variety of reasons, this aspect of Jüngel's thought tends to get overlooked in anglophone secondary studies, not least due to the sway of genealogical theories for mapping intellectual origins. I have tried in this guidebook to stress the *originality* of his programme, arising as it did from the lively environs of Berlin at the turn of the 1960s. Jüngel, I believe, has much to teach younger scholars about how to start a theological career well.

If these are some of Jüngel's signal theological achievements, what are the challenges his work presents to those of us who endeavour to read his theology charitably today? Let me highlight three interrelated themes emerging from the presentation of Jüngel's contribution which unfolded in this book's main chapters. First, for all the praise we might be willing to heap upon Jüngel for the originality of his work, his theological witness is, in certain respects, frustratingly *narrow*. Jüngel does not appear to have substantively broadened his theological bandwidth beyond the patterns of discourse marking his formative Berlin period. Moving forward in his career, he continues to do his work in the same register, addressing a cluster of familiar issues by appealing to a handful of esteemed interlocutors. It is demonstrable that certain aspects of Jüngel's theology evolved over the course of his career. And later on, especially in the 1990s and early 2000s, we find him increasingly interested in themes located in the creedal third article. But such developments unfold quite naturally within the trajectory of Jüngel's programme; they do not appear as real changes of direction or of mind. I am not suggesting here that Jüngel *should* have changed his mind altogether, nor that his programme suffers sheerly for the fact that it lacks a conspicuous sharp turning point. My purpose, rather, is to draw attention to the stark *uniformity* of Jüngel's contribution from beginning to end.

As I indicated earlier, this characteristic of Jüngel's programme comes across especially in his own engagement with secondary sources. His career-long ignorance of contemporaneous anglophone theology surely counts as a major deficiency. We can only speculate how differently his works would have appeared had he interacted with Niebuhr or Hauerwas or Torrance or Gunton or Tracy or Jenson, to name but a few prominent figures from Britain and North America. Jüngel, too, fails to give due attention to key cotemporaneous developments in theology and biblical studies. To recall a glaring instance, while the field of New Testament studies went on from the 1970s to focus on the backgrounds of early Christianity in Second Temple Judaism, Jüngel continued to address exegetical problems by following the tack of hermeneutical theology, which otherwise had become unfashionable once the New Hermeneutic began to wane. To be clear, the problem here is not so much that Jüngel chose one route through the morass instead of another. Rather, his failure to extensively cite key works from, say, the New Perspective suggests that he simply is unaware that an alternate path embarking from a different starting point has been opened.

Second, as readers of this guidebook may have noticed, I remain uneasy with respect to one particular structural commitment marking Jüngel's writings: namely, his persistent appeal to the temporal metaphor of *interruption* (or familial terms) to do the work of depicting the relationship between God and the world, and everything else encompassed beneath that heading. As I have shown elsewhere,[1] one consequence of his abiding focus on the interruptive is a corresponding allergy even to the possibility that some of the things of God occur over time. As a result of this structural motif, he seldom occupies himself with doctrines such as creation and providence, nor does he give sustained attention to the question of the location of Israel within the unfolding of the divine plan. Likewise, doctrines such as pneumatology, ecclesiology and eschatology take awkward shape under the downward pressure of Jüngel's interruptive account of divine agency. Now, perhaps I am being unfair to Jüngel here. After all, throughout this book I have identified him as a practitioner of what Barth called 'irregular' dogmatics, which means, among other things, that his writings often lack the analytical depth and precision normally found in 'regular', comprehensive accounts of Christian divinity. Had Jüngel written, say, a regular ecclesiology, we would expect him to offer an encyclopedic and sophisticated account of how the interruptive word relates to ecclesial continuities. As it stands, the playful use of the metaphor of interruption in an irregular programme for ecclesiology raises more questions than it answers.

With some hesitancy I raise a third item for consideration here. At the time the present book is being written, a host of significant theological conversations are taking place especially in English-speaking countries and in the majority world concerning issues in the vicinity of equality, justice and human rights. Scholars of religious and biblical studies are evaluating with urgency what resources theology might offer for addressing a nexus of problems such as race, 'whiteness', colonialism, poverty, gender identity and sexual orientation. Does Jüngel have anything to contribute to these discussions? To his great credit, Jüngel persistently emphasized themes such as the dignity of the human person, the freedom of the justifying word of God in a world overrun by oppressive hegemonies and the subversive character of theology as an act of public discourse. I therefore would wager that we might discover Jüngel an ally to those doing theology at the margins. But such connections hardly are explicit in his oeuvre. To pry them loose, we need patience and intellectual generosity in healthy doses. Time will tell if Jüngel's work finds a hearing in anglophone theology as the present, complicated century moves forward.

I would argue, though, that Jüngel yet has much to teach us. He faithfully engaged the politics of his own time, and his best writings bear witness to how theology can serve as mode of resistance against the tyranny of powers and principalities. His later writings, especially those in which he addresses issues within the domain of the third article, are just now receiving attention from anglophone scholars. The ongoing work of translating Jüngel into English will aid the reception of his work in Britain and North America considerably. All to say: there is a great deal of labour yet to be done towards assessing his witness and legacy. Finally for now, I submit that theologians today would do well to pay heed to Jüngel's insistence that theology has 'an existential relationship to the pulpit',[2] and that its principal task is to hear the word of God and to reiterate it. So much of what passes for theology today comes across as bureaucratic, sterile and deadly boring, straightjacketed as it is by the scientific demands of the academy. Jüngel's programme stands out and warrants careful reflection insofar as he urges us to consider that theology's proper end is to aid those who bear the church's public witness in the ministry of word and sacrament.

NOTES

Preface

1. Eberhard Jungel, *Leidenschaft*, 21.

2. Jüngel, 'Eberhard Jüngel', in Jürgen Moltmann, ed., *How I Have Changed: Reflections on Thirty Years of Theology* (Harrisburg, PA: Trinity Press International), 4–5.

3. Throughout this book, I employ the locutions 'the gospel', 'the Christian gospel', 'the word of the gospel' and 'the gospel of Jesus Christ' interchangeably to shorthand the message of the death, resurrection and enduring significance of Jesus Christ. I am aware that some of my readers might object to the positive and uncritical use of such language in an academic study of a modern theologian. However, and as I endeavour to show throughout these pages, Jüngel's contribution to the story of modern Christian thought resides in his commitment to the notion that the New Testament message about Jesus Christ lays claim upon those who hear and believe it. To do Christian theology is, for Jüngel, to plunge ever deeper into the mystery opened up in and by the interruptive word of the gospel. For this reason, in order to accurately account for what Jüngel is up to, I cannot shy away from the full-throated usage of these and related expressions.

4. See my prefatory comments in the 2014 editions of *Mystery* and *Justification*.

5. John Webster, *Barth's Earlier Theology: Scripture, Confession and Church* (London and New York: T&T Clark Continuum, 2005).

6. Webster, 'Jesus in the Theology of Eberhard Jüngel', *CTJ* 32 (1997): 43–71. The essay also appears in idem, *Word and Church: Essays in Christian Dogmatics* (Edinburgh and New York: T&T Clark, 2001) under the title, 'Jesus in Modernity: Reflections on Jüngel's Christology'.

7. John wrote two substantive pieces on Jüngel after the appearance of the *CTJ* essay - the introductions to English editions of Jüngel's books *God's Being Is in Becoming* and *Justification*. These introductory pieces, however, are, as a rule, descriptive rather than evaluative.

8. Webster, *Eberhard Jüngel: An Introduction to His Theology* (Cambridge and New York: Cambridge University Press, 1986).

Notes

9. Webster, 'Distinguishing between God and Man – Aspects of the Theology of Eberhard Jüngel' (PhD dissertation, Clare College, University of Cambridge, 1982).

10. It seems worth noting that, up to the last minute, John was preparing to present a paper at the inaugural meeting of the Eberhard Jüngel Research Colloquium, which took place on the morning of Saturday, 22 November 2014, at the Annual Meetings of the American Academy of Religion, and as a joint session with the Karl Barth Society of North America. John had agreed to write a piece titled 'Jüngel: Debts and Questions', detailing points of influence and departure. Regrettably, just weeks prior to the Annual Meetings John emailed to report that he could not make headway into the paper due to illness and needed to decline the invitation to write. It would have been a fascinating, late-career retrospective shedding light upon his complex intellectual and theological relationship with Jüngel.

11. It may be helpful for me to highlight what I consider to be the two most significant points of departure between my reading of Jüngel's theology and that of Webster. First, Webster essentially pioneered the 'genealogical' approach to the origins of Jüngel's thought. He especially is interested in identifying the significance of Karl Barth and Rudolf Bultmann for Jüngel and positions these two figures as Jüngel's dominant theological influences. As I explain in detail in Chapter 2, I have my doubts regarding the utility of genealogical agendas for locating Jüngel's theological contribution and suggest instead that the quest for the origins of his thought must account for the larger discursive patterns marking the theological scene in Germany – particularly, in Berlin – during the late 1950s and early 1960s.

   Second, in several spots Webster dubs Jüngel a 'severely professional theologian'. This judgement, which Webster employs pejoratively, reflects his contention that Jüngel's work finds its home in the high university culture of post-war Germany. I readily acknowledge Jüngel's role as a university theologian of a rather austere and professional ilk. However, I worry that by stressing this aspect of Jüngel's vocation, Webster fails to account for Jüngel's contribution as a *churchman*. Webster rarely mentions the ecclesial settings of Jüngel's key writings. More significantly, Webster seems largely unaware of the importance of *preaching* for Jüngel's work as a theologian. I point out several of these ecclesial and homiletical connections throughout the course of this guidebook.

   I am not, by the way, the first Lutheran to express a little impatience with Webster for failing to appreciate the significance of preaching for Jüngel's theology. See, for instance, Gerhard Forde, Rev. of *Eberhard Jüngel: An Introduction to His Theology*, in *LQ* 2 no. 4 (1988): 531–533.

Chapter 1

1. William Paley, *Natural Theology*, eds. Matthew D. Eddy and David Knight (New York and Oxford: Oxford University Press, 2006), 7–10.

2. Jüngel, 'Eberhard Jüngel', in Jürgen Moltmann, ed., *How I Have Changed: Reflections on Thirty Years of Theology* (Harrisburg, PA: Trinity Press International), 4.

3. Ibid., 4–5.

4. Jüngel, 'Besinnung auf 50 Jahre theologische Existenz', *ThLZ* 128 (2003): 474.

5. Ibid., 475.

6. Eberhard Busch, *Karl Barth: His Life from Letters and Autobiographical Texts*, trans. John Bowden (Grand Rapids, MI: Eerdmans, 1994), 249.

7. Heinrich Vogel, *Gott in Christo. Ein Erkenntnisgang durch die Grundprobleme der Dogmatik* (Berlin: Lettner-Verlag, 1951).

8. Heinrich Vogel, *Consider Your Calling: An Introduction to Theological Study in the Light of the Fundamental Questions It Raises for Ministers and Students of Divinity*, trans. John Penney Smith (Edinburgh and London: Oliver and Boyd, 1962).

9. Jüngel, 'Besinnung auf 50 Jahre theologische Existenz', 475.

10. Ibid., 479.

11. Ibid., 476. The citation is from Ernst Fuchs, *Studies of the Historical Jesus*, trans. Andrew Scobie, Studies in Biblical Theology 41 (London: SCM, 1964), 38.

12. Jüngel, 'Eberhard Jüngel', 8.

13. Jüngel, 'Besinnung auf 50 Jahre theologische Existenz', 480.

14. Ibid.

15. Ibid.

16. Otto Hermann Pesch, 'Das katholische Sakramentsverständnis im Urteil gegenwärtiger evangelische Theologie', in Jüngel, Johannes Wallmann and Wilfrid Werbeck, eds., *Verifikationen. Festschrift für Gerhard Ebeling zum 70. Geburtstag* (Tübingen: Mohr Siebeck, 1982); cited in Jüngel, 'The Church as Sacrament?' in *Essays I*, 191.

17. André Birmelé, 'Eberhard Jüngel and the International Lutheran-Catholic Dialogue', trans. R. David Nelson, in Nelson, ed., *Indicative of Grace – Imperative of Freedom: Essays in Honour of Eberhard Jüngel in His 80th Year* (London: Bloomsbury T&T Clark, 2014), 1.

18. I refer to two series of booklets: *Theologische Existenz heute*, published between 1933 and 1941 by Christian Kaiser Verlag (München); and *Theologische Studien*, published beginning in 1938 and running for over three decades. Karl Barth founded the former series with Eduard Thurneysen, but the Nazis prohibited him from working with Christian Kaiser Verlag beginning in 1937. Barth commenced the latter series with the Swiss publisher TVZ the following year. Jüngel published a host of theological booklets from the start of his career to the mid-1980s, and these texts exhibit strong similarities in style and presentation to the pamphlets released in the two series which had commenced under Barth's editorial direction.

Notes

19. An English translation is available as Hans Dieter Betz, Don Browning, Bernd Janowski and Eberhard Jüngel, eds., *Religion Past and Present*, 14 vols. (Leiden: Brills, 2006–2013).

20. Intrinsic to my commentary here is the judgement that Jüngel is, in fact, doing *Christian dogmatics* in his published output. One might conceivably argue that a number of Jüngel's writings count as contributions to philosophical, rather than dogmatic discourse. In reading such works, however, we discover that Jüngel persistently bends his philosophical insights back upon questions and concerns which are theological in nature. As such, we might say that Jüngel's thought illustrates the creative repurposing of philosophy, both ancient and modern, for the sake of theology. In any event, the reading of Jüngel recommended in this guidebook forefronts the thoroughgoing dogmatic character of his literary yield.

21. Webster, *Eberhard Jüngel – An Introduction to His Theology* (Cambridge and New York: Cambridge University Press, 1986), 5.

22. Ibid., 3.

23. Ibid., 5.

Chapter 2

1. Paul J. DeHart, *Beyond the Necessary God: Trinitarian Faith and Philosophy in the Thought of Eberhard Jüngel*, American Academy of Religion: Reflection and Theory in the Study of Religion, ed. Mary McClintock Fulkerson, no. 15 (Atlanta: Scholars Press, 1999), 5.

2. Ibid. See the entirety of DeHart's sketch of Jüngel's relation to these influences on pages 5–8.

3. Roland Spjuth, *Creation, Contingency and Divine Presence in the Theologies of Thomas F. Torrance and Eberhard Jüngel*, Studia Theologica Ludensia 51 (Lund: Lund University Press, 1995), 42.

4. Mark C. Mattes, *The Role of Justification in Contemporary Theology*, Lutheran Quarterly Books, ed. Paul Rorem (Grand Rapids: Eerdmans, 2004), *passim*.

5. Roland Daniel Zimany, *Vehicle for God: The Metaphorical Theology of Eberhard Jüngel* (Macon, GA: Mercer University Press, 1994), vii.

6. Ibid.

7. Ibid.

8. Paul J. Griffiths, *The Practice of Catholic Theology: A Modest Proposal* (Washington, DC: The Catholic University of America Press, 2016).

9. Ibid., 117.

10. Ibid., 3. See the entirety of his discussion of theology as discursive on pages 2–14.

11. R. David Nelson, 'Prolegomena to Lutheran Theology', *LQ* 31 (2017): 133.

12. Rudolf Bultmann, 'What Is Theology?' trans., Roy A. Harrisville, eds. Eberhard Jüngel and Klaus Müller, *Fortress Texts in Modern Theology* (Minneapolis: Fortress, 1997), 63.

13. Ibid., 73. See the entirety of his discussion in *What Is Theology?* chapters 1–3, pages 23–75.

14. See especially the chapter 'God's Being-as-Object' in *Becoming*, 55–74.

15. Mark Mattes, 'Toward Divine Relationality: Eberhard Jüngel's New Trinitarian, Postmetaphysical Approach' [PhD thesis, University of Chicago, 1995]; Arnold Neufeldt-Fast, 'Eberhard Jüngel's Theological Anthropology in Light of His Christology' [PhD thesis, University of St Michael's College, Toronto, 1996]; and Zimany, *Vehicle for God.*

16. See in particular the essay by Deborah Casewell, 'Reading Heidegger through the Cross: On Eberhard Jüngel's Heideggerian Ontology', *Forum Philosophicum* 21 no. 1 (2016): 95–114.

17. Arnold Neufeldt-Fast, 'Martin Heidegger: Anstoß for Eberhard Jüngel's Theology', in R. David Nelson, ed., *Indicative of Grace – Imperative of Freedom: Essays in Honour of Eberhard Jüngel in His 80th Year* (London: Bloomsbury T&T Clark, 2014), 187–188. The citation within the quote is an allusion to the English translation of the title of Jüngel's autobiographical booklet, *Die Leidenschaft, Gott zu denken.*

18. See, for example, his chapter on 'The Death of a Sinner (Death as the Wages of Sin)', in Iain and Ute Nicol, trans., *Death: The Riddle and the Mystery* (Philadelphia: Westminster, 1974), 59–94. His goal in the chapter is to highlight the incompatibility of different biblical traditions concerning death and the afterlife.

19. Jüngel, *The Freedom of a Christian: Luther's Significance for Contemporary Theology*, trans. Roy A. Harrisville (Minneapolis: Augsburg, 1988).

20. Gerhard Ebeling, *Luther: An Introduction to His Thought*, trans. R.A. Wilson (Philadelphia: Fortress Press, 1970).

21. Jüngel, *Justification*, 212n 145.

22. See the comments in David S. Yeago, 'Theological Impasse and Ecclesial Future', *Lutheran Forum* 26 no. 4 (1992): 36–45.

23. Jüngel, 'Die Theologie als Narr im Haus der Wissenschaften', in Johann Reikerstorfer, ed., *Zum gesellschaftlichen Schicksal der Theologie: ein Wiener Symposium zu Ehren von Johann Baptist Metz* (Münster: LITVerlag, 1999), 60–72.

24. Jüngel, 'Eberhard Jüngel', 9.

25. Nietzsche, *Thus Spoke Zarathustra* 4, LXXIII, 1.

26. For a classic statement, see Jüngel, *Christ, Justice and Peace: Toward a Theology of the State*, trans. D. Bruce Hamill and Alan J. Torrance (London: Bloomsbury T&T Clark, 2014).

Notes

27. See especially Jüngel, 'Säkularisierung – Theologische Anmerkungen zum Begriff einer weltlichen Welt', in *TE II*, 285–289.

28. Jüngel, 'Der Gottesdienst als Fest der Freiheit', in *TE IV*, 330–350.

29. Jüngel, *Karl Barth, A Theological Legacy*, trans. Garrett E. Paul (Philadelphia: The Westminster Press, 1986), 22.

30. Nelson, 'Karl Barth and Eberhard Jüngel', in George Hunsinger and Keith L. Johnson, eds., *Wiley Blackwell Companion to Karl Barth* (Chichester: Wiley Blackwell, 2020).

31. Jüngel, 'Eberhard Jüngel', 10.

32. Karl Barth, Reference Letter for Eberhard Jüngel, 5 July 1958, [Document] Karl Barth-Archiv, Basel.

33. Barth, Letter to Eberhard Jüngel on 13 April 1966, in Karl Barth, *Letters, 1961–1968*, eds. Jürgen Fangmeier and Hinrich Stoevesandt, trans. and ed. Geoffrey W. Bromiley (Grand Rapids, MI: Eerdmans, 1981), 203.

34. Jüngel, 'The Royal Man: A Christological Reflection on Human Dignity in Barth's Theology', in *Karl Barth*, 127–138.

35. See especially Jüngel, 'Gospel and Law: The Relationship of Dogmatics to Ethics', in *Karl Barth*, 105–126.

36. The following comments are a distillation of my research on Jüngel's sacramental theology. On baptism and the Lord's Supper, see especially Nelson, 'Eberhard Jüngel on Baptism and the Lord's Supper: Towards a Hermeneutic for Reading the Texts', in idem, ed., *Indicative of Grace – Imperative of Freedom*, 167–185.

37. Konrad Hammann, *Rudolf Bultmann – A Biography*, trans. Philip E. Devenish (Salem, OR: Polebridge Press, 2013), 326. See the entirety of Hammann's discussion of demythologization on pages 323–336.

38. David W. Congdon, *The Mission of Demythologizing: Rudolf Bultmann's Dialectical Theology* (Minneapolis: Fortress, 2015), 598. Congdon's groundbreaking work on Bultmann's theology has done much to correct a half-century's worth of anglophone mis-readings of demythologization. See also his book *Rudolf Bultmann: A Companion to His Theology*, Cascade Companions (Eugene, OR: Cascade, 2015).

39. Hammann, *Rudolf Bultmann – A Biography*, 338.

40. Ibid., 339.

41. Jüngel, 'Die Wahrheit des Mythos und die Notwendigkeit der Entmythologisierung', in *TE IV*, 40–75.

42. Michael Root, 'Ecumenical Winter', *FT* 286 (October 2018): 33–39.

43. Thomas S. Kuhn, *The Structure of Scientific Revolutions* (Chicago: University of Chicago Press, 1962).

44. Among other things, this exclusive focus on justification by faith as the starting point and criterion for ecumenical engagement gives way to a

somewhat cramped appraisal on his part of Catholic Christianity. Throughout his writings Jüngel draws from a narrow bandwidth of Catholic interlocutors, in nearly every instance bending his exposition of whatever topic is at hand back to the historic dissensus between Protestants and Catholics over justification. While there is much to admire in Jüngel's tenacious ecumenical temperament and his commitment to the difficult task of addressing the doctrines marking the divisions between the Christian churches, his posture towards the Catholic 'other' is open to criticism for its apparent lack of nuance.

45. Jürgen Moltmann, *Theology of Hope: On the Ground and the Implications of a Christian Eschatology*, trans. James W. Leitch (London: SCM, 1967).

46. Wolfhart Pannenberg, ed., *Revelation as History: A Proposal for a More Open, Less Authoritarian View of an Important Theological Concept*, trans. David Granskou (London: Macmillan, 1968).

47. Pannenberg, *Systematic Theology*, 3 volumes, trans. Geoffrey W. Bromiley (Grand Rapids: Eerdmans, 1991–1998).

48. See, for instance, Moltmann's comments on Jüngel in *A Broad Place: An Autobiography*, trans. Margaret Kohl (Minneapolis: Fortress, 2008), *passim*.

49. Moltmann, *The Crucified God: The Cross of Christ as the Foundation and Criticism of Christian Theology*, trans. R.A. Wilson and John Bowden (London: SCM, 1974).

50. Pannenberg, *Jesus – God and Man*, trans. Lewis L. Wilkins and Duane A. Priebe (Philadelphia: Westminster Press, 1968).

51. Pannenberg, *Theology and the Philosophy of Science*, trans. Francis McDonagh (Louisville, KY: Westminster John Knox Press, 1985).

52. Pannenberg, *Anthropology in Theological Perspective*, trans. Matthew J. O'Connell (Louisville, KY: Westminster John Knox Press, 1976).

53. Jüngel, 'Das Dilemma der natürlichen Theologie und die Wahrheit ihres Problems: Überlegungen für ein Gespräch mit Wolfhart Pannenberg', in *TE II*, 158–177.

54. Eberhard Jüngel and Karl Rahner, *Was ist ein Sakrament? Vorstöße zur Verständigung*, Ökumenische Forschungen. Ergänzende Abteilung. Kleine ökumenische Schriften 6 (Freiburg: Herder, 1971).

55. Hans Küng, *Justification: The Doctrine of Karl Barth and a Catholic Reflection*, 40th anniversary ed. (Louisville: Westminster John Knox, 2004).

56. Küng, *Infallible? An Inquiry*, trans. Edward Quinn (New York: Doubleday, 1971).

57. Jüngel, 'Irren ist menschlich: Zur Kontroverse um Hans Küngs Buch "Unfehbar? Eine Anfrage"', in *TE I*, 75–80.

58. Jüngel, '*Caritas fide formata*: die erste Ekzyklika Benedikt XVI – gelesen mit den Augen eines evangelischen Christenmenschen', *IKaZ* 35 no. 6 (2006): 595–614.

Notes

Chapter 3

1. In English-language literature on Jüngel, the only sustained engagements with *Paulus und Jesus* are found in two pieces by Webster, *Eberhard Jüngel*, 6–15; and idem, 'Jesus in the Theology of Eberhard Jüngel,' *CTJ* 32 (1997): 43–71.

2. See, for instance, the essays translated and anthologized in Fuchs, *Studies of the Historical Jesus*, especially 'What Is a "Language Event" – a Letter?' (207–212); and 'The Essence of "Language-Event" and Christology' (213–228). Fuchs's prose (even in German) is notoriously opaque, and he assumes that his reader is thoroughly familiar with contemporaneous discussions in exegesis, hermeneutics and theology. Students of Jüngel's work, though, would do well to read some of Fuchs's short pieces from the late 1950s and 1960s. Readers will note some striking rhetorical parallels between Fuchs and Jüngel.

3. On the theme of Jesus's parables of the kingdom, see the entirety of Jüngel's argument in *P&J*, 139–142.

4. See Jülicher, *Die Gleichnisreden Jesu*, vol. 1 (Freiburg, IB: J.C.B. Mohr, 1899), 44–81. Regrettably, Jülicher's study has never been translated into English. A helpful and succinct review of Jülicher's contribution and the ensuing dispute its publication caused can be found in Klyne Snodgrass, *Stories with Intent: A Comprehensive Guide to the Parables of Jesus* (Grand Rapids, MI: Eerdmans, 2008), 4–7.

5. Fuchs, 'The Essence of "Language-event" and Christology', 224.

6. Webster, 'Jesus in the Theology of Eberhard Jüngel', 49.

7. See, for instance, Jüngel's introductory comments in *P&J*, 3–5.

8. For a fascinating demonstration of how this line of reasoning might appear when carried through to its logical conclusion, see Roland Zimany, 'God with Intermittent Being', *CThMi* 14 (1987): 1–13. Inspired by Jüngel and a handful of others we have encountered in this guidebook, Zimany argues that God does not have being beyond the interruptive word of proclamation.

9. The book was first made available in English in 1976 under the title *The Doctrine of the Trinity*, giving the impression that Jüngel is offering a constructive doctrine of God and not a paraphrase of Barth. See Jüngel, *The Doctrine of the Trinity: God's Being Is in Becoming*, trans. Horton Harris, Monograph Supplements to the *Scottish Journal of Theology*, eds. Thomas F. Torrance and J.K.S. Reid (Edinburgh: Scottish Academic Press, 1976). While Horton's translation did much to introduce anglophone readers to Jüngel's theology, throughout this guide I refer readers to Webster's superior translation from 2001.

10. For a masterful summary statement of this view, see Bruce L. McCormack, 'Grace and Being: The Role of God's Gracious Election in Karl Barth's Theological Ontology', in *Orthodox and Modern: Studies in the Theology of Karl Barth* (Grand Rapids, MI: Baker Academic, 2008), 183–200.

11. George Hunsinger articulates this position in *Reading Barth with Charity: A Hermeneutical Proposal* (Grand Rapids, MI: Baker Academic, 2015).

12. Letter from Bruce L. McCormack dated 4 October 2004, in Wolfgang Eck and Dirk Evers, Hgs., *Für Eberhard Jüngel: Eine Festgabe* (Stuttgart: Radius-Verlag, 2004), 78.

13. In the background of Jüngel's comments on the relation of God's existence and essence is his dispute with Helmut Gollwitzer's doctrine of God as stated in Gollwitzer, *The Existence of God as Confessed by Faith*, trans. James W. Leitch (Philadelphia: Westminster, 1965). See also the analyses of this dispute in Bruce L. McCormack, 'God Is His Decision: The Jüngel-Gollwitzer "Debate" Revisited', in Bruce L. McCormack and Kimlyn Bender, eds., *Theology as Conversation: The Significance of Dialogue in Historical and Contemporary Theology* (Grand Rapids, MI: Eerdmans, 2009), 48–66; and Akke van der Kooi, 'Election and the Lived Life: Considerations on Gollwitzer's Reading of Karl Barth in *CD* II/2 as a Contribution to Actual Discussions on Trinity and Election', *ZDTh* 4 Supplement (2010): 67–82.

14. While acknowledging the ungainliness of the terms, I will use 'temporal history' and 'primal history' in the following section. These idioms are taken from the argument of *God's Being Is in Becoming* and are crucial for my analysis, as they encapsulate Jüngel's insistence that both created time as a chronology of past, present and future and eternity as the perichoretic life of God as Father, Son and Holy Spirit are *histories*.

15. Webster, 'Translator's Introduction', in *Becoming*, xii. Joseph Mangina strikes a similar chord when he remarks that Jüngel takes pains here to avoid a 'featureless Sabellian deity, aloof from history and human suffering'. See Mangina, Rev. of *God's Being Is in Becoming*, by Eberhard Jüngel, *IJST* 5 no. 1 (2003): 89.

16. For Jüngel's analysis of the identity of the 'economic' and 'immanent' trinities, see the important essay, 'The Relationship between "Economic" and "Immanent" Trinity', *ThD* 24 no 2 (1976): 179–184. I survey this essay, which is an abridgement of the original, in Chapter 4. For reasons explained momentarily, readers of this essay may wish to consult the longer German text, available in *TE II*, 265–275.

17. See the single, dense paragraph in *Becoming*, 13–15, for Jüngel's introduction to this Christological solution to the question of the relations of God's essence and existence, immanent life and economic activity, and so on.

18. While the Western–Augustinian origins of Jüngel's doctrine of the trinity are conspicuous, it should be noted that, as a rule, he resists employing 'classical' trinitarian jargon – e.g. 'hypostasis', 'ousia' and so on. By invoking the concept of hypostasis here, I am suggesting that a connection between Jüngel's exposition and the classical tradition of trinitarian discourse operates tacitly in the argument of *God's Being Is in Becoming*.

19. See Jüngel, 'The Relationship between "Economic" and "Immanent" Trinity', 183; cf. *TE II*, 273. I have adjusted the translation and added emphasis.

Notes

20. Jüngel, 'The Relationship between "Economic" and "Immanent" Trinity', 184; cf. *TE II*, 275. The anonymous translator of the English edition of the essay renders the phrases '*Gott kommt von Gott*', '*Gott kommt zu Gott*' and '*Gott kommt als Gott*' as 'God *proceeds* from God', and so on, instead of the literal 'God *comes* from God', etc. The former rendering is certainly apt and also alludes to the classical trinitarian concept of divine *processions*; the literal rendering more directly squares with Jüngel's numerous other statements from the same period concerning the *advent* of God – the coming of God to the world. I am slightly cautious about the translator's decision, as I find no evidence that would suggest that Jüngel is invested in the classical account of divine processions. If we are to take the verb '*kommen*' as 'to proceed', we must bear in mind that Jüngel is not using this language in dialogue with classical trinitarian discourse.

21. Jüngel, 'The Royal Man', 130.

22. These are Luther's terms for the essence ('what-being') and existence ('that-being') of God, cited by Jüngel in *Mystery*, 124ft. 53.

23. Jüngel, 'God – as a Word of Our Language: For Helmut Gollwitzer on His Sixtieth Birthday', trans. Robert T. Osborn, in Fredrick Herzog, ed., *Theology of the Liberating Word: In Memory of Karl Barth, 1886–1968 – Four Articles from Evangelische Theologie* (Nashville: Abingdon, 1971), 29.

24. See the entirety of the second section, 'Is God Necessary?', in *Mystery*, 14–35.

25. Garrett Green, 'The Mystery of Eberhard Jüngel: A Review of His Theological Program', *RelSRev* 5 no. 1 (1979): 34.

26. Ibid., 38.

27. Three widely available sources are especially helpful here: John A. Radano, *Lutheran and Catholic Reconciliation on Justification: A Chronology of the Holy See's Contributions, 1961–1999, to a New Relationship between Lutherans and Catholics and to Steps Leading to the* 'Joint Declaration on the Doctrine of Justification' (Grand Rapids, MI: Eerdmans, 2009); Christopher J. Malloy, *Engrafted into Christ: A Critique of the* Joint Declaration (New York: Peter Lang, 2005), 219–266; and William G. Rusch, ed., *Justification and the Future of the Ecumenical Movement: The* Joint Declaration on the Doctrine of Justification (Collegeville, MN: Liturgical Press, 2003).

28. Jüngel, *Das Evangelium von der Rechtfertigung des Gottlosen als Zentrum des christlichen Glaubens. Eine theologische Studie in ökumenischer Absicht* (Tübingen: Mohr Siebeck, 1998). At present, the Mohr Siebeck text is in its sixth (unrevised) edition.

29. See especially the introduction to the section 'By the word alone (*solo verbo*)', in *Justification*, 198–204.

30. Comments on the fundamental passivity of the recipient of the justifying word are found throughout the monograph. For a particularly clear expression of the insight, see Jüngel's remarks on 'mere passivity' in *Justification*, 181–182, including the long footnote that extends over those pages.

31. Of note here is Jüngel's exposition of God's 'Yes' in *Justification*, 104–108.

32. Root, 'Ecumenical Winter', 33–39.

33. Walter Cardinal Kasper, *Harvesting the Fruits: Basic Aspects of Christian Faith in Ecumenical Dialogue* (London and New York: Continuum, 2009), 2.

34. See the entirety of Cardinal Kasper's argument in *Harvesting the Fruits*, but especially the introduction, pages 1–9.

35. The two best studies of the *Grunddifferenz* debate continue to be Robert W. Jenson, *Unbaptized God: The Basic Flaw in Ecumenical Theology* (Minneapolis: Fortress, 1992); and André Birmelé, *La communion ecclésiale. Progrès œcuméniques et enjeux méthodologiques* (Paris: Le Cerf, 2000). See also my summary of the problem in R. David Nelson and Charles Raith II, *Ecumenism: A Guide for the Perplexed* (London: Bloomsbury T&T Clark, 2017), 101–126.

Chapter 4

1. Jüngel, 'God – as a Word in Our Language', in Frederick Herzog, ed., *Theology of the Liberating Word: In Memory of Karl Barth, 1886–1968 - Four Articles from* Evangelische Theologie (Nashville: Abingdon, 1971), 24–45.

2. Jüngel, 'The Truth of Life: Observations on Truth as the Interruption of the Continuity of Life', in Richard W.A. McKinney, ed., *Creation, Christ and Culture: Studies in Honour of T.F.Torrance* (Edinburgh: T&T Clark, 1976), 231–236.

3. Jüngel, 'The Christian Understanding of Suffering', *JTSA* 65 (1988): 3–13.

4. Jüngel, 'The Last Judgment as an Act of Grace', *LS* 14 (1990): 389–405.

5. Jungel, '*Caritas fide formata*: die erste Enzyklika Benedikt XVI - gelesen mit den Augen eines evangelischen Christenmenschen', *IKaZ* 35 (2006): 595–614.

6. Hans Urs von Balthasar, *The Theology of Karl Barth*, 3rd ed., trans. Edward T. Oakes, S.J. (San Francisco: Ignatius Press, 1992).

7. Ibid., 382.

8. Karl Barth, Letter to Eberhard Jüngel on 3 November 1962, in Barth, *Letters, 1961–1968*, 71.

9. Barth, Letter to Eberhard Jüngel on 13 April 1966, in *Letters*, 203.

10. Jüngel, 'The Relationship between "Economic" and "Immanent" Trinity', 179–184. The translator of the essay is not identified. For reasons detailed in Chapter 3, the reader is advised to consult the German text, available in *TE II*, 265–275.

11. Karl Rahner, *The Trinity*, trans. Joseph Donceel, Milestones in Catholic Theology (New York: Crossroad Herder, 1970).

12. Ibid., 22.

Notes

13. Jüngel, 'The Relationship between "Economic" and "Immanent" Trinity', 179.

14. Ibid., 180.

15. Ibid., 181.

16. As I indicated, above, I am uneasy with the translator's rendering of 'kommen' as 'proceeds' for the simple reason that Jüngel does not in the essay engage the classical tradition of trinitarian discourse. To my mind, the verb 'kommen' seems suggestive of the idiosyncratic locutions 'kommen-zur-Sprache', which recurs with some frequency in Jüngel's writings from the period. It is worth noting, too, that Rahner expresses his preference for the concept of *communication* to that of procession. See, for instance, his comments in *The Trinity*, 67–68.

17. Jüngel, 'The Relationship between "Economic" and "Immanent" Trinity', 184.

18. Ibid.

19. See Hans-Georg Gadamer, *Truth and Method*, 2nd Rev. ed., trans. Joel Weinsheimer and Donald G. Marshall (New York: Continuum, 2003), 300–307.

20. See Nelson, *The Interruptive Word: Eberhard Jüngel on the Sacramental Structure of God's Relation to the World*, T&T Clark Studies in Systematic Theology 24, eds. John Webster, Ian A. McFarland and Ivor Davidson (London: Bloomsbury T&T Clark, 2013), 87–111. For the expression of a similar concern, see also Webster, 'Jesus in the Theology of Eberhard Jüngel', *CJT* 32 (1997): 64–65.

21. In addition to the essay at hand, and also the 1997 article 'Um Gottes willen – Klarheit!' and the book *Justification*, both of which we examine in this guidebook, the following short pieces reflect Jüngel's interest in ecumenical work between Lutherans and Catholics: Jüngel, 'amica Exegesis: einer römischen Note', *ZThK* 95 (1998): 252–279; Jüngel, 'Kardinale Probleme', *Stimmen der Zeit* 11 (1999): 727–739; Jüngel, 'Paradoxe Ökumene. Ende der Höflichkeiten bei wachsender Nähe', *zeitzeichen* 11 (2000): 1–6; Jüngel, 'Church Unity Is Already Happening: The Path toward Eucharistic Community', trans. Richard P. Schenk *dialog* 44 no. 1 (2005): 30–37. For a summary of such contributions, see Birmelé, 'Eberhard Jüngel and the International Lutheran-Catholic Dialogue', 1–12.

22. On this progress, see the survey in John A. Radano, *Lutheran & Catholic Reconciliation on Justification: A Chronology of the Holy See's Contributions, 1961–1999, to a New Relationship between Lutherans & Catholics and to Steps Leading to the* 'Joint Declaration on the Doctrine of Justification' (Grand Rapids, MI: Eerdmans, 2009), particularly pages 31–52.

23. On this point, see also Jenson's discussion in *Unbaptized God*, 90–94.

24. See especially Jüngel's comments in *Essays*, 190n 5, and 191.

25. See here the entirety of Jüngel's reading of the Catholic doctrine of sacrament in *Essays*, 197–199.

26. The essay was originally published as "'Meine Theologie" – kurz gefaßt', in Johannes B. Bauer, ed., *Entwürfe der Theologie* (Köln: Styria Verlag, 1985), 163–179. Other participants in the collection include Yves Congar, Gerhard Ebeling, Hans Küng, Johann Baptist Metz, Jürgen Moltmann and Helmut Thielicke.

27. Jüngel, *Essays II*, 14. The translator renders the German word *wohltätig* as 'wholesomely'. I am not sure that this choice quite captures the sense of Jüngel's original, as *wohltätig* typically is translated as 'benevolently' or 'charitably' and conveys the giving of gifts. Hence, Jüngel seems to be saying here that idolatry confuses and mixes what the Creator, by divine grace, gives in a differentiated way within creation.

28. Notably in the little book *El Ser Sacramental: En Perspectiva Evangélica* (Salamanca: Ediciones Sígueme, 2007), 85–97.

29. Martin Luther, 'Preface to the Wittenberg Edition of Luther's German Writings', *LW* 34, 285–287.

30. Albert Schweitzer, *The Quest of the Historical Jesus: The First Complete Edition*, ed. and trans. John Bowden (Minneapolis: Fortress Press, 2001).

31. Webster, 'Jesus in the Theology of Eberhard Jüngel', 46.

32. In addition to the essay by Webster just cited, see Nelson, *The Interruptive Word*, 87–111, for a critical evaluation of Jüngel's Christology, including a survey of 'Dogmatic Significance'. As with my comments on 'The Effectiveness of Christ Withdrawn', above, I will not foreground my concerns in this guidebook. Rather, I simply will remark that 'Dogmatic Significance' raises questions about the relation between Jesus Christ and time which are never suitably addressed in the essay itself – and nor should we expect them to be, given the limited scope of the essay as a piece of irregular dogmatics. Since Jüngel never attempted a full-fledged, regular statement on Christology, in which, presumably, he would have addressed these and other concerns, we must leave the questions dangling.

33. Interestingly, an anthology of Kuhn's writings on the same topic, published in English under the title, *The Essential Tension: Selected Studies in Scientific Tradition and Change* (Chicago: University of Chicago Press, 1977), appeared in German with the title, *Die Entstehung des Neuen*; lit. *The Emergence of the New* [Kuhn, *Die Entstehung des Neuen: Studien zur Struktur der Wissenschaftsgeschichte*, hg. Lorenz Krüger (Frankfurt: Suhrkamp Verlag, 1977)]. While Jüngel appears to have borrowed his essay's title from the Kuhn anthology, in the piece he engages only with *Structure*.

34. Boethius, *The Consolation of Philosophy* 5.VI, trans. Scott Goins and Barbara H. Wyman, Ignatius Critical Editions, ed. Joseph Pearce (San Francisco: Ignatius, 2012), 167.

35. Jüngel, 'New – Old – New: Theological Aphorisms', trans. R. David Nelson, in R. David Nelson, Darren Sarisky and Justin Stratis, eds., *Theological*

Notes

Theology: Essays in Honour of John Webster (London & New York: Bloomsbury T&T Clark, 2015), 131–135.

36. Jüngel, 'Um Gottes willen – Klarheit! Kritische Bemerkungen zur Verharmlosung der kriteriologischen Funktion des Rechtfertigungsartikles – aus Anlass einer ökumenischen »gemeinsamen Erklärung zur Rechtfertigungslehre«', *ZThK* 94 (1997): 394–406.

37. For a summary of the issues at stake, couched within a thoroughgoing defence of the criteriological use of the doctrine of justification, see Mark C. Mattes, *The Role of Justification in Contemporary Theology*, Lutheran Quarterly Books, ed. Paul Rorem (Grand Rapids, MI: Eerdmans, 2004).

38. Walter Kasper, 'In allem Christus bekennen Einig in der Rechtfertigungslehre als Mitte und Kriterium des christlichen Glaubens?' *Katholische Nachrichten-Agentur* 32 (12 August 1997): 5–7.

39. Jüngel summarizes this segment of the history of the document in 'Um Gottes willen – Klarheit', 395.

40. Ibid.

41. The definition derives from Gloege, *Gnade für die Welt*, 34–35. Jüngel cites the statement in 'Um Gottes willen – Klarheit', 404.

42. 'No Consensus on the *"Joint Declaration on the Doctrine of Justification."* A Critical Evaluation by Professors of Protestant Theology', trans. Oliver K. Olson, *LQ* 12 (1998): 193–196.

43. Ibid., 193.

44. Notably in Nelson, *The Interruptive Word*. See also idem, 'Eberhard Jüngels Theologie der Sakramente', trans. Sven Ensminger, in Dirk Evers and Malte Krüger, eds., *Eberhard Jüngels Theologie. Kontexte, Themen und Perspektiven* (Tübingen: Mohr Siebeck, 2020).

45. On this point, see the entirety of Jüngel's argument in 'Sakrament und Repräsentation', 278–279.

46. Jüngel, 'Church Unity Is Already Happening', 32.

47. The distinction is found in Schleiermacher, *Sämmtliche Werke*, Abth. 1, Bd. 13, *Die praktische Theologie, nach den Grundsätzen der evangelischen Kirche im Zusammenhange dargestellt* (Charleston, SC: Nabu Press Reprints, 2010), 69–71. See also Jüngel's comments in the essay, 'Gottesdienst als Fest der Freiheit – Der theologische Ort des Gottesdienstes nach Friedrich Schleiermacher', in *TE IV*, 330–350.

48. Jüngel, 'Church Unity Is Already Happening', 33.

49. Jüngel, '*Credere in ecclesiam.* Eine ökumenische Besinnung', *ZThK* 99 (2002): 177–195. An abridged version of this essay is available in translation as Jüngel, 'Belief in the One Holy, Catholic and Apostolic Church', in Hans-Peter Grosshans, ed., *One Holy, Catholic and Apostolic Church: Some Lutheran and Ecumenical Perspectives*, LWF Studies 2009 (Geneva: Lutheran University

Press and the Lutheran World Federation, 2009), 21–32. Due to some concerns about this unattributed translation, in the following comments I rely on my own English rendering of key passages from the essay.

50. Jüngel, 'Credere in ecclesiam', 180.

51. For more on this, see the helpful discussion of *credere ecclesiam* and *credere in ecclesiam* in Benoît-Dominique de la Soujeole, OP, *Introduction to the Mystery of the Church*, trans. Michael J. Miller (Washington, DC: Catholic University of America Press, 2014), 296–301.

52. Jüngel, 'Credere in ecclesiam', 181. Jüngel references here the *Catechismus Romanus* of Trent, which likewise identifies the church as an object of faith and not of knowledge.

53. Jüngel, 'Credere in ecclesiam', 182. Jüngel cites the following paragraph from the *Catechism*: 'The Church is both visible and spiritual, a hierarchical society and the Mystical Body of Christ. She is one, yet formed of two components, human and divine. That is her mystery, which only faith can accept.' See *Catechism of the Catholic Church*, 2nd edition (2003), no. 779. http://www.vatican.va/archive/ccc_css/archive/catechism/p123a9p1.htm.

54. Jüngel, 'Credere in ecclesiam', 182.

55. Webster, 'The Self-Organizing Power of the Gospel of Christ: Episcopacy and Community Formation', in *Word and Church: Essays in Christian Dogmatics* (Edinburgh: T&T Clark, 2001), 197. The citation within the quote comes from Christoph Schwöbel, 'The Creature of the Word: Recovering the Ecclesiology of the Reformers', in Colin Gunton and Daniel Hardy, eds., *On Being the Church: Essays on the Christian Community* (Edinburgh: T&T Clark, 1989), 131.

56. Jüngel, 'Credere in ecclesiam', 179.

57. Ibid., 183.

58. Ibid., 185.

59. Ibid., 186.

60. Ibid., 186–187.

61. Ibid., 187.

Conclusion

1. In R. David Nelson, *The Interruptive Word: Eberhard Jüngel on the Sacramental Structure of God's Relation to the World*, T&T Clark Studies in Systematic Theology 24, eds. John Webster, Ian A. McFarland, and Ivor Davidson (London: Bloomsbury T&T Clark, 2013).

2. Jüngel, *Christ, Justice and Peace: Toward a Theology of the State*, trans. D. Bruce Hamill and Alan J. Torrance (Bloomsbury T&T Clark, 2014), 8.

SELECTED BIBLIOGRAPHY

I have organized this selected bibliography with anglophone students of Jüngel's theology in mind, prioritizing English translations and listing only key primary sources in German. I also identify some significant secondary studies available in English. Readers interested in exhaustive bibliographic information should consult the lists compiled by Hans-Peter Großhans (in Ingolf U. Dalferth, Johannes Fischer and Hans-Peter Großhans, eds., *Denkwürdiges Geheimnis: Beiträge zur Gotteslehre. Festschrift für Eberhard Jüngel zum 70. Geburtstag* [Tübingen: Mohr Siebeck, 2004], 605–649) and Piotr J. Małysz (in R. David Nelson, ed., *Indicative of Grace – Imperative of Freedom: Essays in Honour of Eberhard Jüngel in His 80th Year* [London: Bloomsbury T&T Clark, 2014], 267–287).

Translations of Jüngel's works available in English

1. Monographs

1974   *Death: The Riddle and the Mystery*, trans. Iain and Ute Nicol (Edinburgh: St. Andrew Press; Philadelphia: The Westminster Press, 1975).

1976   *The Doctrine of the Trinity: God's Being Is in Becoming*, trans. Horton Harris (Edinburgh: Scottish Academic Press; Grand Rapids: Wm. B. Eerdmans, 1976).

1983   *God as the Mystery of the World: On the Foundation of the Theology of the Crucified One in the Dispute between Theism and Atheism*, trans. Darrell L. Guder (Edinburgh: T&T Clark; Grand Rapids: Wm. B. Eerdmans, 1983). Reprint, with a Foreword by R. David Nelson (London: Bloomsbury T&T Clark, 2014).

1988   *The Freedom of a Christian: Luther's Significance for Contemporary Theology*, trans. Roy A. Harrisville (Minneapolis: Augsburg).

1992   *Christ, Justice and Peace: Toward a Theology of the State in Dialogue with the Barmen Declaration*, trans. D. Bruce Hamill and Alan J. Torrance (Edinburgh: T&T Clark). Reprint, with a Foreword by Philip G. Ziegler (London: Bloomsbury T&T Clark, 2014).

2001   *God's Being Is in Becoming: The Trinitarian Being of God in the Theology of Karl Barth – A Paraphrase*, trans. John B. Webster (Edinburgh: T&T Clark). Reprint (London: Bloomsbury T&T Clark, 2014).

2001   *Justification: The Heart of the Christian Faith*, trans. Jeffrey F. Cayzer, with an Introduction by John Webster (Edinburgh: T&T Clark). Reprint, with a Foreword by R. David Nelson (London: Bloomsbury T&T Clark, 2014).

2. Collections

1986   *Karl Barth: A Theological Legacy*, trans. Garrett E. Paul (Philadelphia: Westminster).

1989   *Theological Essays*, trans. J. B. Webster (Edinburgh: T&T Clark). Reprint, with a new Foreword by John Webster (London: Bloomsbury T&T Clark, 2014).

1994   *Theological Essays II*, trans. Arnold Neufeldt-Fast, ed. John Webster (Edinburgh: T&T Clark). Reprint, with a new Foreword by John Webster (London: Bloomsbury T&T Clark, 2014).

3. Essays and short pieces

1969   'Four Preliminary Considerations on the Concept of Authority', *ER* 21 no. 2 (1969): 150–166.

1969   'Review of *CD* IV/4 Fragment, by Karl Barth', *Literature Survey: A Review of Recent Theological Publications* 1 (1969): 78–83.

1971   'God – as a Word of Our Language', Frederick Herzog (ed.), *Theology of the Liberating Word* (Nashville: Abingdon), 24–45.

1976   'The Relationship between "Economic" and "Immanent" Trinity', *TD* 24 (1976): 179–184.

1976   'The Truth of Life: Observations on Truth as the Interruption of the Continuity of Life', Richard W.A. McKinney (ed.),

Creation, Christ, and Culture: Studies in Honour of T. F. Torrance (Edinburgh: T&T Clark), 231–236.

1988   'The Christian Understanding of Suffering', *JTSA* 65 (1988): 3–13.

1989   'Response to Josef Blank', Hans Kung and David Tracy (eds.), *Paradigm Change in Theology: A Symposium for the Future* (Edinburgh: T&T Clark), 297–304.

1989   'What Does It Mean to Say, "God Is Love"?' Trevor A. Hart and Daniel P. Thimell (eds.), *Christ in Our Place: The Humanity of God in Christ for the Reconciliation of the World. Essays Presented to Prof. James Torrance* (Exeter, UK: Paternoster), 294–312.

1990   'The Last Judgment as an Act of Grace', *LS* 14 (1990): 389–405.

1991   'Life after Death? A Response to Theology's Silence about Eternal Life', *WW* 11 (1991): 5–8.

1991   'Toward the Heart of the Matter', *CCe* 108 no. 7 (27 February 1991): 228–233.

1993   'The Gospel and the Protestant Churches of Europe: Christian Responsibility for Europe from a Protestant Perspective', *RelSoc* 21 no. 2 (1993): 137–149.

1998   'Trinitarian Prayers for Christian Worship', *WW* 18 (1998): 244–253.

1999   'On the Doctrine of Justification', *IJST* 1 no. 1 (1999): 24–52.

2000   'To Tell the World about God: The Task for the Mission of the Church on the Threshold of the Third Millennium', *IRM* (30 April, 2000): 203–215.

2001   'Theses on the Relation of the Existence, Essence and Attributes of God', *TJT* 17 no. 1 (2001): 55–74.

2005   'Church Unity Is Already Happening: The Path toward Eucharistic Community', *Di* 44 no. 1 (2005): 30–37.

2006   'Theses on the Eternality of Eternal Life', *TJT* 22 no. 2 (2006): 163–169.

2015   'New – Old – New: Theological Aphorisms', R. David Nelson, Darren Sarisky, and Justin Stratis (eds.), *Theological Theology: Essays in Honour of John Webster* (London: Bloomsbury T&T Clark, 2015), 131–136.

Primary Sources in German

1. Monographs

1962   *Paulus und Jesus. Eine Untersuchung zur Präzisierung der Frage nach dem Ursprung der Christologie* (Tübingen: Mohr Siebeck; 7th ed., 2004).

1964   *Zum Ursprung der Analogie bei Parmenides und Heraklit* (Berlin: de Gruyter).

1965   *Gottes Sein ist im Werden. Verantwortliche Rede vom Sein Gottes bei Karl Barth. Eine Paraphrase* (Tübingen: Mohr Siebeck; 4th ed., 1986).

1971   *Tod* (Stuttgart, Kreuz Verlag; 4th ed., Gütersloh: Mohn, 1990).

1977   *Gott als Geheimnis der Welt. Zur Begründung der Theologie des Gekreuzigten im Streit zwischen Theismus und Atheismus* (Tübingen: Mohr Siebeck; 8th ed., 2010).

1978   *Zur Freiheit eines Christenmenschen. Eine Erinnerung an Luthers Schrift* (München: Chr. Kaiser).

1998   *Das Evangelium von der Rechtfertigung des Gottlosen als Zentrum des christlichen Glaubens. Eine theologische Studie in ökumenischer Absicht* (Tübingen: Mohr Siebeck; 6th ed., 2011).

2. Essay and paper collections

1972   *Unterwegs zur Sache. Theologische Erörterungen I* (Tübingen: Mohr Siebeck; 3rd ed., 2000).

1976   *Von Zeit zu Zeit. Betrachtungen zu den Festzeiten im Kirchenjahr* [Kaiser-Traktate 22] (München: Chr. Kaiser).

1976   *Anfechtung und Gewißheit des Glaubens – oder, Wie die Kirche wieder zu ihrer Sache kommt. Zwei Vorträge* [Kaiser-Traktate 23] (München: Chr. Kaiser).

1977   *Der Wahrheit zum Recht verhelfen* (Stuttgart: Kreuz Verlag; 2nd ed., 1977).

1979   *Reden für die Stadt. zum Verhältnis von Christengemeinde und Bürgergemeinde* [Kaiser-Traktate 38] (München: Chr. Kaiser).

1980   *Entsprechungen: Gott – Wahrheit – Mensch. Theologische Erörterungen II* (Tübingen: Mohr Siebeck; 3rd ed., 2002).

1982   *Barth-Studien* [Ökumenische Theologie 9] (Zürich: Benziger; Gütersloh: Mohn; Reprint ed., Tübingen: Mohr Siebeck, 2003).

1990   *Wertlose Wahrheit: Zur Identität und Relevanz des christlichen Glaubens. Theologische Erörterungen III* (Tübingen: Mohr Siebeck; 2nd ed., 2003).

2000   *Indikative der Gnade – Imperative der Freiheit. Theologische Erörterungen IV* (Tübingen: Mohr Siebeck).

2002   *Beziehungsreich. Perspektiven des Glaubens* (Stuttgart: Radius-Verlag).

2003   *Anfänger. Herkunft und Zukunft christlicher Existenz* (Stuttgart: Radius-Verlag).

2003   *Ganz Werden. Theologische Erörterungen V* (Tübingen: Mohr Siebeck).

2008   *Erfahrungen mit der Erfahrung. Unterwegs bemerkt* (Stuttgart: Radius-Verlag).

2009   *Die Leidenschaft, Gott zu denken* (Zürich: Theologischer Verlag).

2011   *Außer sich. Theologische Texte* (Stuttgart: Radius-Verlag).

3. Sermon collections

1968   *Predigten. Mit einem Anhang: Was hat die Predigt mit dem Text zu tun?* (München: Chr. Kaiser; Reprint ed., Stuttgart: Radius-Verlag, 2003 [as *... weil ein gesprochenes Wort war ... Predigten 1*, without "Anhang"]).

1974   *Geistesgegenwart. Predigten* (München: Chr. Kaiser; Reprint ed., Stuttgart: Radius-Verlag, 2003 [as *Geistesgegenwart. Predigten 2*]).

1976   *Gott – für den ganzen Menschen* [Theologische Meditationen 39] (Einsiedeln/Zürich/Köln: Benziger).

1983   *Schmecken und Sehen. Predigten III* (München: Chr. Kaiser; Reprint ed., Stuttgart: Radius-Verlag, 2003 [as *Schmecken und Sehen. Predigten 3*]).

1989   *Unterbrechungen. Predigten IV* (München: Chr. Kaiser; Reprint ed., Stuttgart: Radius-Verlag, 2003 [as *Unterbrechungen. Predigten 4*]).

2005   *… eine bisschen meschugge … Predigten 5* (Stuttgart: Radius-Verlag).

2004   *Zum Staunen geboren. Predigten 6* (Stuttgart: Radius-Verlag).

2005   *Unterwegs im Kirchenjahr. Predigten zu Advent, Weihnachten, Silvester, Epiphanias, Fastnacht, Karfreitag, Ostern, Pfingsten, Reformation, Totensonn* (Stuttgart: Radius-Verlag).

2009   *Allerneuernde Klarheit. Predigten 7* (Stuttgart: Radius-Verlag).

4. Miscellaneous unanthologized essays and short pieces

1971   'Das Sakrament – Was ist das? Versuch einer Antwort', Eberhard Jüngel und Karl Rahner (ed.), *Was ist ein Sakrament? Vorstöße zur Verständigung* (Freiburg: Herder), 7–61.

1974   'Redlich von Gott reden. Bemerkungen zur Klarheit der Theologie Rudolf Bultmanns', *EK* 7 (1974): 475–477.

1977   'Gott entsprechendes schweigen? Theologie in der Nachbarschaft des Denkens von Martin Heidegger', Jürgen Busche (ed.), *Martin Heidegger. Fragen an sein Werk: Ein Symposion* (Stuttgart: Philipp Reclam), 37–45.

1978   'Die Wirksamkeit des Entzogenen. Zum Vorgang geschichtlichen Verstehens als Einführung in die Christologie', Barbara Aland (ed.), *Gnosis. Festschrift für Hans Jonas* (Göttingen: Vandenhoeck & Ruprecht), 15–32.

1978   'Zur Lehre von den Zeichen der Kirche', Günther Metzger (ed.), *Zukunft aus dem Wort. Helmut Class zum 65. Geburtstag* (Stuttgart: Calwer), 113–118.

1981   (with Ingolf U. Dalferth) 'Person und Gottebenbildlichkeit', Franz Böckle, Franz-Xaver Kaufmann, Karl Rahner, SJ, Bernhard Welte and Robert Scherer (eds.), *Christlicher Glaube in moderner Gesellschaft* (Freiburg: Herder), 57–99.

1983   'Zur Lehre vom heiligen Geist. Thesen', Ulrich Luz and Hans Weder (eds.), *Die Mitte des Neuen Testaments: Einheit und Vielfalt neutestamentlicher Theologie. Festschrift für Eduard Schweizer zum siebzigsten Geburtstag* (Göttingen: Vandenhoeck & Ruprecht), 97–118.

1986   '"Jedermann sei untertan der Obrigkeit …": Eine Bibelarbeit über Römer 13: 1–7', Eberhard Jüngel, Roman Herzog und Helmut

Simon (eds.), *Evangelische Christen in unserer Demokratie: Beiträge aus der Synode der Evangelischen Kirche* (Gütersloh: Gütersloher Verlagshaus Mohn), 8–37.

1987   'Ordnung gibt der Freiheit einen Raum', *Evangelische Freiheit – kirchliche Ordnung: Beiträge zum Selbstverständnis der Kirche* (Stuttgart: Quell), 105–119.

1989   'Nihil divinitatis, ubi non fides. Ist christliche Dogmatik in rein theoretischer Perspektive möglich? Bemerkungen zu einem theologischen Entwurf von Rang', *ZThK* 86 (1989): 204–235.

1989   'Zum Begriff der Offenbarung', Gerhard Besier and Eduard Lohse (eds.), *Glaube – Bekenntnis – Kirchenrecht* (Hannover: Lutherisches Verlaghaus), 215–221.

1997   'Die Freiheit eines Christenmenschen: Freiheit als Summe des Christentums', Michael Beintker, Eberhard Jüngel and Wolf Krötke (eds.), *Wege zum Einverständnis. Festschrift für Christoph Demke* (Leipzig: Evangelische Verlagsanstalt), 118–137.

1997   'Um Gottes willen – Klarheit! Kritische Bemerkungen zur Verharmlosung der kriteriologischen Funktion des Rechtfertigungsartikels – aus Anlaß einer ökumenischen, "Gemeinsamen Erklärung zur Rechtfertigungslehre"', *ZThK* 94 (1997): 394–406.

1998   'Amica Exegesis einer römischen Note', *ZThK*, Beiheft 10 (1998): 252–279.

1998   'Zum Gewissen', *CV* 40 no. 1 (1998): 33–43.

1999   'Gemeinsamkeiten und Differenzen: Ein Brief von Eberhard Jüngel zum Rechtfertigungsstreit', *HerKorr* 53 no. 3 (1999): 154–157.

1999   'Hoffnung: Bemerkungen zum christlichen Verständnis des Begriffs', *Edith-Stein-Jahrbuch* 5 (1999): 55–62.

1999   'Kardinale Probleme', *StZ* 217 no. 11 (November 1999): 727–735.

1999   'Die Theologie als Narr im Haus der Wissenschaften', Johann Reikerstorfer (ed.), *Zum gesellschaftlichen Schicksal der Theologie. Ein Wiener Symposium zu Ehren von Johann Baptist Metz* (Münster: Lit), 60–72.

2000   'Das Amt in der Kirche nach evangelischem Verständnis', Konrad Raiser and Dorothea Sattler (eds.), *Ökumene vor neuen Zeiten. Festschrift für Theodor Schneider zum 70. Geburtstag* (Freiburg: Herder, 2000), 267–274.

2000   'Paradoxe Ökumene: Ende der Höflichkeiten bei wachsender Nahe', *Zeitzeichen* 1 no. 11 (2000): 1–6.

2001   'Der Geist der Liebe als Gemeinschaftsgeist. Zur pneumatologischen Begründung der christlichen Kirche', Albert Raffelt (ed.), *Weg und Weite. Festschrift für Karl Lehmann* (Freiburg: Herder), 549–562.

2002   '*Credere in ecclesiam*: eine ökumenische Besinnung', *ZThK* 99 (2002): 177–195.

2002   'Ökumenische Anläufe', *StZ* 220 no. 10 (October 2002): 662–670.

2003   'Besinnung auf 50 Jahre theologische Existenz', *ThLZ* 128 no. 5 (2003): 471–484.

2004   'Der Mensch – im Schnittpunkt von Wissen, Glauben, Tun und Hoffen: Die theologische Fakultät im Streit mit der durch Immanuel Kant repräsentierten philosophischen Fakultät', *ZThK* 101 (2004): 315–345.

2005   'Provozierende Theologie: zur theologischen Existenz Karl Barths (1921-1935), 'Michael Beintker, Christian Link and Michael Trowitzsch (eds.), *Karl Barth in Deutschland (1921-1935): Aufbruch – Klärung – Widerstand* [Beiträge zum Internationalen Symposion vom 1. bis 4. Mai 2003 in der Johannes a Lasco Bibliothek Emden] (Zürich: Theologischer Verlag), 41–55.

2005   'Religion, Zivilreligion und christlicher Glaube: das Christentum in einer pluralistischen Gesellschaft', Burkhard Kämper (ed.), *Religionen in Deutschland und das Staatskirchenrecht* (Münster: Aschendorff), 53–100.

2006   *Caritas fide formata*: die erste Enzyklika Benedikt XVI. - gelesen mit den Augen eines evangelischen Christenmenschen', *IKaD* 35 no. 6 (November/December 2006): 595–614.

2006   'Gott selbst im Ereignis seiner Offenbarung: Thesen zur trinitarischen Fassung der christlichen Rede von Gott', Michael Welker and Miroslav Volf (eds.), *Der lebendige Gott als Trinität:*

Selected Bibliography

Jürgen Moltmann zum 80. Geburtstag (Gütersloh: Gütersloher Verlagshaus), 23–33.

2008   'Glaube und Vernunft', George Augustin and Klaus Krämer (eds.), *Gott denken und bezeugen. Festschrift für Kardinal Walter Kasper zum 75. Geburtstag* (Freiburg: Herder), 15–32.

2008   '"Was ist er inwerds?" Bemerkungen zu einem bemerkenswerten Aufsatze', *ZThK* 105 (2008): 443–455.

Selected secondary literature on Jüngel in English

Case, Jonathan P., 'The Death of Jesus and the Truth of the Triune God in Wolfhart Pannenberg and Eberhard Jüngel', *JCTR* 9 (2004): 1–13.

Casewell, Deborah, 'Reading Heidegger through the Cross: On Eberhard Jüngel's Heideggerian Ontology', *Forum Philosophicum* 21 no. 1 (2016): 95–114.

Davidson, Ivor J., '*Crux probat omnia*: Eberhard Jüngel and the Theology of the Crucified One', *SJT* 50 no. 2 (1997): 157–190.

DeHart, Paul, *Divine Simplicity: Theistic Reconstruction in Eberhard Jüngel's Trinitarian Glaubenslehre* (PhD dissertation, University of Chicago, 1997).

DeHart, Paul, 'Eberhard Jüngel on the Structure of Theology', *ThSt* 57 (1996): 46–64.

DeHart, Paul, *Beyond the Necessary God: Trinitarian Faith and Philosophy in the Thought of Eberhard Jüngel* [AAR Reflection and Theory in the Study of Religion] (Atlanta, GA: Scholars Press, 1999).

DeHart, Paul, 'The Ambiguous Infinite: Jungel, Marion, and the God of Descartes', *JR* 82 no. 1 (January 2002): 75–96.

Ellis, Daryl, 'God's Hiddenness as Trinitarian Grace and Miracle: A Response to Christopher R. J. Holmes's Critique of Eberhard Jüngel's Conception of Divine Hiddenness', *NZSThR* 52 no. 1 (2010): 82–101.

Green, Garrett, 'The Mystery of Eberhard Jüngel: A Review of His Theological Program', *RelSRev* 5 no. 1 (1979): 34–40.

Holmes, Christopher, 'Disclosure without Reservation: Re-evaluating Divine Hiddenness', *NZSThR* 48 no. 3 (2006): 367–379.

Holmes, Christopher, 'The Glory of God in the Theology of Eberhard Jüngel', *IJST* 8 no. 4 (October 2006): 342–355.

Holmes, Christopher, *Revisiting the Doctrine of the Divine Attributes: In Dialogue with Karl Barth, Eberhard Jüngel, and Wolf Krötke* (Bern: Peter Lang Publishing, 2006).

Holmes, Christopher, 'Locating the Divine Being: On the Presence of Dietrich Bonhoeffer in the Theology of Eberhard Jüngel', Matthew D. Kirkpatrick, (ed.), *Engaging Bonhoeffer: The Impact and Influence of Bonhoeffer's Life and Thought* (Minneapolis: Fortress, 2016), 221–237.

Kelsey, David H., 'Two Theologies of Death: Anthropological Gleanings', *MoTh* 13 no. 3 (July 1997): 347–370.

Małysz, Piotr J., 'Elementally Interrupted': Divine and Human Freedom in the
    Thought of Eberhard Jüngel (PhD dissertation, Harvard University, 2011).

Małysz, Piotr J., Trinity, Freedom, and Love: An Engagement with the Theology of
    Eberhard Jüngel [T&T Clark Studies in Systematic Theology 18] (London: T&T
    Clark/ Continuum, 2012).

Mattes, Mark C., Toward Divine Relationality: Eberhard Jüngel's New Trinitarian,
    Postmetaphysical Approach (unpublished PhD dissertation, University of
    Chicago, 1995).

Mattes, Mark C., The Role of Justification in Contemporary Theology (Grand Rapids:
    Eerdmans, 2004).

McCormack, Bruce, 'God Is His Decision: The Jüngel-Gollwitzer "Debate"
    Revisited', Bruce L. McCormack and Kimlyn J. Bender (eds.), Theology as
    Conversation: The Significance of Dialogue in Historical and Contemporary
    Theology. A Festschrift for Daniel L. Migliore (Grand Rapids: Eerdmans, 2009),
    48–66.

Nelson, Derek, 'The Indicative of Grace and the Imperative of Freedom: An
    Invitation to the Theology of Eberhard Jüngel', Di 44 no. 2 (2005): 164–180.

Nelson, R. David, The Interruptive Word: Eberhard Jüngel on the Sacramental
    Structure of God's Relation to the World [T&T Clark Studies in Systematic
    Theology 24] (London: Bloomsbury T&T Clark, 2013).

Nelson, R. David, (ed.), Indicative of Grace – Imperative of Freedom: Essays in
    Honour of Eberhard Jüngel in His 80th Year (London: Bloomsbury T&T Clark,
    2014).

Neufeldt-Fast, Arnold V., Eberhard Jüngel's Theological Anthropology in Light of His
    Christology (unpublished PhD dissertation, University of St. Michael's College,
    Toronto, 1996).

O'Donovan, Leo J., S.J., 'The Mystery of God as a History of Love: Eberhard
    Jüngel's Doctrine of God', ThSt 42 (1981): 251–271.

Palakeel, Joseph, The Use of Analogy in Theological Discourse: An Investigation in
    Ecumenical Perspective (Rome: Gregorian University, 1995).

Pambrun, James R., 'Eberhard Jüngel's Gott als Geheimnis der Welt. An
    Interpretation', EeT 15 (1984): 321–146.

Paulson, Steven D., Analogy and Proclamation: The Struggle over God's Hiddenness
    in the Theology of Martin Luther and Eberhard Jüngel (unpublished ThD
    dissertation, Lutheran School of Theology, Chicago, 1992).

Rolnick, Philip A., Analogical Possibilities: How Words Refer to God [American
    Academy of Religion Academy Series 81] (Atlanta: Scholar's Press, 1993).

Schott, Faye E., 'Comparing Eberhard Jüngel and Wolfhart Pannenberg on
    Theological Method and Religious Pluralism', Di 31 no. 2 (Spring 1992):
    129–135.

Spencer, Archie, The Analogy of Faith: The Quest for God's Speakability [Strategic
    Initiatives in Evangelical Theology] (Downers Grove, IL: IVP Academic, 2015).

Spjuth, Roland, Creation, Contingency and Divine Presence in the Theologies of
    Thomas F. Torrance and Eberhard Jüngel (unpublished ThD dissertation, Lunds
    Universitet, Sweden, 1995).

Selected Bibliography

Spjuth, Roland, 'Redemption without Actuality: A Critical Interrelation between Eberhard Jüngel's and John Milbank's Ontological Endeavours', *MoTh* 14 no. 4 (October 1998): 505–522.

Watts, Graham John, *Revelation and the Spirit: A Comparative Study of the Relationship between the Doctrine of Revelation and Pneumatology in the Theology of Eberhard Jüngel and Wolfhart Pannenberg* (Milton Keynes, UK; Waynesboro, GA: Paternoster, 2005).

Webster, John, 'Distinguishing between God and Man – Aspects of the Theology of Eberhard Jüngel' (PhD dissertation, University of Cambridge, 1982).

Webster, John, 'Eberhard Jüngel: The Humanity of God and the Humanity of Man', *Evangel* (Spring 1984): 4–6.

Webster, John, 'Eberhard Jüngel on the Language of Faith', *MoTh* 1 no. 3 (1985): 253–276.

Webster, John, 'Bibliography: The Theology of Eberhard Jungel', *MC* 28 no. 3 (1986): 41–44.

Webster, John, *Eberhard Jüngel: An Introduction to His Theology* (Cambridge: Cambridge University Press, 1986).

Webster, John, (ed.), *The Possibilities of Theology: Studies in the Theology of Eberhard Jüngel in His Sixtieth Year* (Edinburgh: T&T Clark, 1994).

Webster, John, 'Jesus Speech, God's Word: An Introduction to Eberhard Jüngel (I)', *CCe* 112 no. 35 (6 December, 1995): 1174–1178.

Webster, John, 'Who God Is, Who We Are: An Introduction to Eberhard Jüngel (II)', *CCe* 112 no. 36 (13 December, 1995): 1217–1220.

Webster, John, 'Jesus in the Theology of Eberhard Jüngel', *CTJ* 32 no. 1 (April 1997): 43–71.

Webster, John, 'Jesus in Modernity: Reflections on Jüngel's Christology', *Word and Church: Essays in Christian Dogmatics* (Edinburgh: T&T Clark, 2001), 151–190.

Wigley, Stephen D., 'Karl Barth on St Anselm: The Influence of Anselm's 'Theological Scheme' on T. F. Torrance and Eberhard Jüngel', *SJT* 46 no. 1 (1993): 79–97.

Zeitz, James V., 'God's Mystery in Christ: Reflections on Erich Przywara and Eberhard Jüngel', *Communio* 12 (Summer 1985): 158–172.

Zimany, Roland D., *Eberhard Jüngel's Synthesis of Barth and Heidegger* (PhD dissertation, Duke University, 1980).

Zimany, Roland D., *Vehicle for God: The Metaphorical Theology of Eberhard Jüngel* (Macon, GA: Mercer University Press, 1994).

AUTHOR INDEX

Author Index

SUBJECT INDEX

Subject Index